I0644771

POSTCARD HISTORY SERIES

Eastern Montgomery County

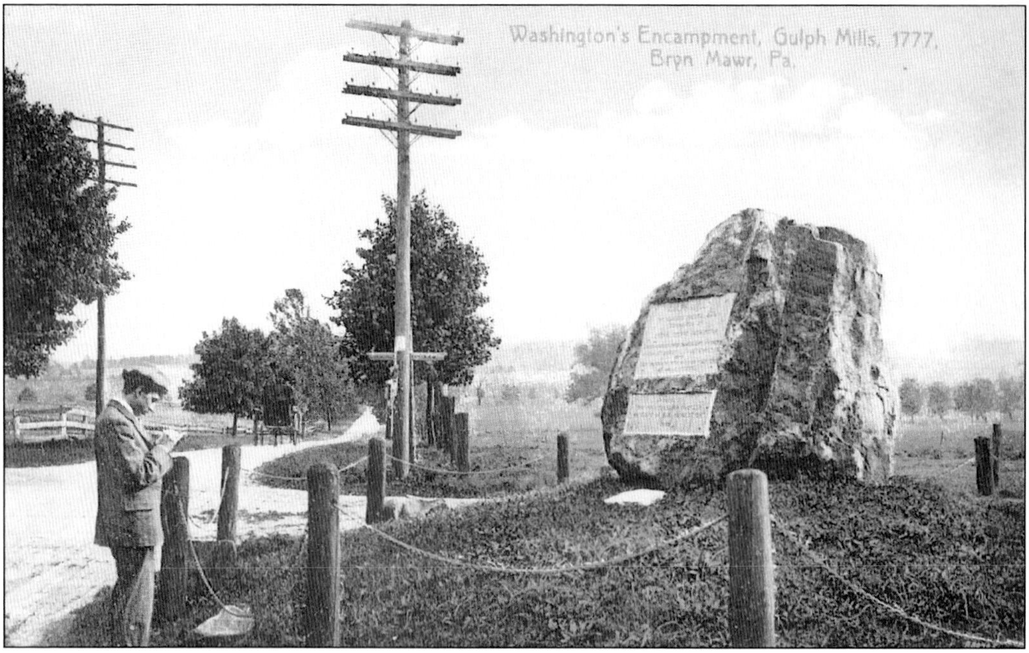

WASHINGTON'S ENCAMPMENT, BRYN MAWR, 1777. A young man pauses in front of Memorial Rock at the corner of Gulph and Upper Gulph Roads in Gulph Mills *c.* 1910. This marks the spot of General Washington's encampment prior to Valley Forge. (Moore postcard.)

POSTCARD HISTORY SERIES

Eastern Montgomery County

Andrew Mark Herman

ARCADIA PUBLISHING

ISBN 978-0-7385-0190-1

Published by Arcadia Publishing
Charleston, South Carolina

Printed in the United States of America

For all general information, contact Arcadia Publishing:
Telephone 843-853-2070
Fax 843-853-0044
E-mail sales@arcadiapublishing.com
For customer service and orders:
Toll-free 1-888-313-2665

Visit us on the Internet at www.arcadiapublishing.com

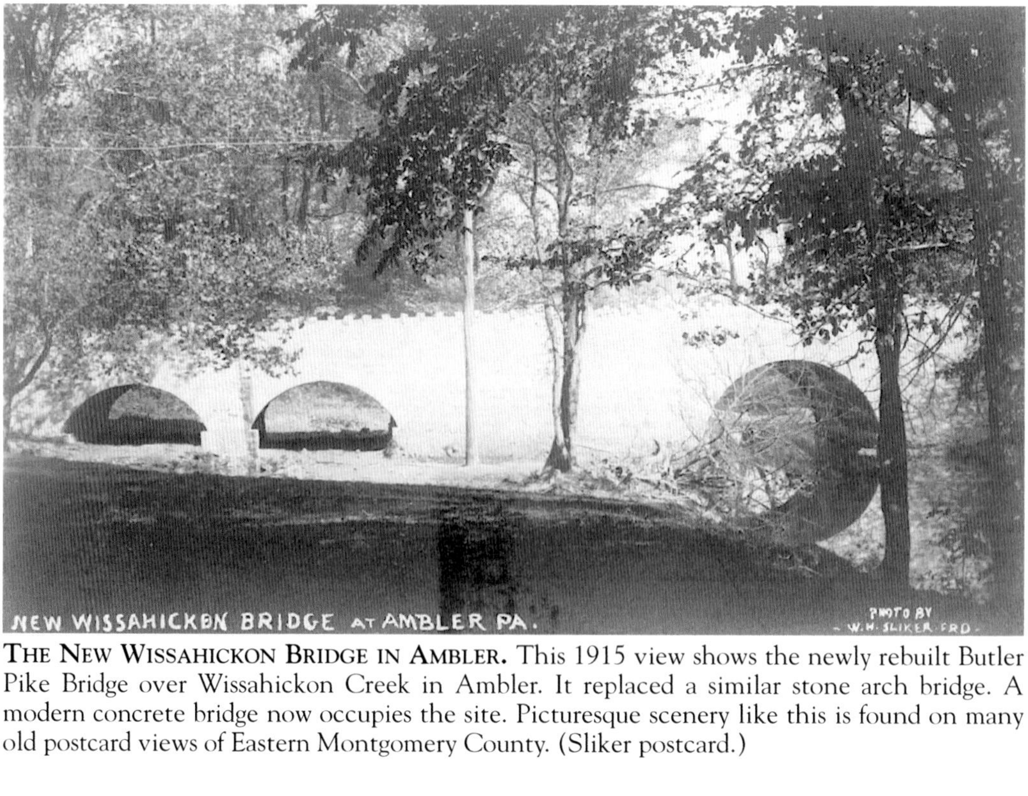

THE NEW WISSAHICKON BRIDGE IN AMBLER. This 1915 view shows the newly rebuilt Butler Pike Bridge over Wissahickon Creek in Ambler. It replaced a similar stone arch bridge. A modern concrete bridge now occupies the site. Picturesque scenery like this is found on many old postcard views of Eastern Montgomery County. (Sliker postcard.)

Contents

ACKNOWLEDGMENTS AND BIBLIOGRAPHY

I am grateful for the knowledge, assistance, and expertise of the following individuals: Henry Scholz of Ambler, PA; Joyce Root, Edith Prout, and especially Mary Washington of The Old York Road Historical Society, Jenkintown, PA; my wife, Claudia, for her hours of assistance in preparation of this book; and my children, Lauren, Allison, and Madeleine, to whom this book is dedicated.

Elaine W. Rothchild. *A History of Cheltenham Township*. N.p.: Cheltenham Township Historical Commission, 1976.

H.W. Kriebel. *A Brief History of Montgomery County Pennsylvania*. Norristown, PA: Norristown Herald Printing and Publishing Company, 1923.

Helen L. Shaffer. *A Tour of Old Abington*. N.p., 1976.

Lower Merion Historical Society. *Lower Merion—A History*. Broomall, PA: Havertown Printing Co., 1988.

Ray Thompson. *Washington at Whitemarsh*. Fort Washington, Pennsylvania: The Bicentennial Press, 1974.

Sarah C. Pinkerton. *250th Anniversary of Hatboro*. The Robinson Publishing Company, 1955.

Sylvia M. Fesmire. *Window on the Past, A History of the Huntingdon Valley Area and Bryn Athyn*. Huntingdon Valley, PA: The Pennickpacka Historical Society, 1977.

Phil Johnson Ruth. *Fairland, Gwynedd*. Souderton, PA: Indian Valley Printing, Ltd., 1991.

Velma Thorne Carter. *Penns' Manor of Springfield*. Wyndmoor, PA: The Township of Springfield, Montgomery County Pennsylvania, N.p., 1976.

W.F. Collins. *Bicentennial Conshohocken, March to Valley Forge*. Conshohocken Bicentennial Committee, Inc., N.p., 1976.

Whitpain Township Bicentennial Commission. *Whitpain, Crossroads in Time*. N.p., 1977.

INTRODUCTION

Montgomery County is situated in southeastern Pennsylvania, northwest of the city and county of Philadelphia. Although Montgomery County was not one of the three original counties in Pennsylvania (Bucks, Chester, and Philadelphia), its area was part of the original land grants and settlements of William Penn and his landholders in 1681. The Montgomery County we know today was part of Philadelphia County. In 1784, the western and northern sections of the immensely huge Philadelphia County were made separate, and Montgomery County was created.

Between 1681 and 1700, five townships were created—Cheltenham, Merion, Moreland, Plymouth, and Springfield. Between 1701 and 1720 an additional eight townships were established—Whitpain, Gwynedd, Skippack, Abington, Whitemarsh, Montgomery, Horsham, and Upper Dublin. In the 1800s and early 1900s, boroughs were created out of these original townships. These include Ambler, Bridgeport, Bryn Athyn, Conshohocken, Hatboro, Jenkintown, Narberth, Norristown, and Rockledge. It is these townships and boroughs, or mainly places to the east and south of the present Route 202 (Dekalb Pike), that make up the approximate area of eastern Montgomery County, which will be the area of focus for this book. It is this section of the county that is older and more historically significant, having many structures that pre-date the 1784 founding of the county.

Having once been a part of Philadelphia, Montgomery County has an abundance of historically significant places that are not only associated with the founding of Pennsylvania, but the nation as well. The county remained rural until the mid-20th century. Philadelphia's influence on art, architecture, learning institutions, industry, and wealth helped Montgomery County develop and prosper in the early years and today. The postcards in this book will illustrate a historically and architecturally rich area noted for its scenic beauty.

Old hotels, mills, stores, and fine residences have always been located on or near highways. Old roads fan out from the center of Philadelphia like spokes of a wheel. Many of these important roads traverse eastern Montgomery County and were traveled on by a number of famous leaders, including George Washington, Lafayette, and Benjamin Franklin.

This book will allow us to travel along these roads, using old picture postcards, starting near the Philadelphia boundary and heading to the north and west points. Each chapter is devoted to a specific road and its associated places, including Old York Road, Bethlehem Pike, Germantown Pike, Ridge Pike, Huntingdon Pike, Easton Road, and Lancaster Pike/Old Gulph Road.

The greater Philadelphia region had an abundance of local card publishers during the early 20th century. Montgomery County had several prolific postcard photographers and publishers. John Bartholomew (1863–1943) of Lansdale published many real photo cards of eastern and central Montgomery County, as did W.W. Miller (1885–1960) of North Wales. Graham and Johnson of Conshohocken and Rees C. Roberts of Ambler published extensive views of their locales.

Philadelphia supplied several publishers of Montgomery County views. The World Post Card Company produced over 100 cards of the eastern part of the county. Phillip H. Moore of Germantown also concentrated on the eastern part of the county. But William H. Sliker of the Bridesburg section of Philadelphia produced the most detailed photographic images that make up this region. He appears to not only have captured the major landmarks of the region, but the obscure as well. It is because of these photographers that, today, we can see a world and a time gone by. Their dedication to producing wonderful views deserves our praise and admiration.

This book is not meant to be a history of eastern Montgomery County, but rather an illustrated look at early-20th-century postcards of the area. Careful consideration and organization was used in selecting the images. Not every place had postcard images made and some towns are not depicted in the author's collection of over 1,000 images. *Eastern Montgomery County Postcards* represents the best possible selection of views illustrating a variety of themes, including historic homes, street scenes, stores, hotels, creeks, and parks. It is hoped that readers will gain a better understanding and appreciation of the rare, unique, and historic region in which we live.

One

HUNTINGDON PIKE

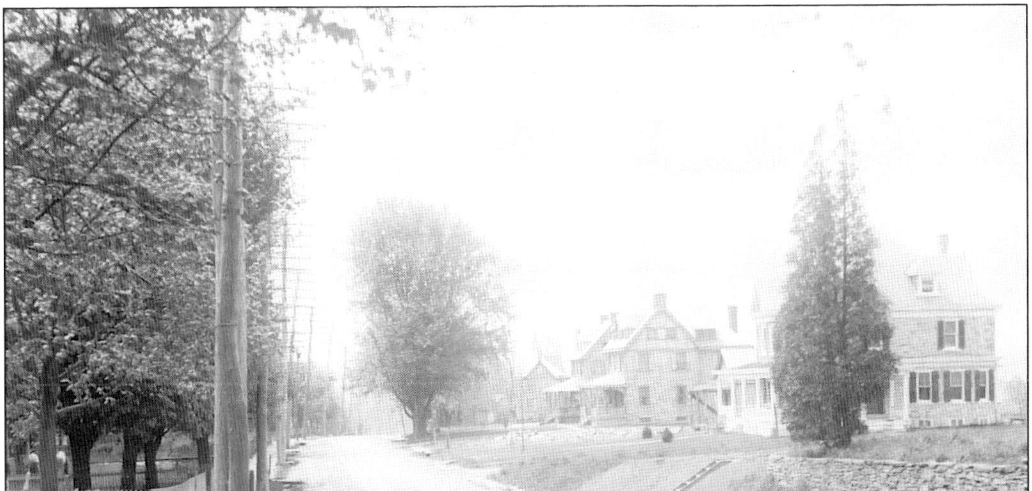

SECOND STREET PIKE LOOKING NORTH. This is a 1908 view of Huntingdon (Second Street) Pike north of Welsh Road. Many old buildings in Huntingdon Valley are still standing today. (Sliker postcard.)

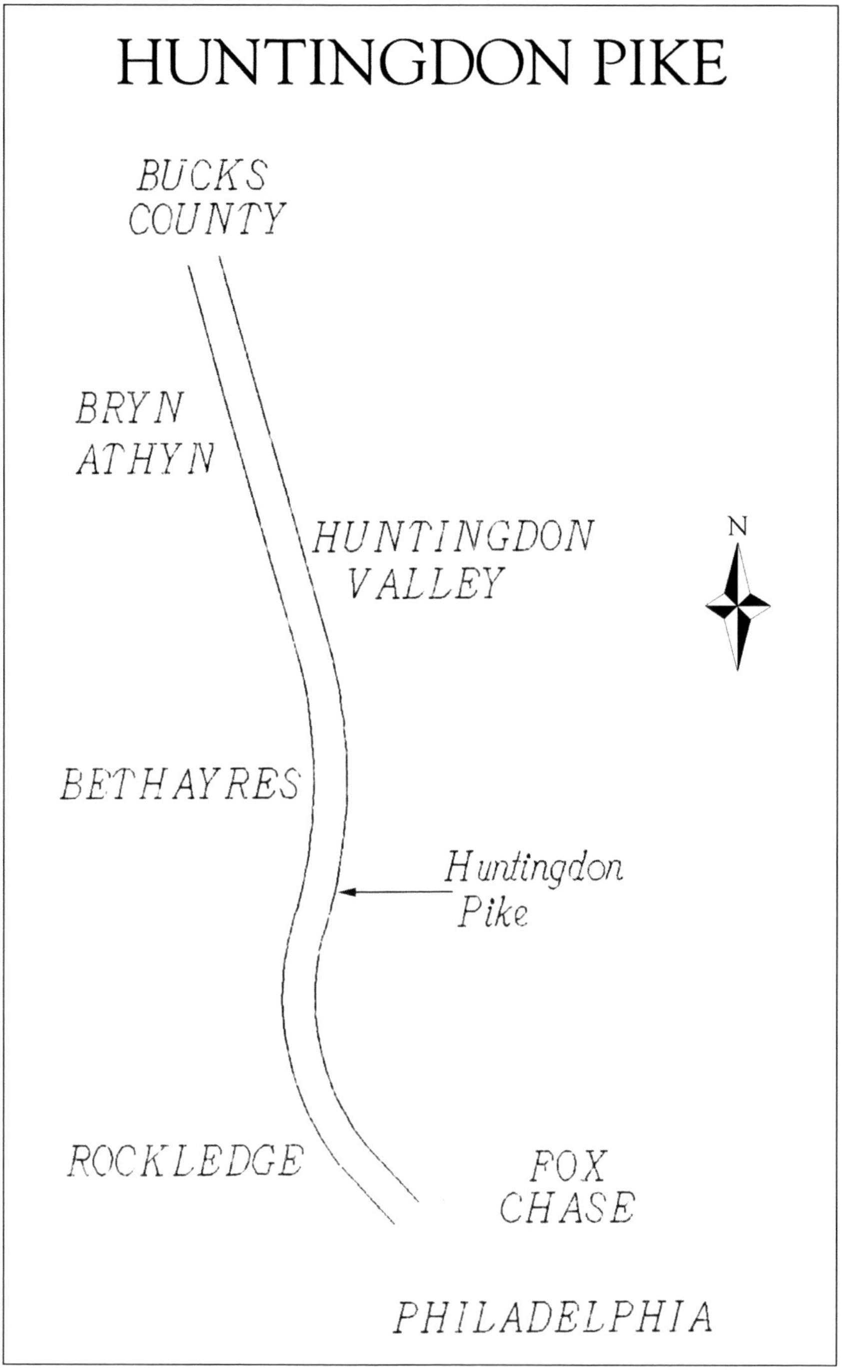

HUNTINGDON PIKE. Huntingdon Pike runs from Rockledge to County Line Road in Montgomery County. Sections of this road have been known as Oxford Avenue, Oxford Pike, and Oxford Turnpike, which is south of Rockledge in Philadelphia where it begins at Frankford Avenue. North of the city it was known as the Fox Chase-Huntingdon Turnpike. In Colonial times, it was referred to as the Middle Road because of its position between Bustleton Pike and Old York Road.

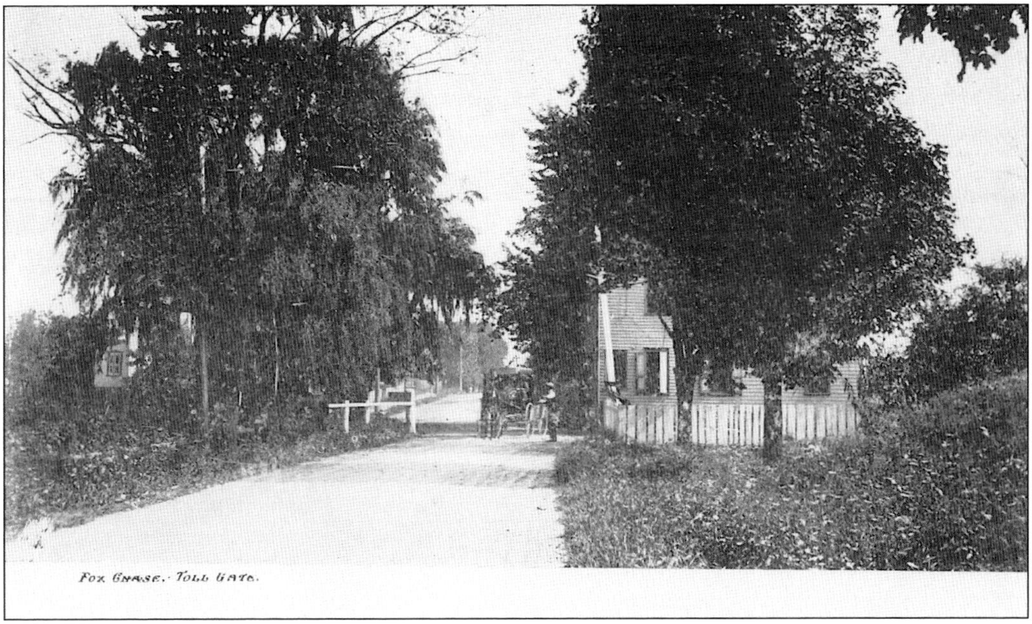

THE FOX CHASE TOLLGATE. This tollgate stood just inside the county boundaries and collected a toll to ride on the Fox Chase-Huntingdon Turnpike. Built in the early 1800s, it was discontinued as a tollhouse prior to 1920. This view is looking east on Huntingdon Pike at Central Avenue in Rockledge Borough. Today, the Lawnview Cemetery Entrance occupies the site. (World Post Card Company postcard.)

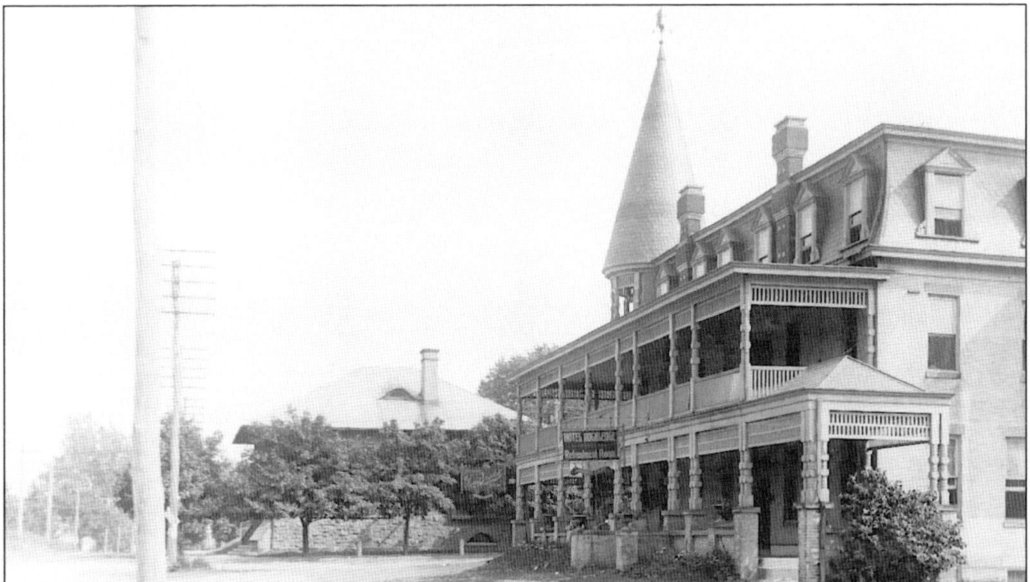

FOX CHASE BANK AND HOTEL ROCKLEDGE. The intersection of Huntingdon Pike at Fillmore Street is shown here in a view looking toward Philadelphia. Built in the 1890s, the hotel closed in the early 1900s and was used for other purposes until it was torn down. Today, a building of the Fox Chase Cancer Center occupies the site. (Sliker postcard.)

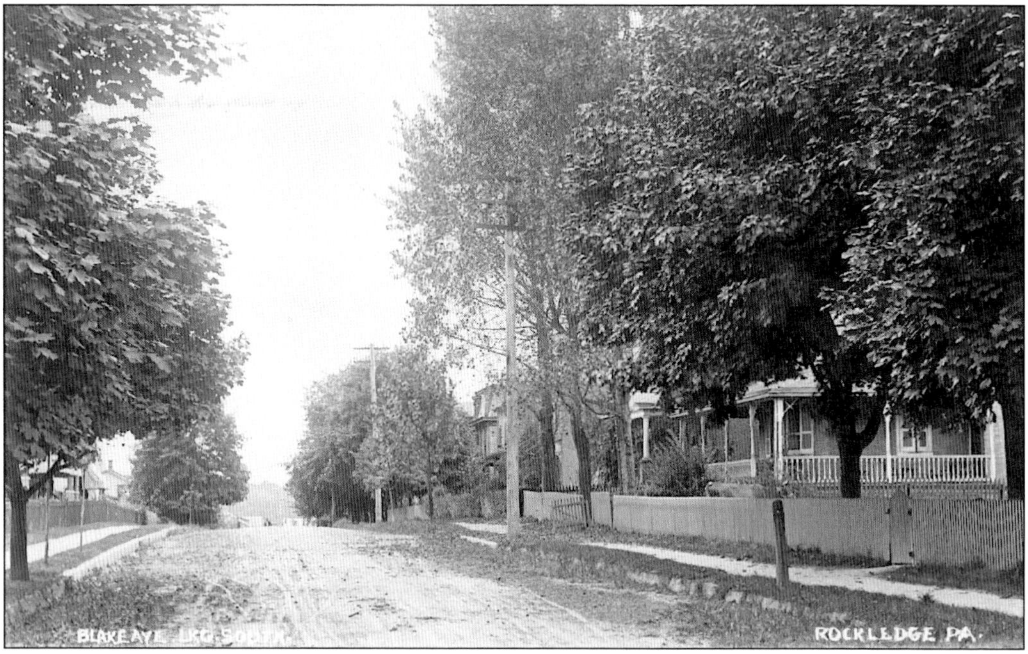

BLAKE AVENUE LOOKING SOUTH. This is Blake Avenue in Rockledge Borough when the beautiful tree-lined street was a dirt road. The borough was created from Abington Township in 1893 and is still noted for its lovely residential streets, which are lined with varying architectural styles. (Sliker postcard.)

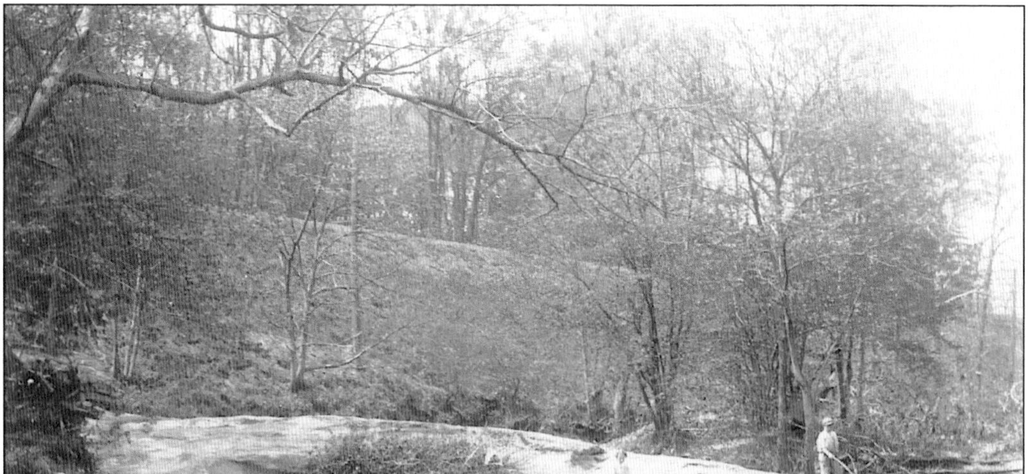

FLAT ROCK, WALNUT HILL. Walnut Hill occupies a rural area of Abington Township near Moredon Road and east of Huntingdon Pike. This view shows interesting rock formations along Pennypack Creek. When the Sliker postcard was mailed in 1912, many local residents enjoyed the wonderful natural scenery of the area. Fortunately, today, this area is preserved in Lorimer County Park.

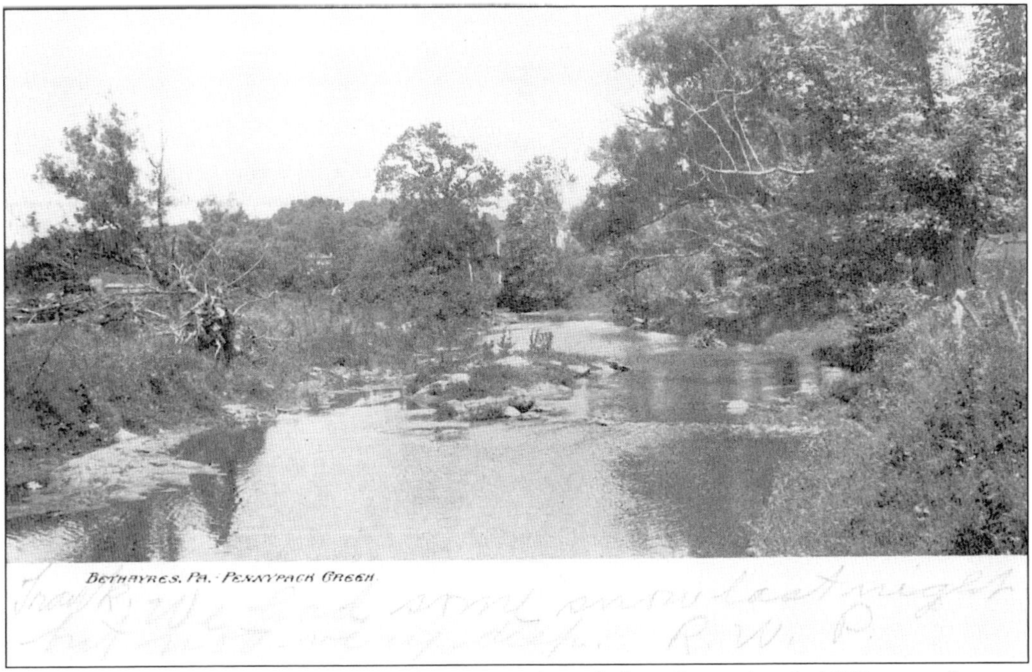

PENNYPACK CREEK IN BETHAYRES. This postcard, mailed on December 2, 1907, states ". . . we had some snow last night." The scenic area around Pennypack was popular for postcard views. (World Post Card Company postcard.)

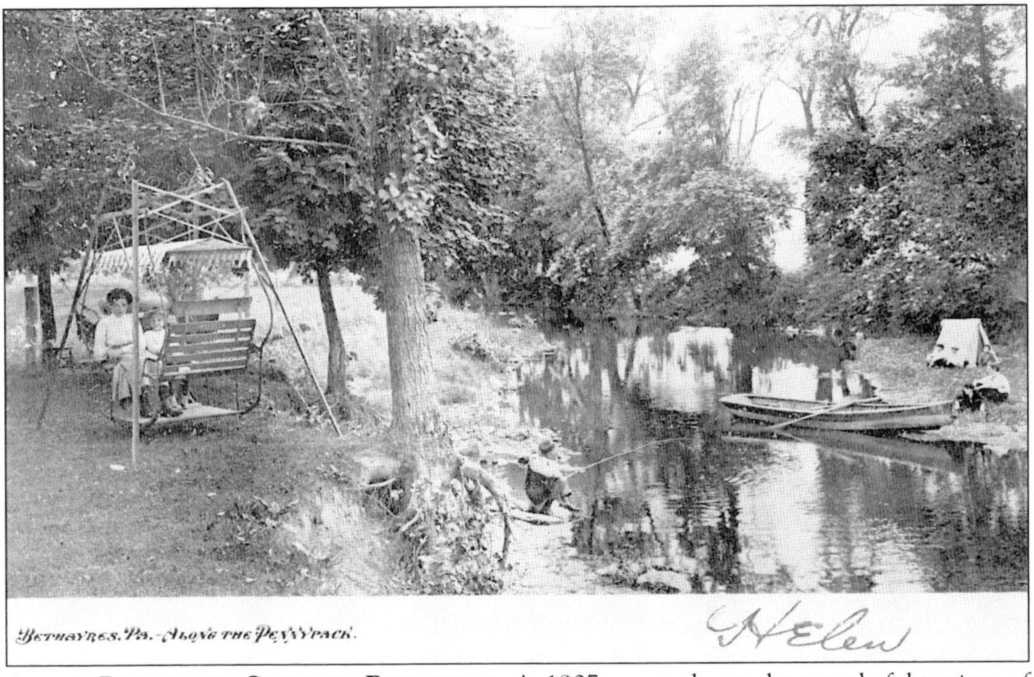

ALONG PENNYPACK CREEK IN BETHAYRES. A 1907 scene shows the wonderful variety of pleasures found along picturesque Pennypack Creek. A small boat, a swing, a fisherman, and a camping tent all indicate the intimacy shared between people and nature early in the 20th century. (World Post Card Company postcard.)

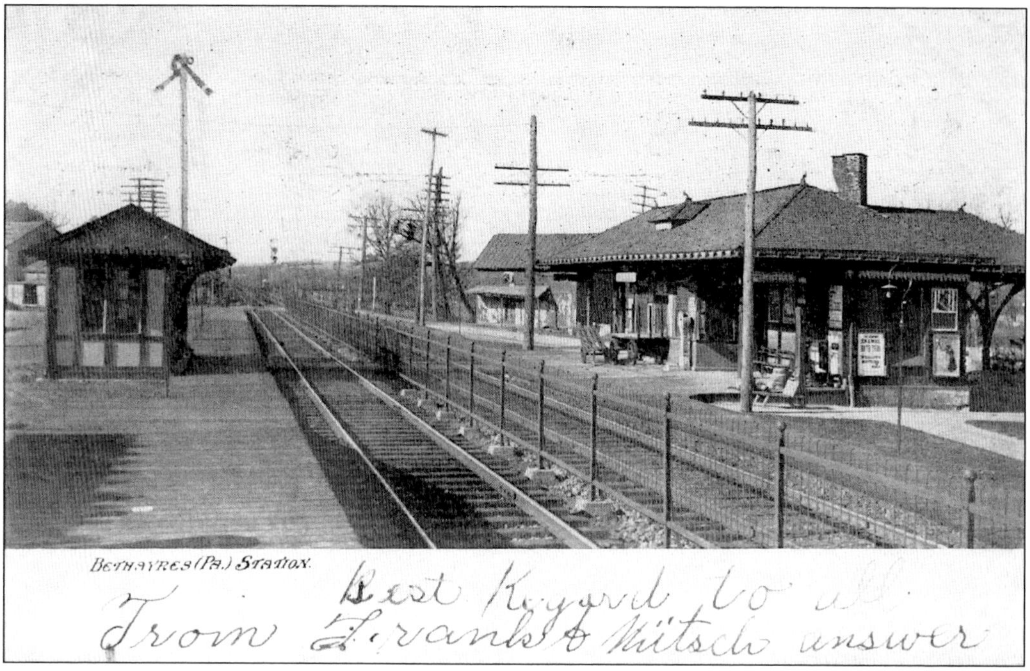

THE BETHAYRES RAILROAD STATION. Built in 1883 on the Newtown Branch of the North Pennsylvania Railroad, the station is still in use today. The mother of the president of the railroad was Elizabeth Ayres—hence the name of the station. (World Post Card Company postcard.)

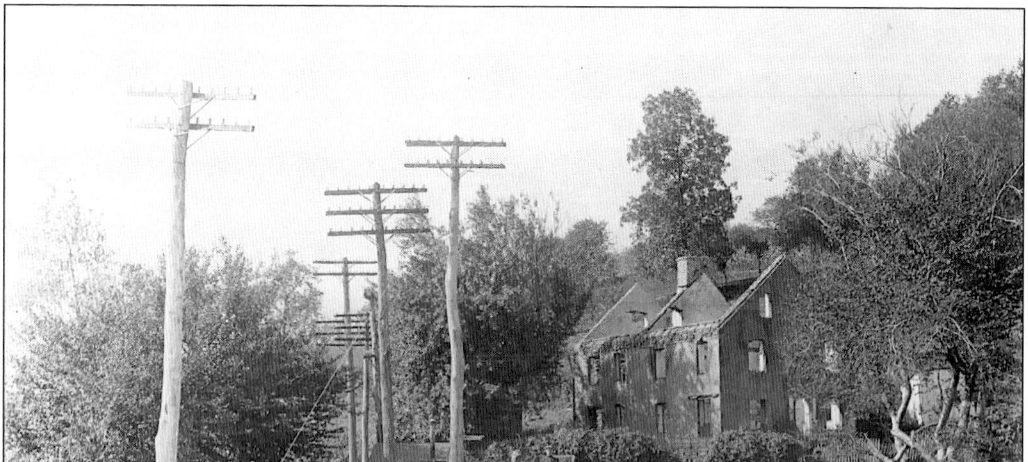

THE NEWTOWN BRANCH RAILROAD STATION, HUNTINGDON VALLEY. This scene shows the intersection of Welsh and Terwood Roads. The Newtown Branch Railroad crosses these roads here, as does Pennypack Creek—shown by the bridge on Welsh Road. Welsh Road has been widened and the curve has been straightened so that this view no longer exists today. (Sliker postcard.)

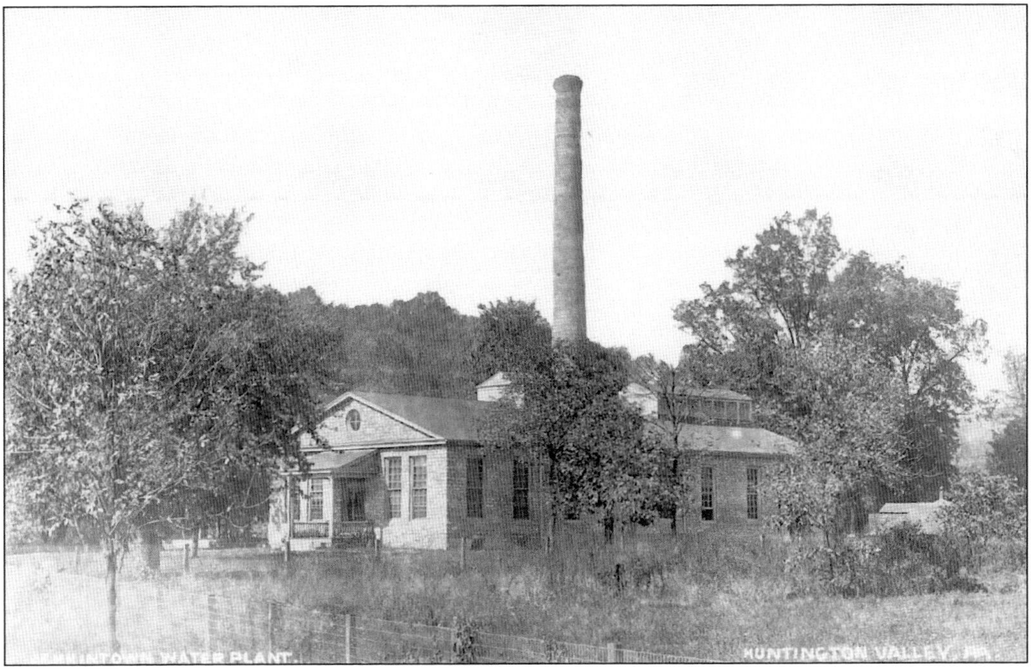

The Jenkintown Water Plant in Huntingdon Valley. Pennypack Creek provided water for even its earliest inhabitants. The plant still stands on Welsh Road near Terwood Road along Pennypack Creek. (Sliker postcard.)

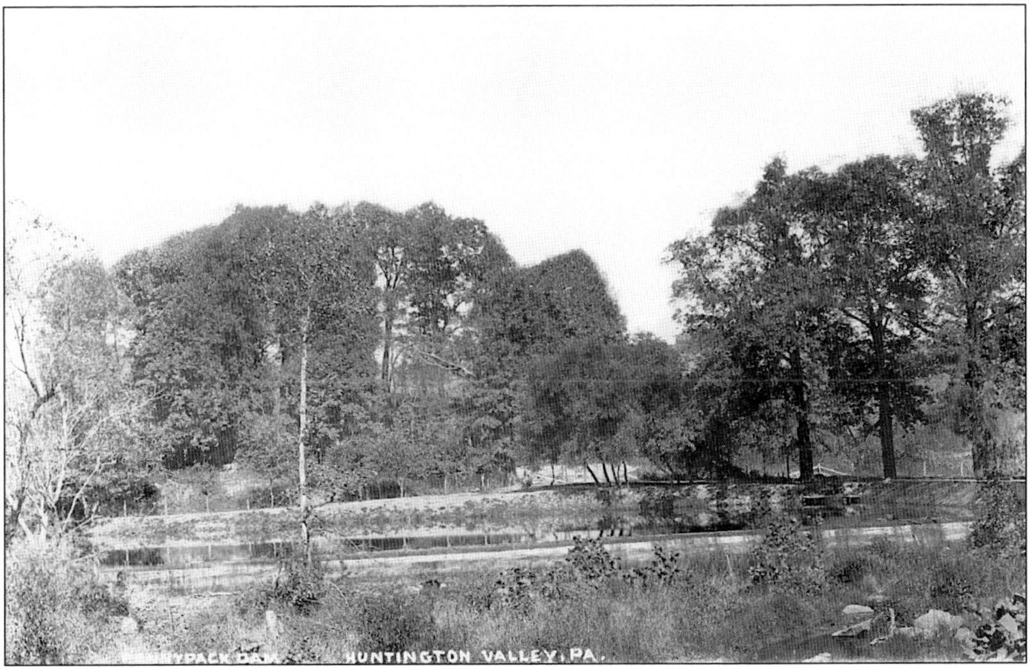

The Pennypack Dam in Huntingdon Valley. This dam provided water to the pumping station. (Sliker postcard, 1910.)

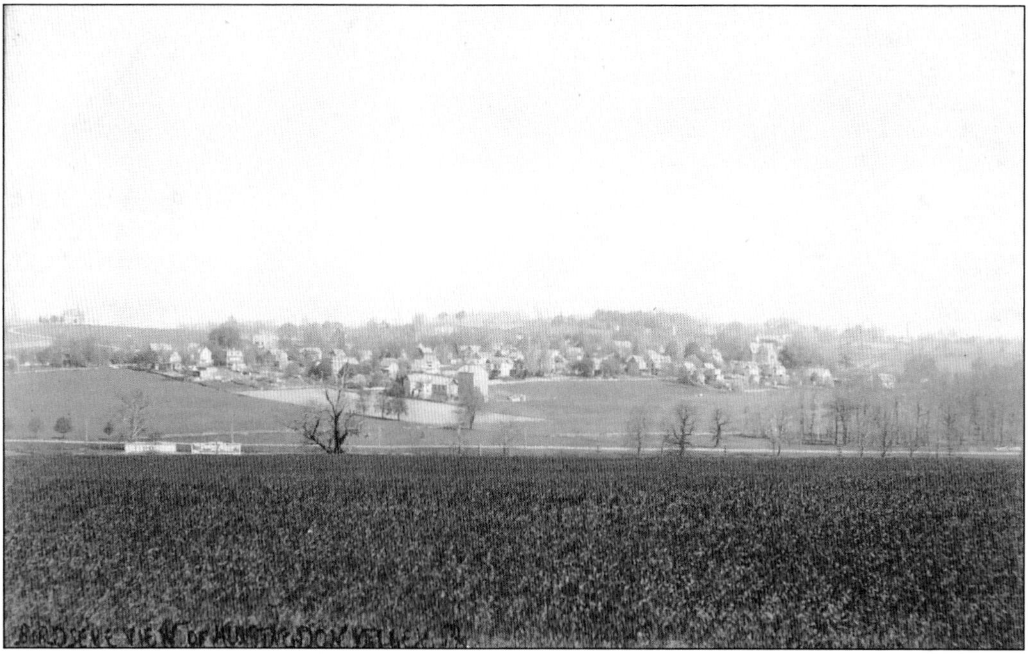

A Bird's-Eye View of Huntingdon Valley. The area of Huntingdon Valley is along the Huntingdon Pike where it crosses old and important roads. From the south, the pike intersects with, respectively, Welsh Road, Fetters Mill, Red Lion Road, Byberry Road, and finally, the county line. This view shows Huntingdon Valley occupying a ridge between Pennypack Creek and Huntingdon Valley Creek. (Sliker postcard.)

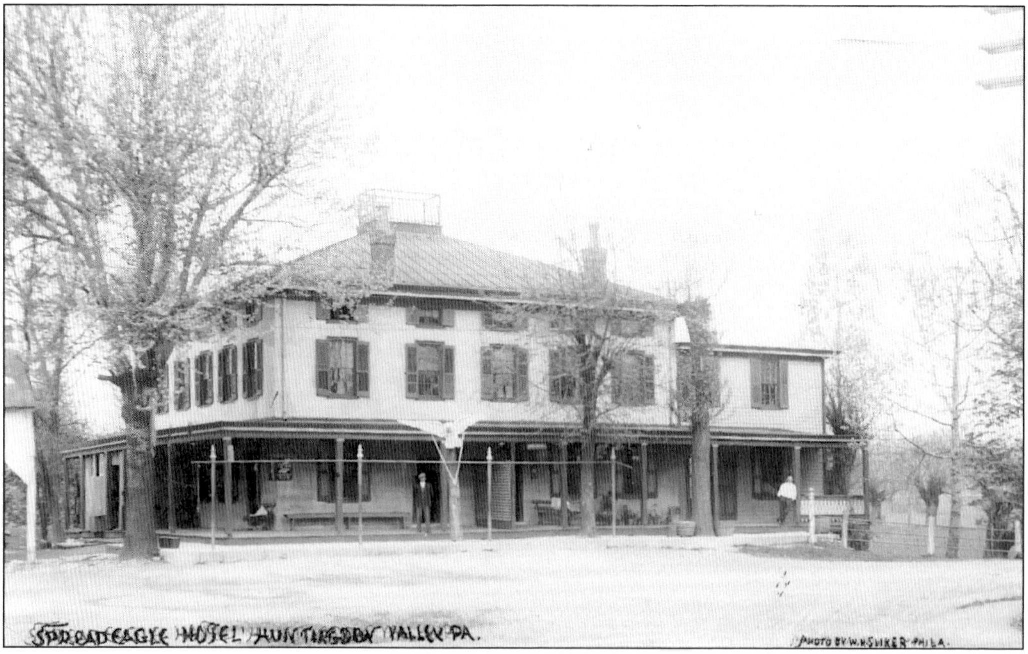

The Spread Eagle Hotel in Huntingdon Valley. The inn was built in 1793 and stood along the west side of Huntingdon Pike, near Pennypack Creek and the railroad. In 1936, the hotel was torn down to make way for a new bridge over the railroad. (Sliker postcard.)

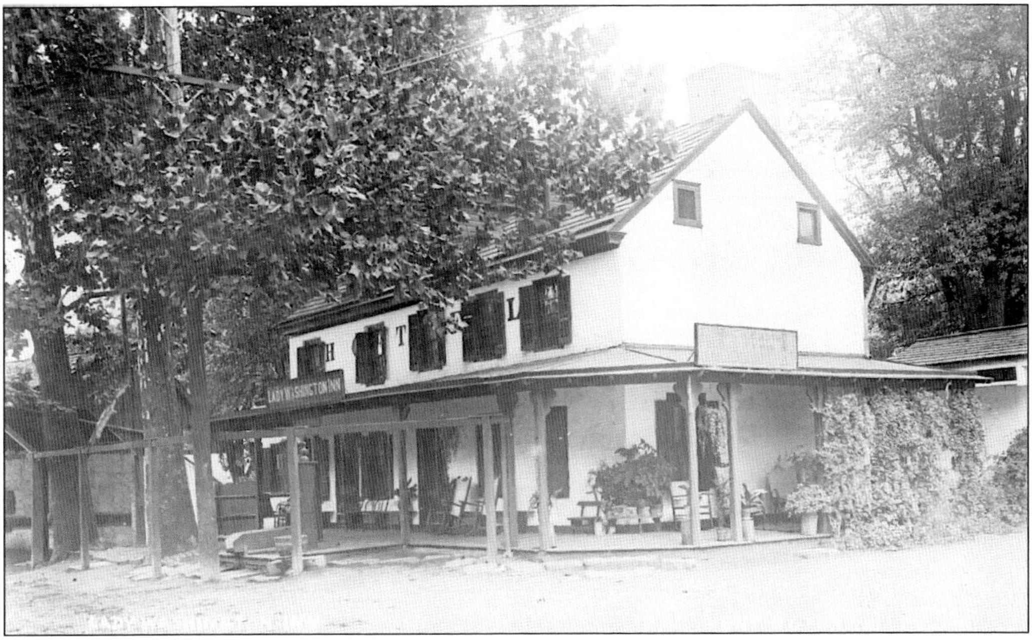

THE LADY WASHINGTON INN IN HUNTINGDON VALLEY. The Lady Washington Inn was built in 1761 at the southwest corner of Huntingdon Pike and Fetters Mill Road. This postcard by W. Sliker was mailed in 1910. At that time the inn still functioned as a hotel, though it later became a private home. It still stands on the pike below the bank at Fetters Mill Road.

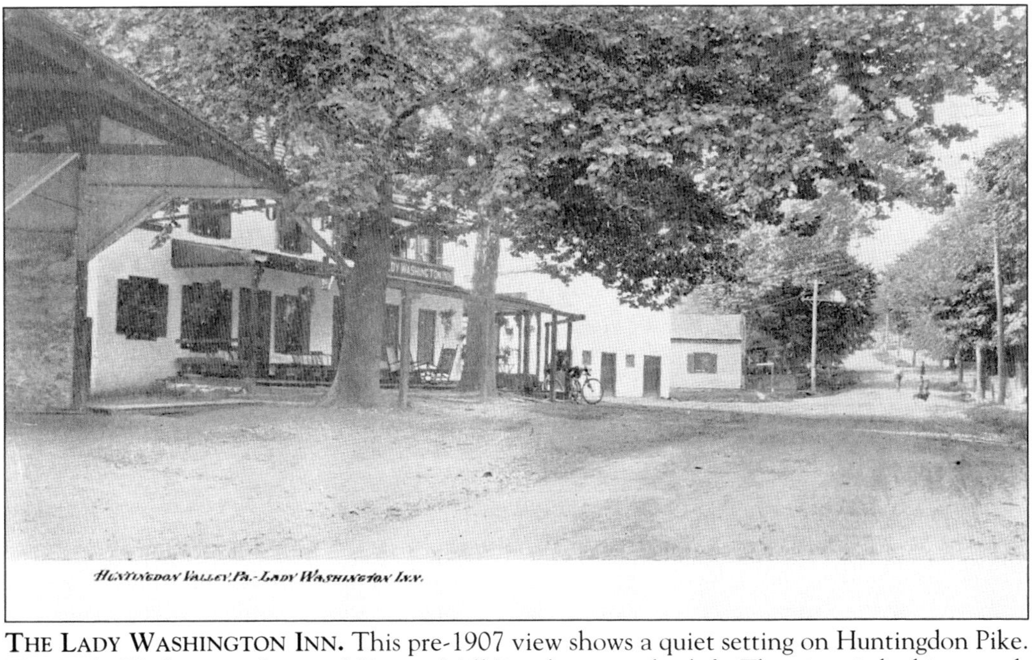

THE LADY WASHINGTON INN. This pre-1907 view shows a quiet setting on Huntingdon Pike. The Lady Washington Inn and Fetters Mill Road are on the left. The view is looking north toward Red Lion Road. It is quite a picturesque scene. (World Post Card Company postcard.)

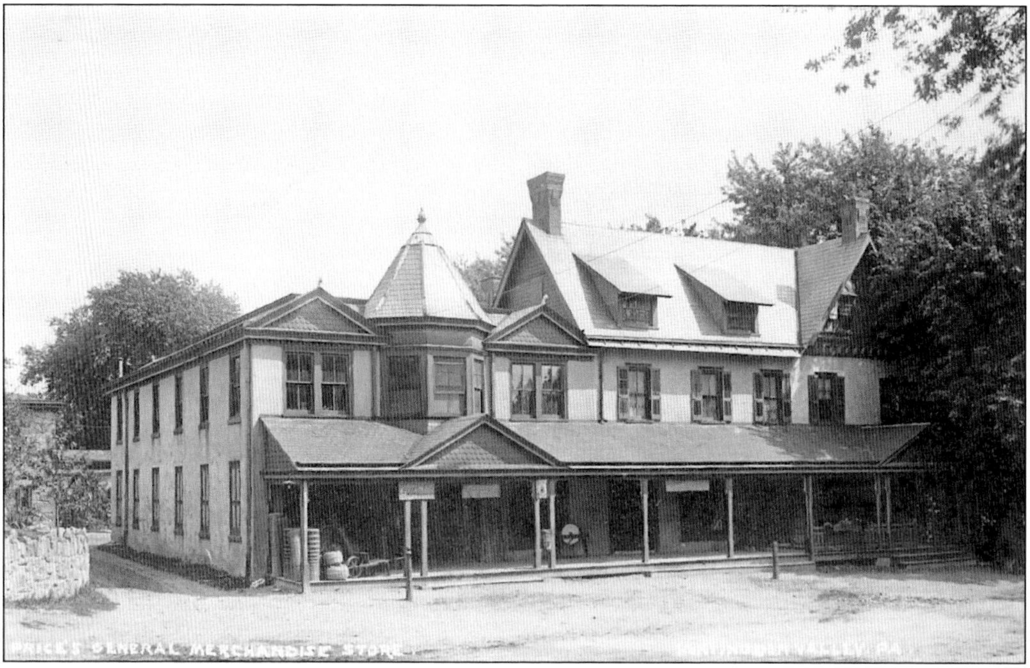

PRICE'S GENERAL STORE IN HUNTINGDON VALLEY. Most locales had general stores, including Huntingdon Valley. Built in the late 1800s by Andrew Erwin, this store was later owned by Charles Price. Located at the corner of Red Lion Road and Huntingdon Pike, it saw a number of uses during the 20th century. It is no longer standing. (Sliker postcard.)

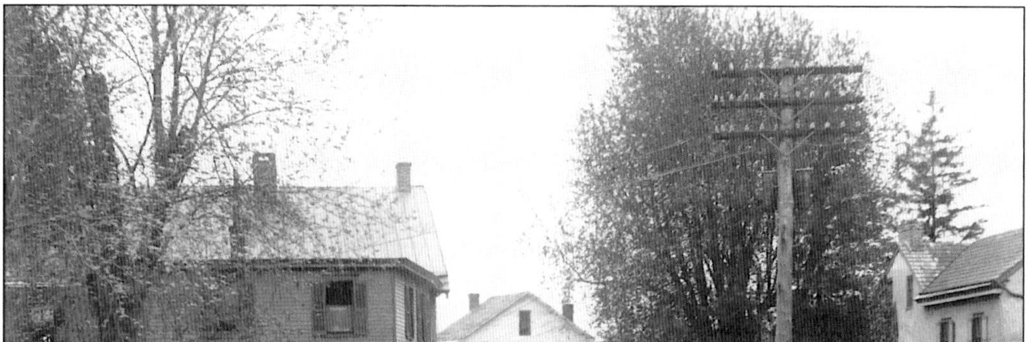

WELSH ROAD SHOWING THE TOLLGATE IN HUNTINGDON VALLEY. This view is looking east on Welsh Road toward Huntingdon Pike where today it also intersects with Philmont Avenue. The tollhouse is usually referred to as the Bethayres Toll House. All of the buildings shown here are no longer standing. (Sliker postcard.)

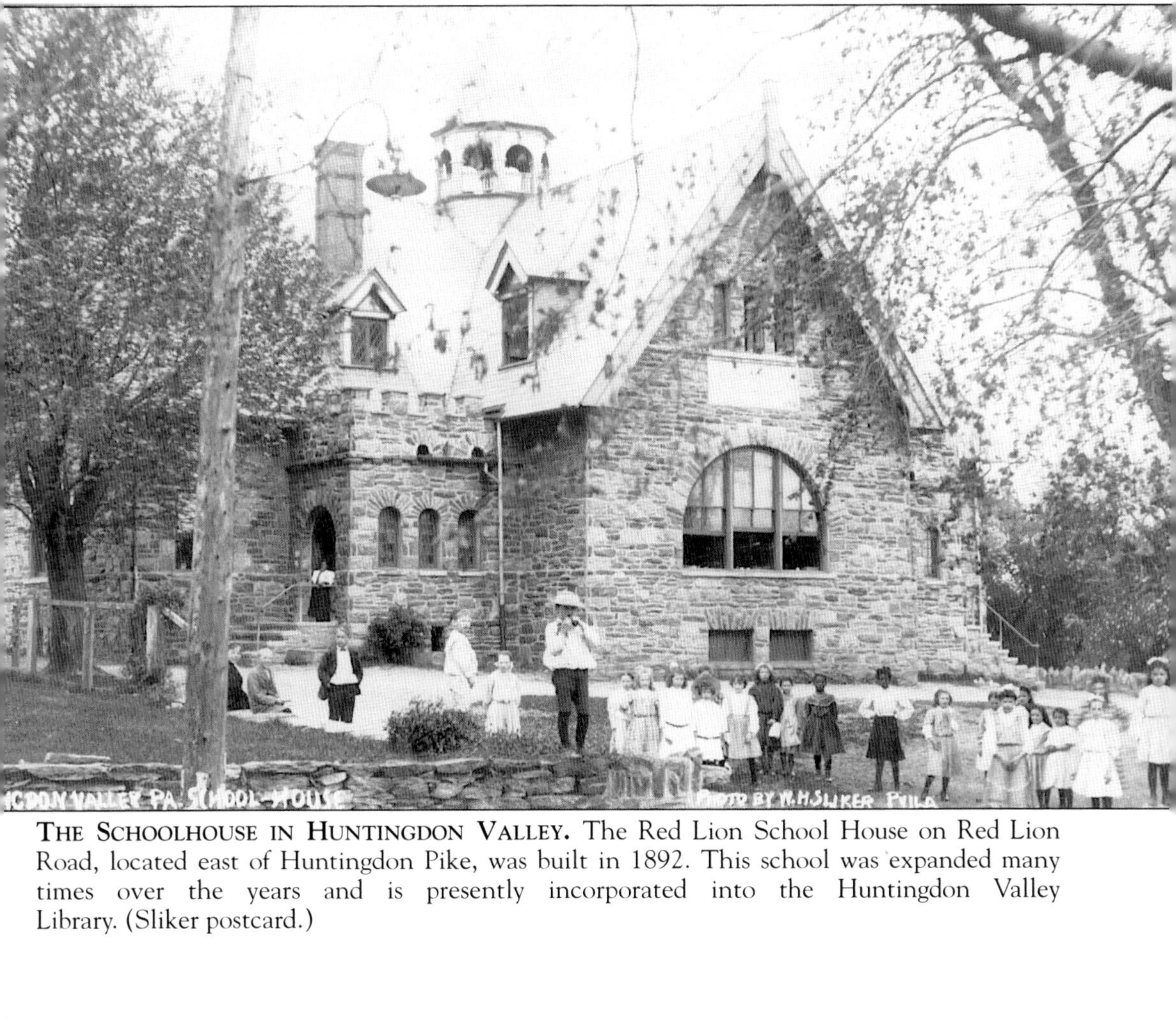

The Schoolhouse in Huntingdon Valley. The Red Lion School House on Red Lion Road, located east of Huntingdon Pike, was built in 1892. This school was expanded many times over the years and is presently incorporated into the Huntingdon Valley Library. (Sliker postcard.)

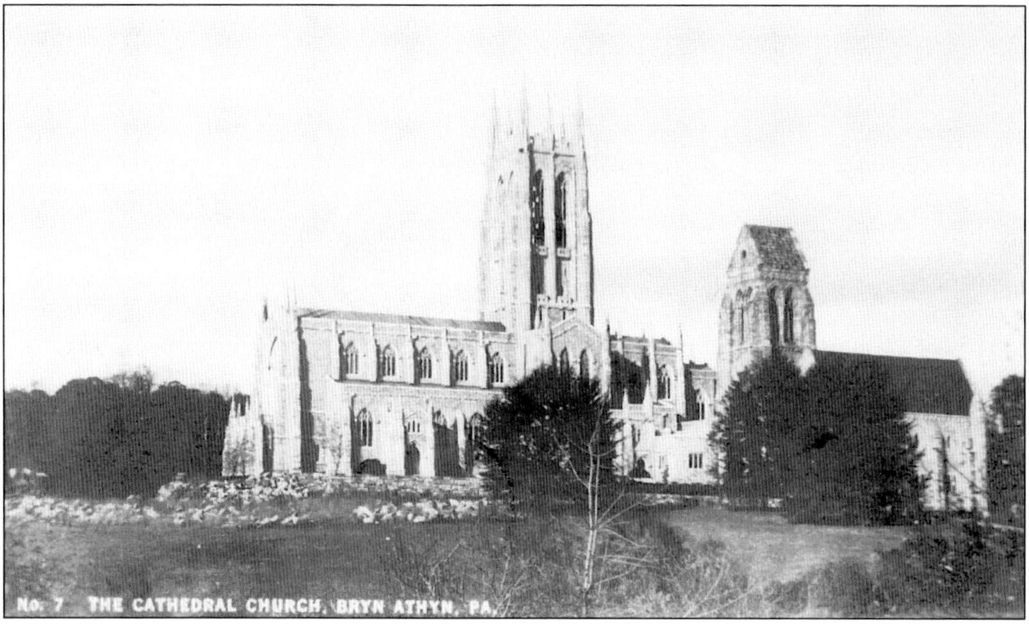

THE CATHEDRAL CHURCH, BRYN ATHYN. North of Huntingdon Valley, Huntingdon Pike goes through Bryn Athyn Borough. Bryn Athyn is Welsh for "hill of cohesion" and it was incorporated as a borough in 1916. The cathedral complex was begun in 1913 and was first used in 1915.

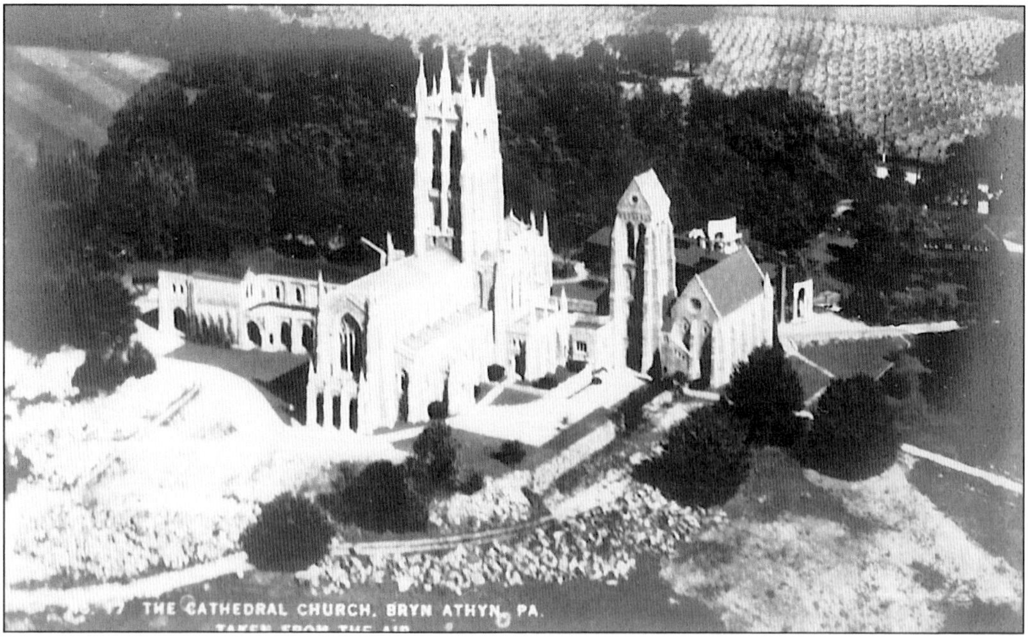

AN AERIAL VIEW OF THE CATHEDRAL CHURCH. The cathedral is associated with the Church of New Jerusalem and the Swedenborgian Church. It is modeled after the Gothic style of architecture that dates back to the 13th through the 15th centuries. Tours of this complex, which includes other buildings, blend religion with incredible architecture and make for a truly unique experience.

Two

Old York Road

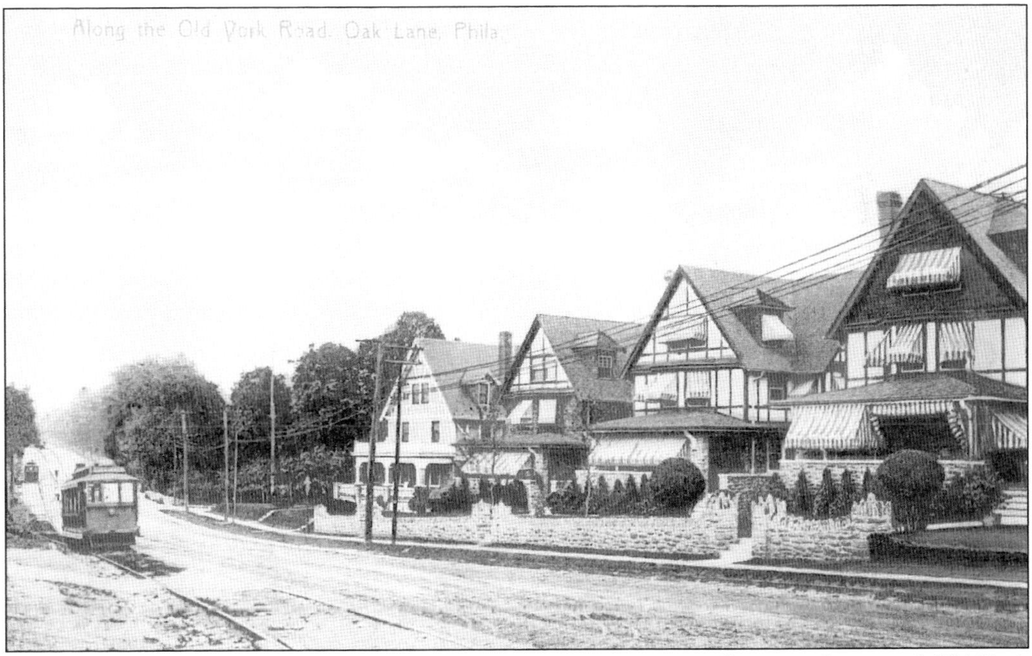

Along the Old York Road in Oak Lane, Philadelphia. This is a glimpse of Old York Road in Philadelphia, south of the Montgomery County line, *c.* 1912. Oak Lane is a large section in northwest Philadelphia and a small area in Cheltenham Township. The trolley was heading north toward Jenkintown and Willow Grove. (Moore postcard.)

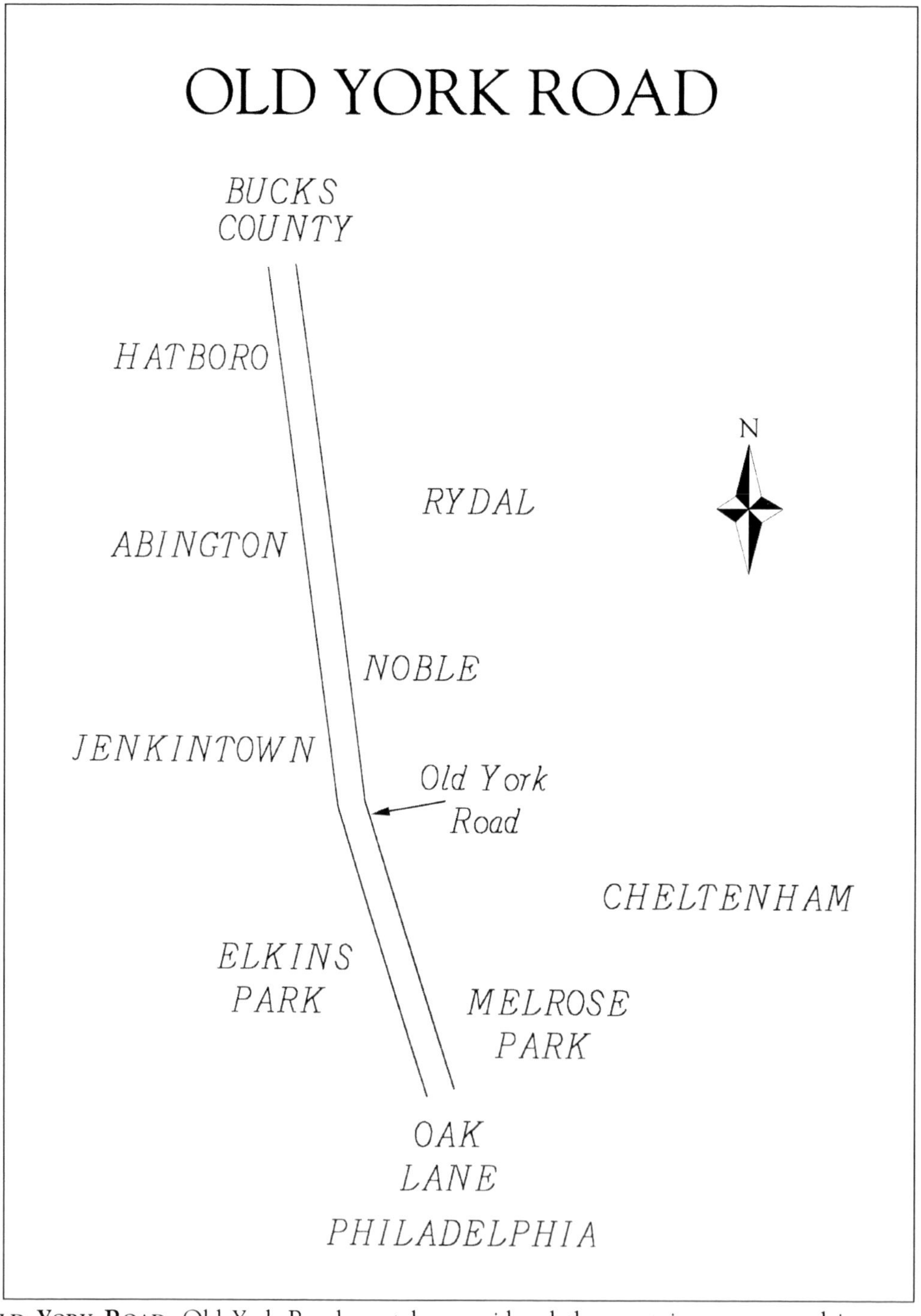

OLD YORK ROAD. Old York Road must be considered the most important road in eastern Montgomery County. It was, and still is today, the "Main Street" of the area. By 1769, it was the main stagecoach route between Philadelphia and New York. It was first authorized as a road in 1693 and linked the Abington Meeting to Philadelphia. Around 1697 it was extended to Moreland Township and, in 1711, it reached the Delaware River above New Hope.

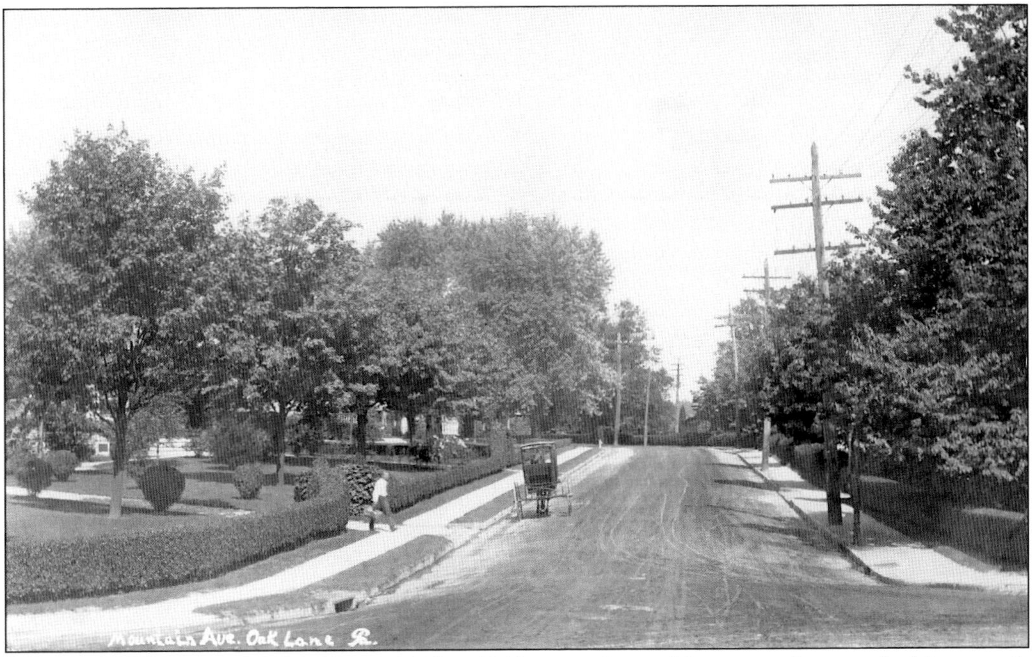

MOUNTAIN AVENUE IN OAK LANE. This 1910 view shows Mountain Avenue looking north from Valley Road in Oak Lane, Cheltenham Township. Now known as Melrose Park, very little has changed at the intersection today. (Sliker postcard.)

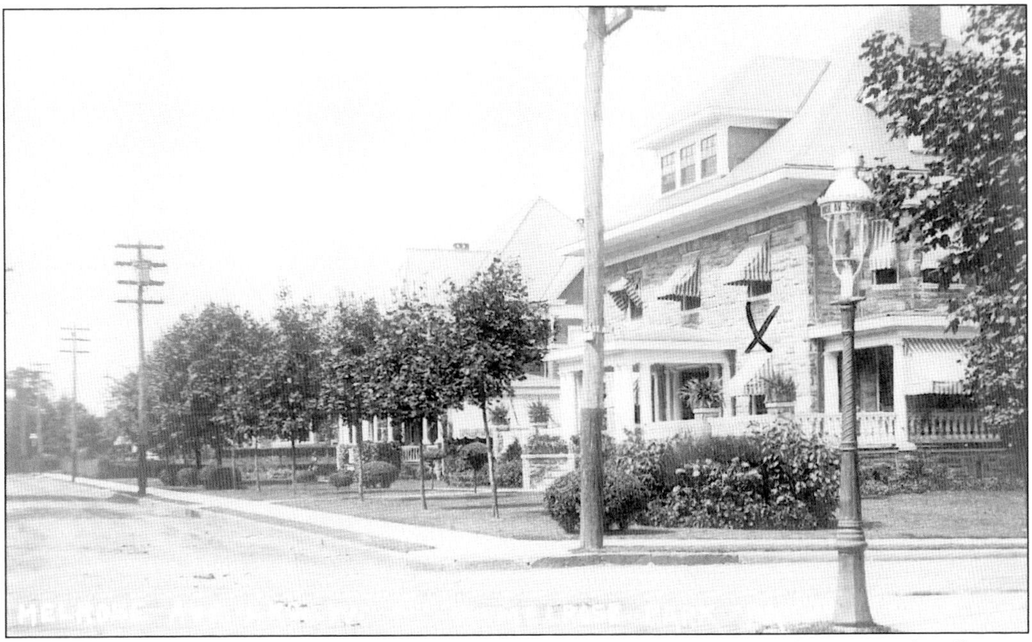

MELROSE AVENUE LOOKING WEST IN MELROSE PARK. Melrose Park was, and still is, a fashionable and attractive community in Cheltenham Township. Pictured here is Melrose Avenue looking west from Spring Avenue, just two blocks east of York Road. These fine homes still stand. (Sliker postcard.)

MRS. BLACK'S RESIDENCE IN MELROSE PARK. The residence of Mrs. Black and the grocery store of George Haney was located on Valley Road at Mill Road in Melrose Park. This view is looking west, with the railroad overpass to the left. The building is still standing. (Sliker postcard.)

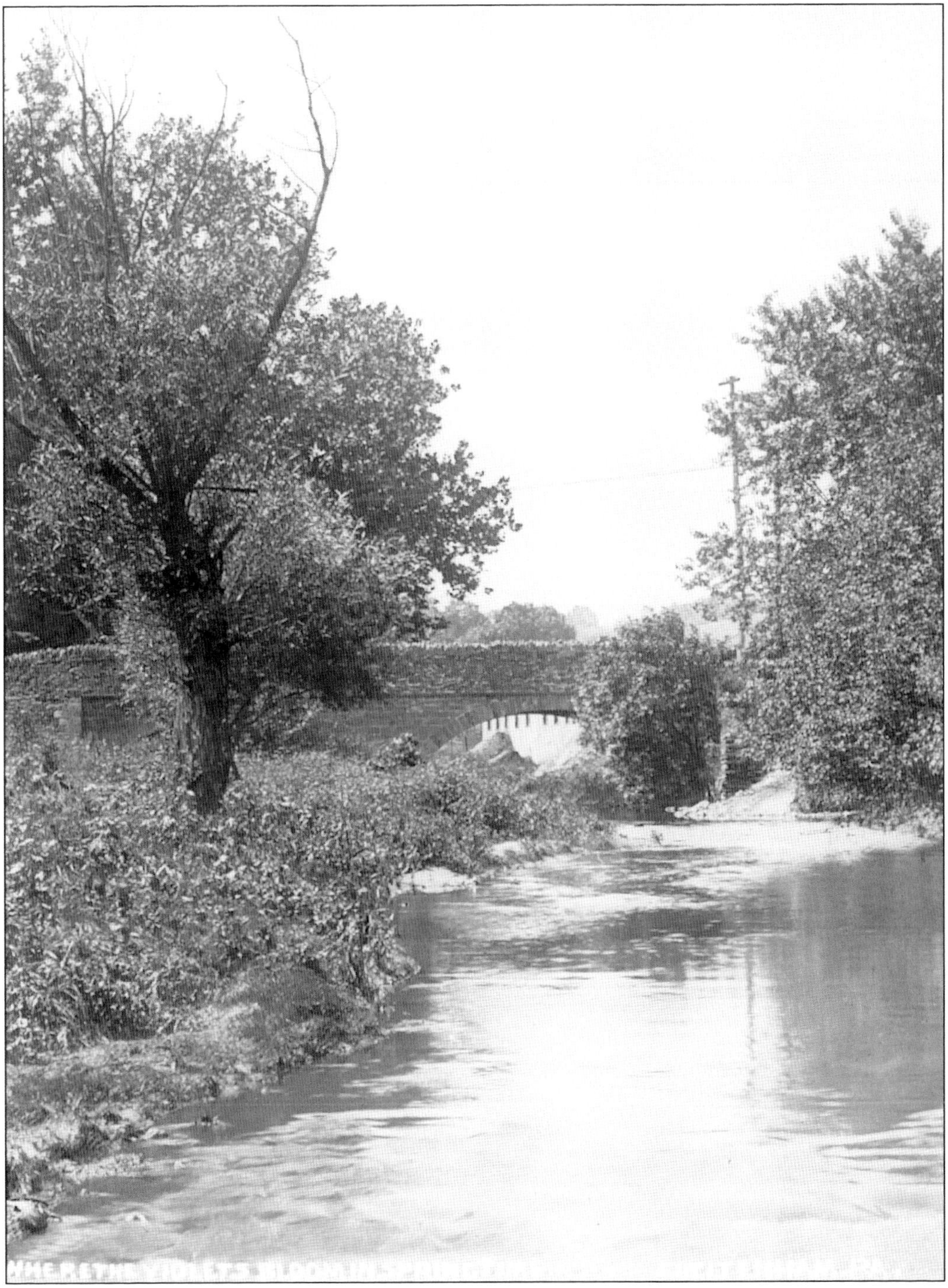

WHERE VIOLETS BLOOM IN SPRINGTIME, CHELTENHAM. From the time the first Europeans arrived in Pennsylvania, Tacony (or Tookany) Creek has supplied power for many mills, and in part, helped settle the Cheltenham area. This view shows one of the many old stone arch bridges that crossed the stream. Fortunately, much of this attractive area is preserved in Tookany Creek Park today. (Sliker postcard.)

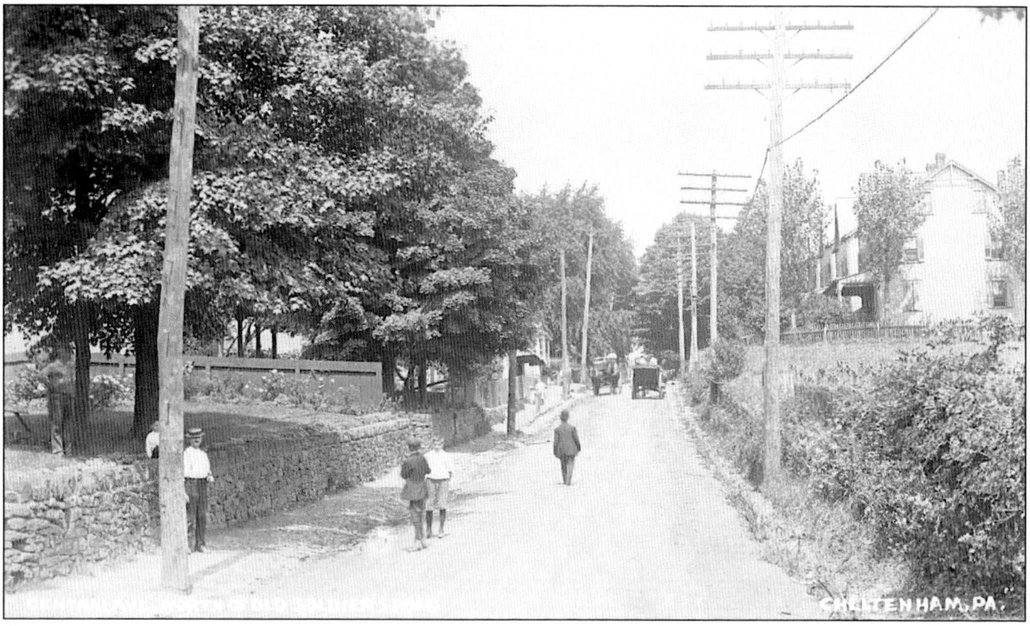

CENTRAL AVENUE, NORTH OF OLD SOLDIERS ROAD IN CHELTENHAM. This postcard, mailed in 1910, shows a busy scene along Central Avenue in Cheltenham Village. Many old homes in the village survive today. (Sliker postcard.)

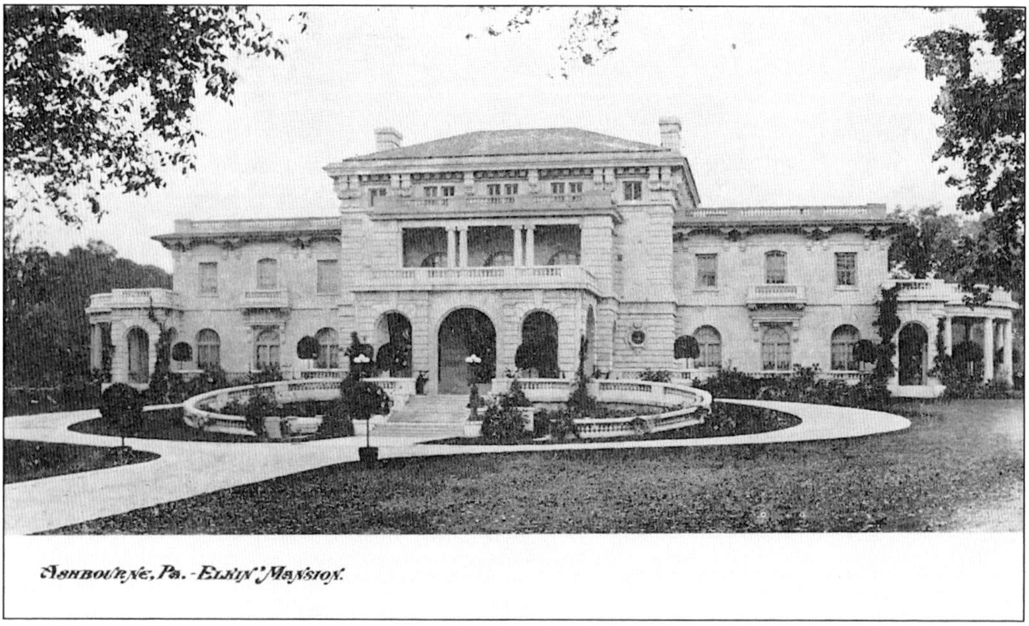

THE ELKINS MANSION IN ASHBOURNE. The home of William L. Elkins, who owned traction companies, built Elstowe Manor. Its style was influenced by the architecture of Italian villas. Erected in 1899 and still standing on Ashbourne Road near Lynnewood Hall, it is presently a retreat for a Dominican Order Convent. Elkins, in his lifetime, helped finance many projects in Cheltenham, including a railroad station. The area would later adopt his name and become Elkins Park. (World Post Card Company postcard.)

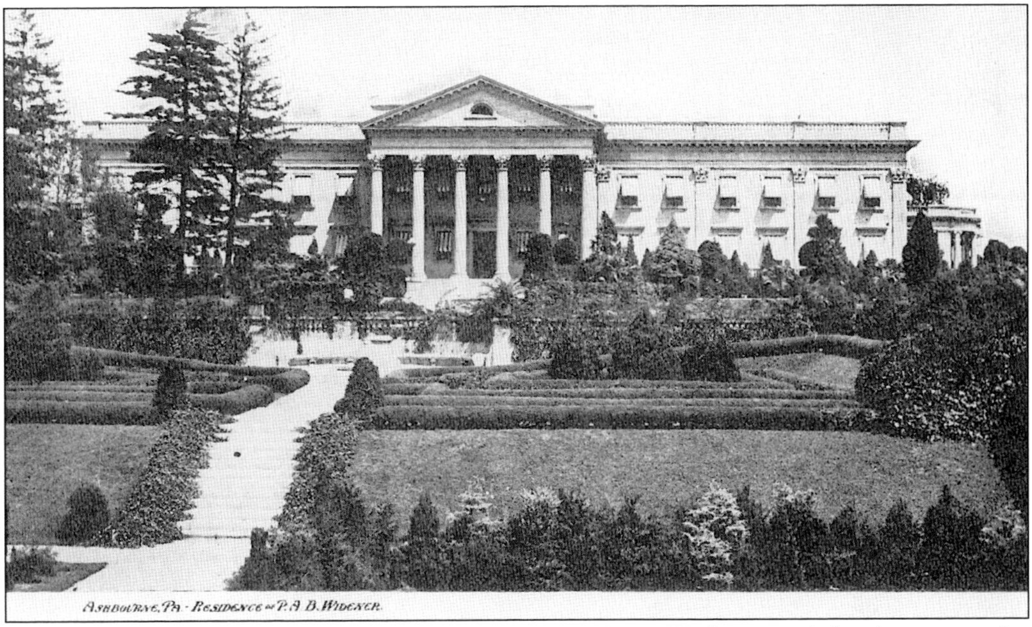

The Residence of P.A.B. Widener in Ashbourne. Peter Widener made his fortunes in the late 1800s and early 1900s in railroads in the East and Midwest, and in the Philadelphia rail system. He, along with other entrepreneurs, represented the new wealth from the Industrial Revolution. In 1908, Lynnewood Hall, shown above, was completed at a staggering cost of $8 million. Modeled after the palace of Versailles in France, it contains over 100 rooms. At one point, it contained the finest private art collection known to exist. The mansion and lavish grounds were sold to a seminary in 1952. (World Post Card Company postcard.)

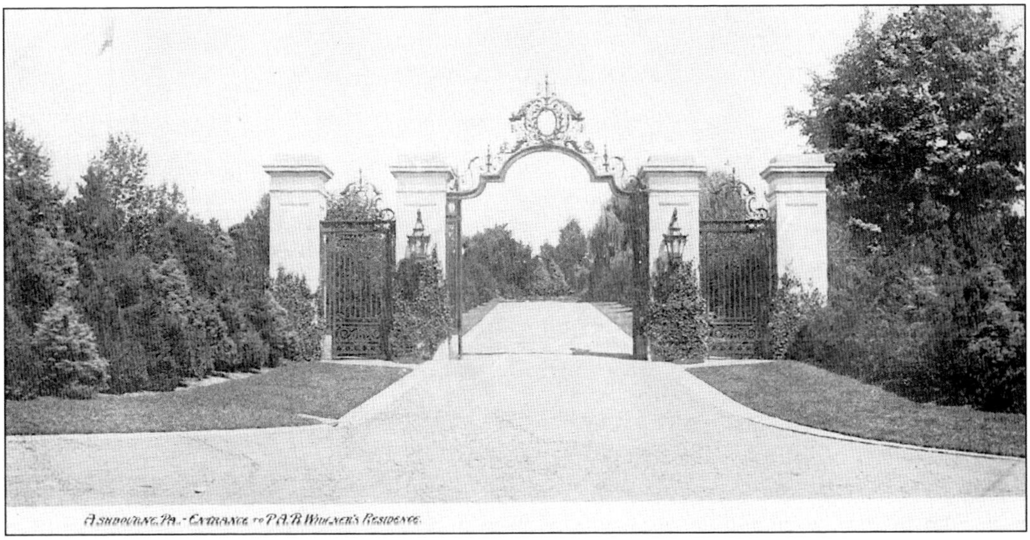

The Entrance to the P.A.B. Widener Residence in Ashbourne. This view illustrates the beautiful entrance and grounds on Ashbourne Road. Though still standing, the Philadelphia region's most elaborate and expensive estate has in recent years been stripped of its priceless interiors and is a mere shell of its former self. The grounds and gardens have also suffered badly. Still, it is today an impressive site in size and grandeur. (World Post Card Company postcard.)

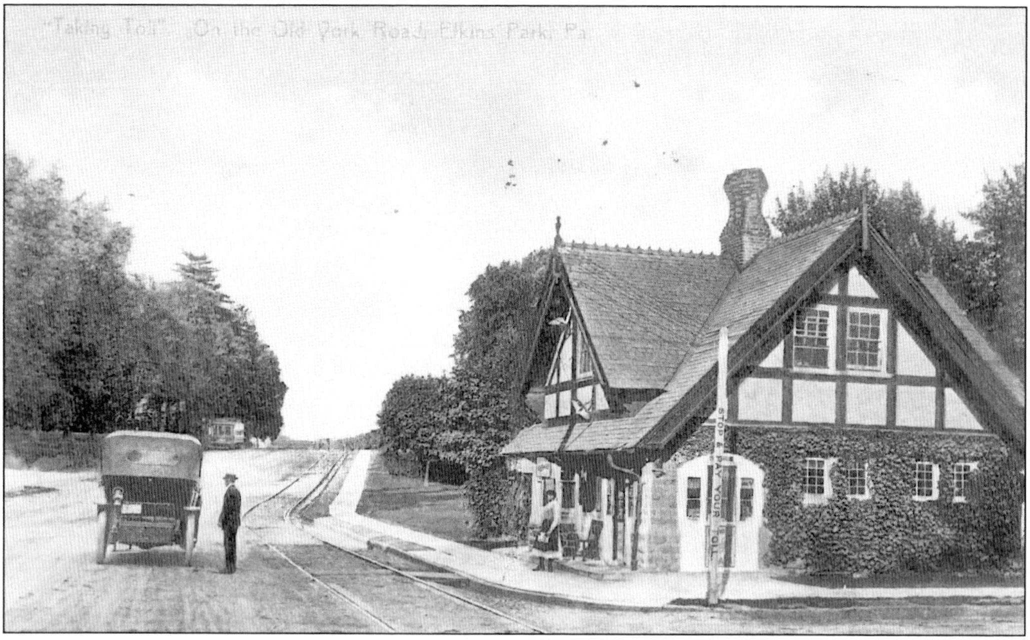

TAKING A TOLL ON OLD YORK ROAD IN ELKINS PARK. This postcard by Philip Moore shows a tollgate in Elkins Park on the northeast corner of Old York Road and Spring Avenue. The building is no longer standing.

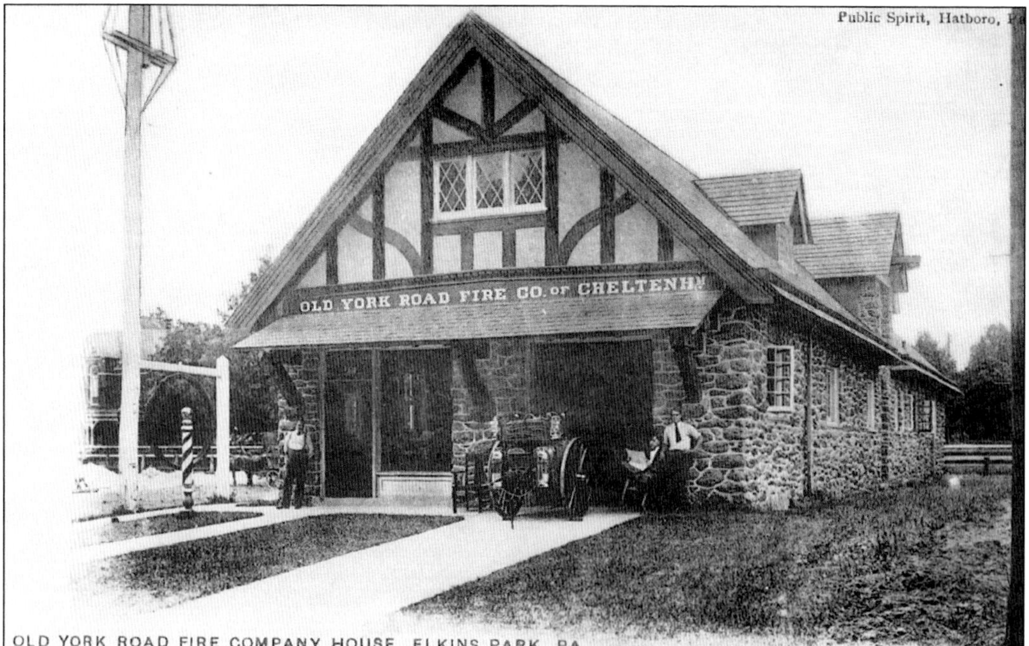

THE OLD YORK ROAD FIRE COMPANY HOUSE IN ELKINS PARK. Oddly, the Old York Road Fire Company is not located on Old York Road, but is found on Montgomery Avenue in Elkins Park. In 1926, the name was changed to the Elkins Park Fire Company. This building, altered and enlarged through the years to accommodate larger fire trucks, still serves the local community. (Postcard published by the *Public Spirit of Hatboro.*)

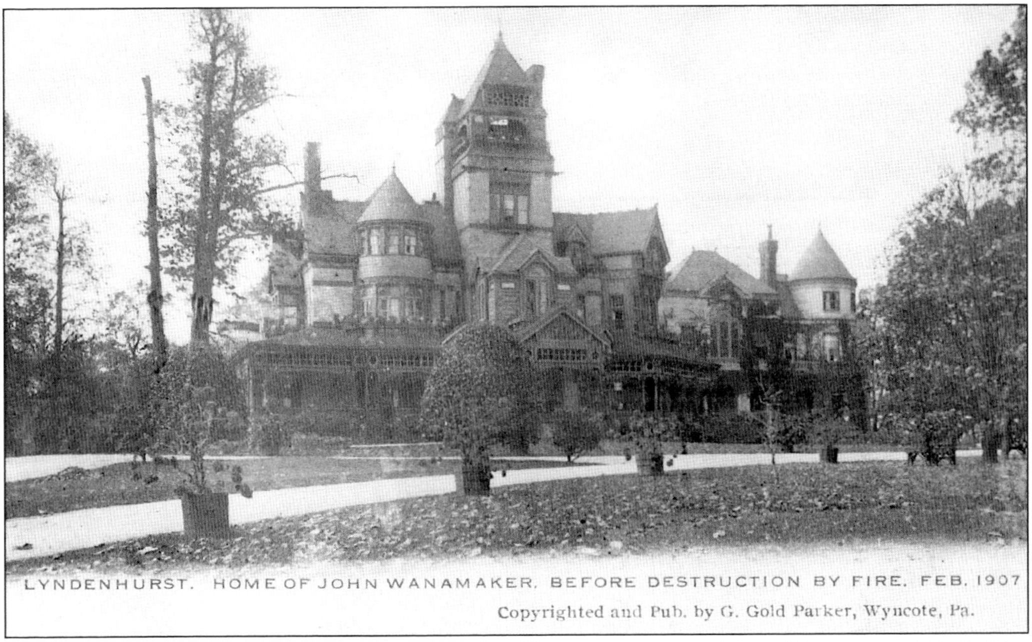

THE HOME OF JOHN WANAMAKER BEFORE ITS DESTRUCTION BY FIRE, FEBRUARY 1907. The Cheltenham and Jenkintown areas became home to the newly rich merchants and industrialists of the 19th century. John Wanamaker, the pioneer department store founder, built a lavish home with beautiful gardens and contained a priceless art collection. On February 16, 1907, the house was destroyed by fire, as noted on the postcard by G. Gold Parker of Wyncote.

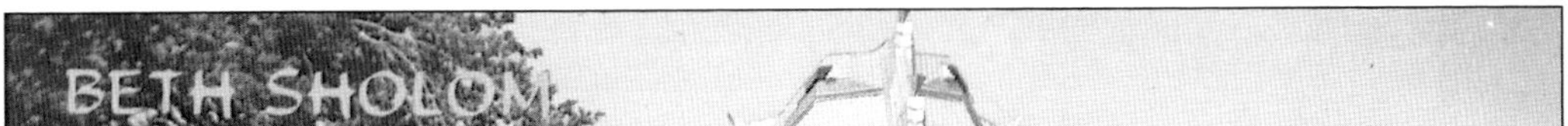

BETH SHOLOM. The Beth Sholom Synagogue was founded in 1909 in the Logan section of North Philadelphia. It moved in the 1950s into this building on Old York Road in Elkins Park. It was dedicated in the fall of 1959. Designed by world-renowned architect Frank Lloyd Wright, it is his only synagogue and is considered to be a masterpiece, different from anything else he built.

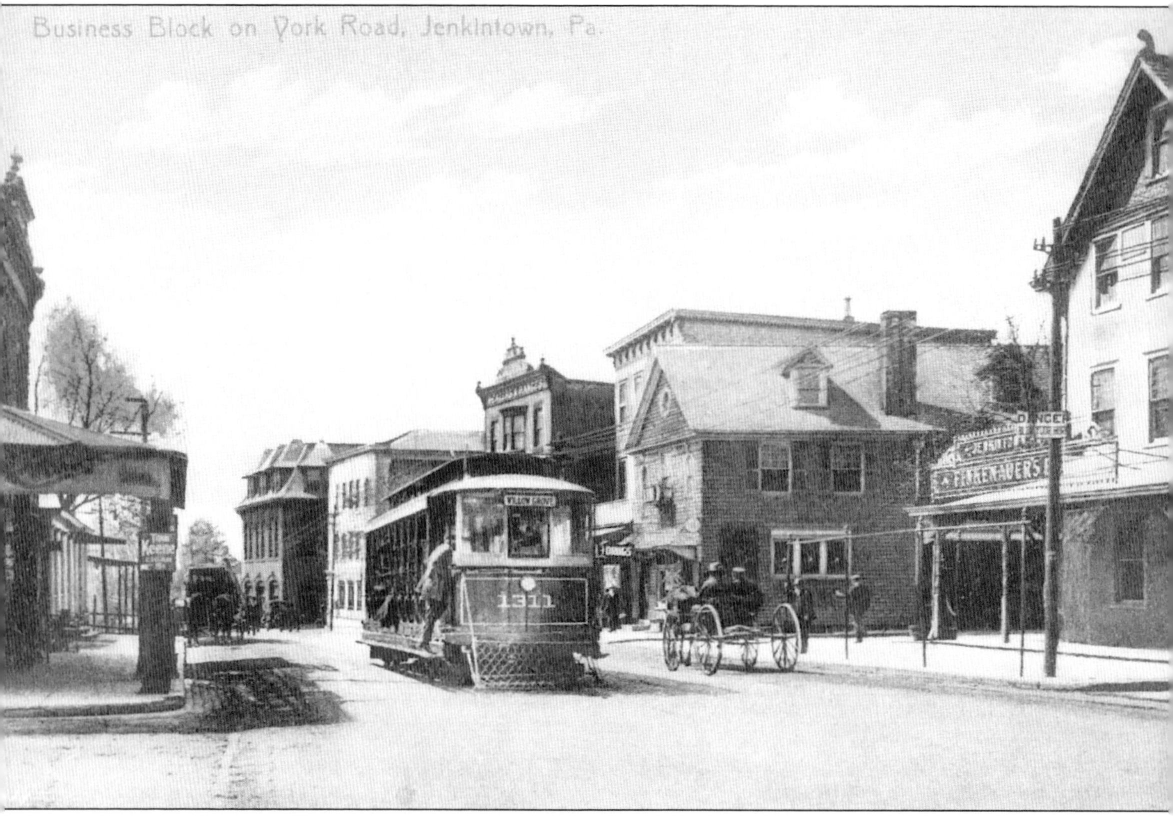

THE BUSINESS BLOCK ON OLD YORK ROAD IN JENKINTOWN. This Philip Moore postcard shows a wonderful view of the center of Jenkintown Borough. That is the Willow Grove Trolley heading north on Old York Road c. 1910. Trolleys ran on Old York Road from 1895 to 1940.

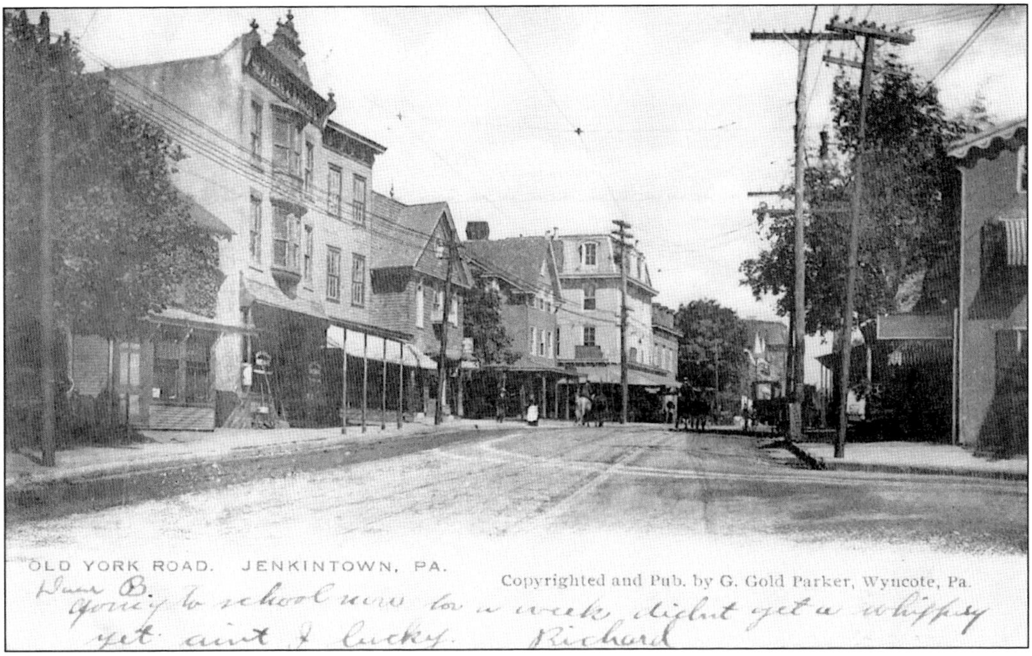

OLD YORK ROAD IN JENKINTOWN. A much quieter and simpler pace is shown in this 1905 view of Old York Road in the center of Jenkintown looking north. (Parker postcard.)

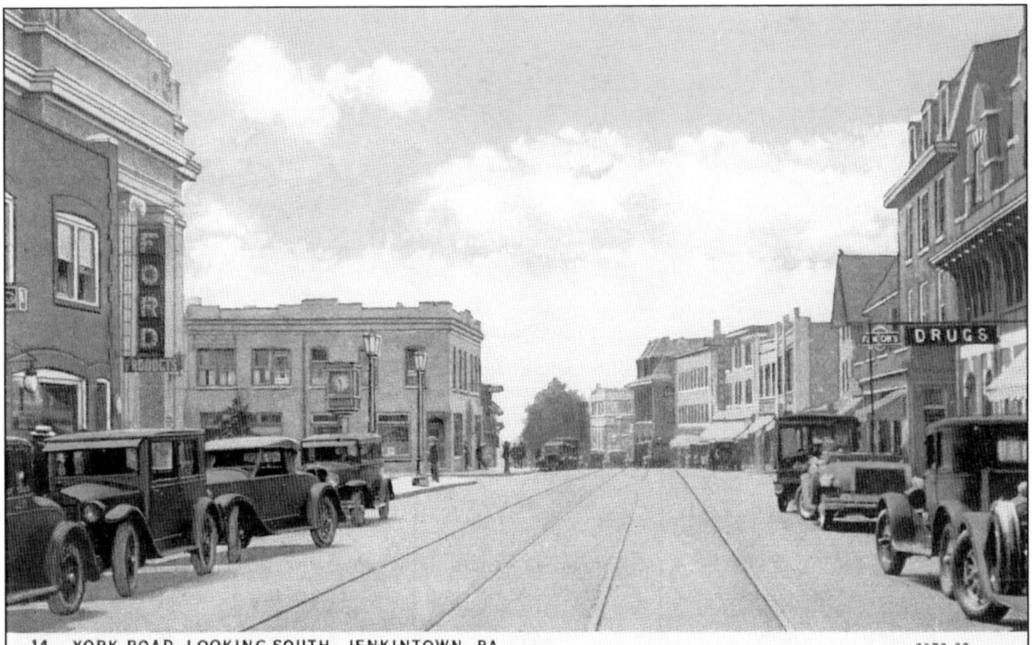

YORK ROAD, LOOKING SOUTH. This 1920s view shows the center of Jenkintown on York Road. This decade saw vast changes with some older buildings being replaced by new commercial ones.

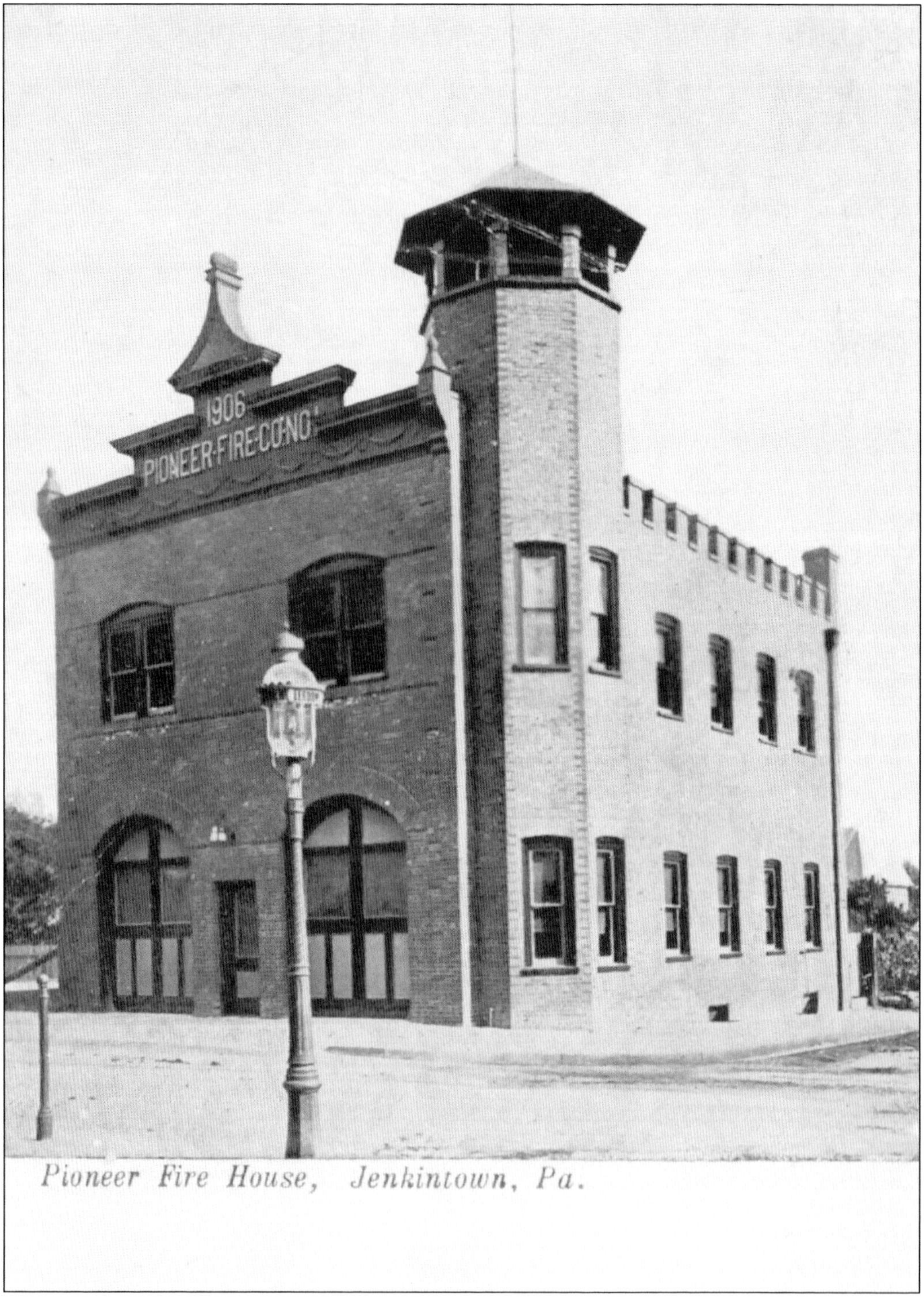

THE PIONEER FIREHOUSE IN JENKINTOWN, C. 1910. The Pioneer Fire Company, located at Greenwood and Leedom Avenues, was founded in 1884. Built in 1906, it still stands today, though its appearance has been modernized.

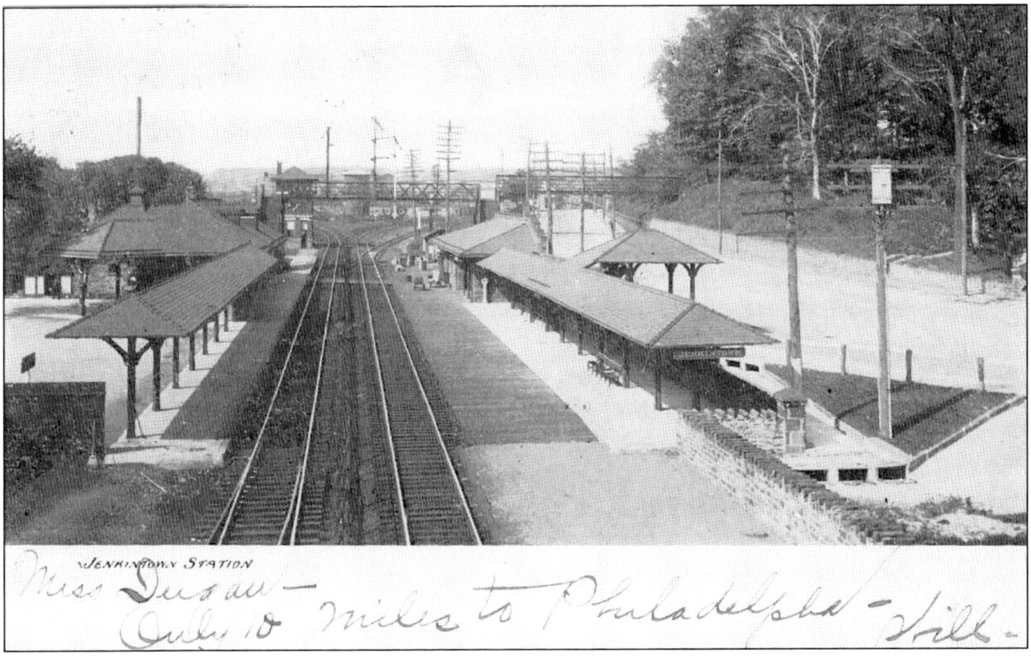

JENKINTOWN STATION. This view is taken from atop the Greenwood Avenue bridge looking west. Compared to other stations in the area, Jenkintown, built in 1872, appears to be one of the largest. Today, it is one of the busiest in the suburbs and also contains a popular restaurant. (World Post Card Company postcard.)

THE ABINGTON LIBRARY IN JENKINTOWN. The Abington Library dates back to 1803. After moving to many locations, it moved to this building, The Lyceum, in 1909, and still occupies it today. The Jenkintown Lyceum building was built on York Road in 1839. (Moore postcard, mailed in 1911.)

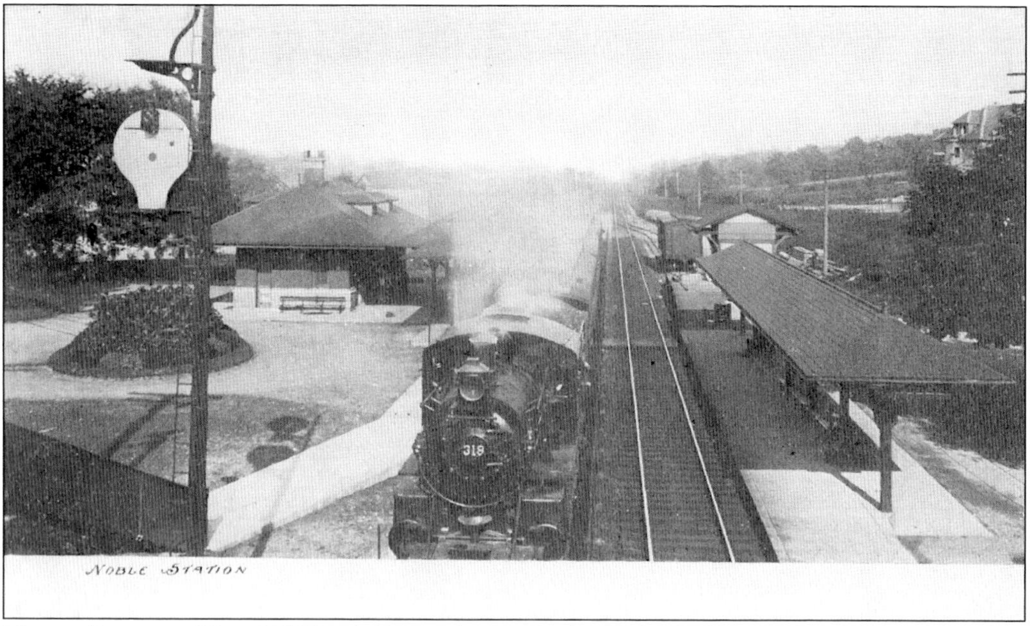

NOBLE STATION. The Old North Pennsylvania Railroad, later the Reading Railroad, crossed Old York Road immediately north of Jenkintown in what is called Noble. Noble Station, named after Samuel Noble's estate, was built in 1873. The view shows an inbound train to Philadelphia, looking east from atop the Old York Road overpass. The station is still in use. (World Post Card Company postcard.)

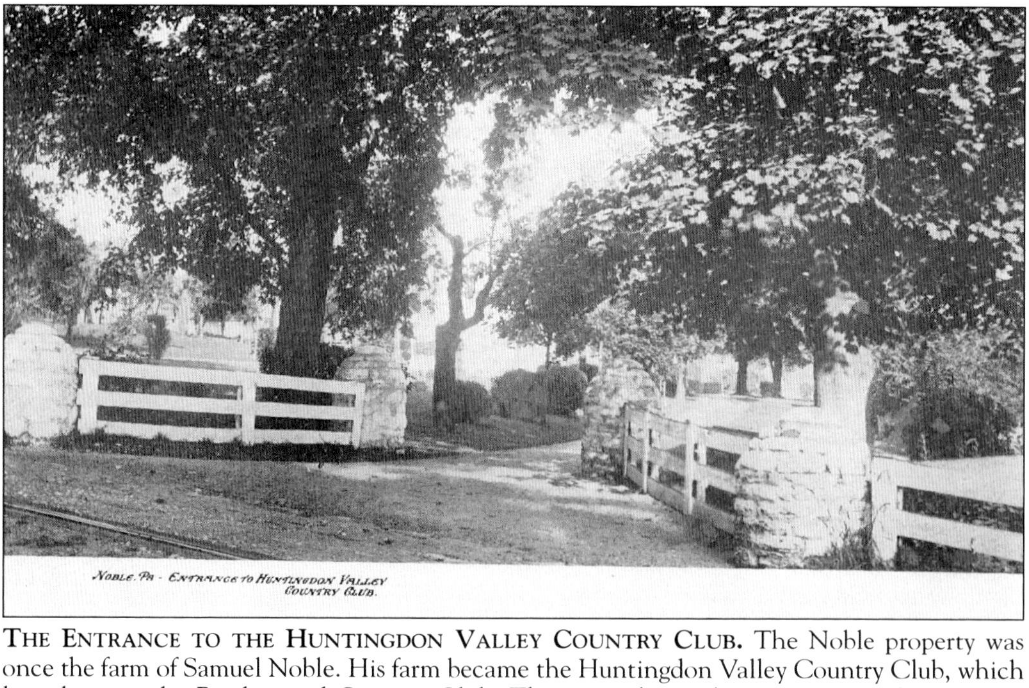

THE ENTRANCE TO THE HUNTINGDON VALLEY COUNTRY CLUB. The Noble property was once the farm of Samuel Noble. His farm became the Huntingdon Valley Country Club, which later became the Baederwood Country Club. This view shows the entrance to the property along the east side of York Road where, for years, the John Wanamaker Store stood. Nothing remains of the country club today. (World Post Card Company postcard.)

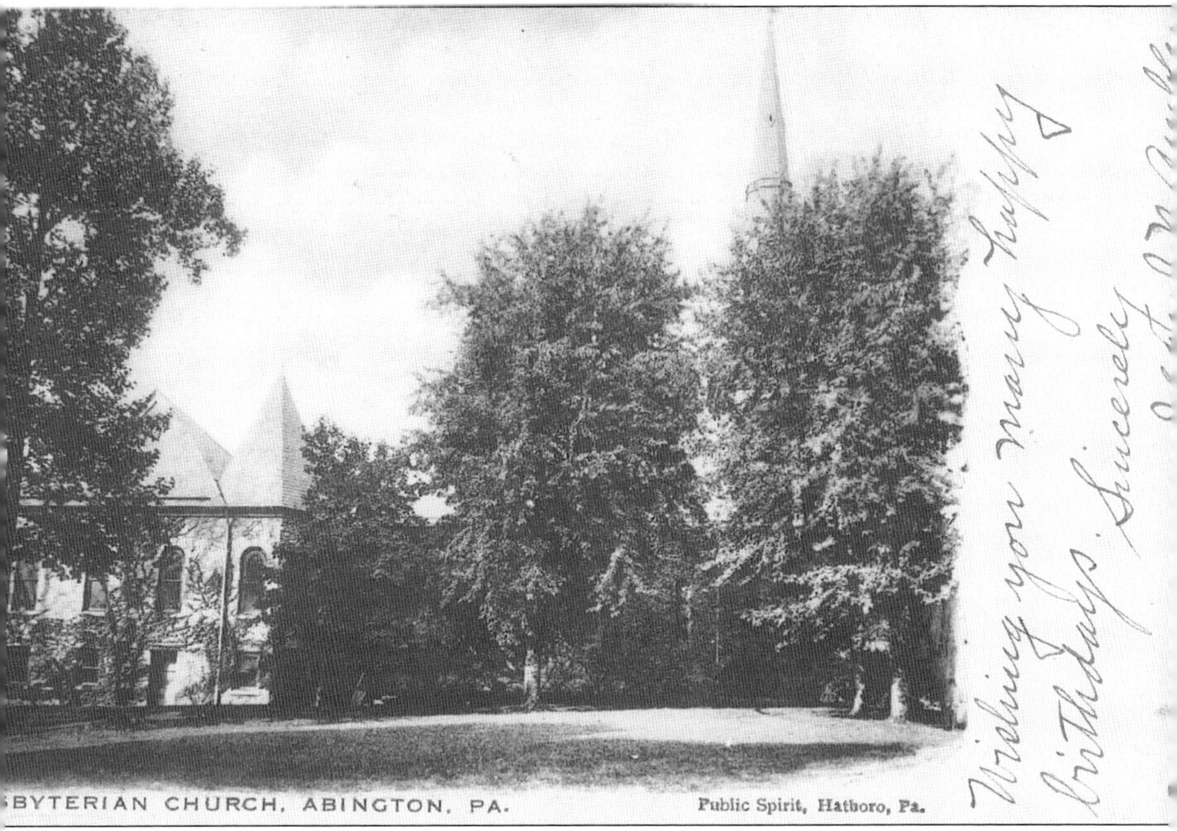

THE PRESBYTERIAN CHURCH IN ABINGTON. At the corner of Old York and Susquehanna Roads stands the Abington Presbyterian Church. Founded in 1714, its original building was completed in 1719. A stone church, built in 1793, was rebuilt and enlarged throughout the years. It was destroyed by fire in 1895 but was rebuilt the following year. Today, its tall steeple and old cemetery are landmarks along the Old York Road. (Postcard published by *The Public Spirit of Hatboro.*)

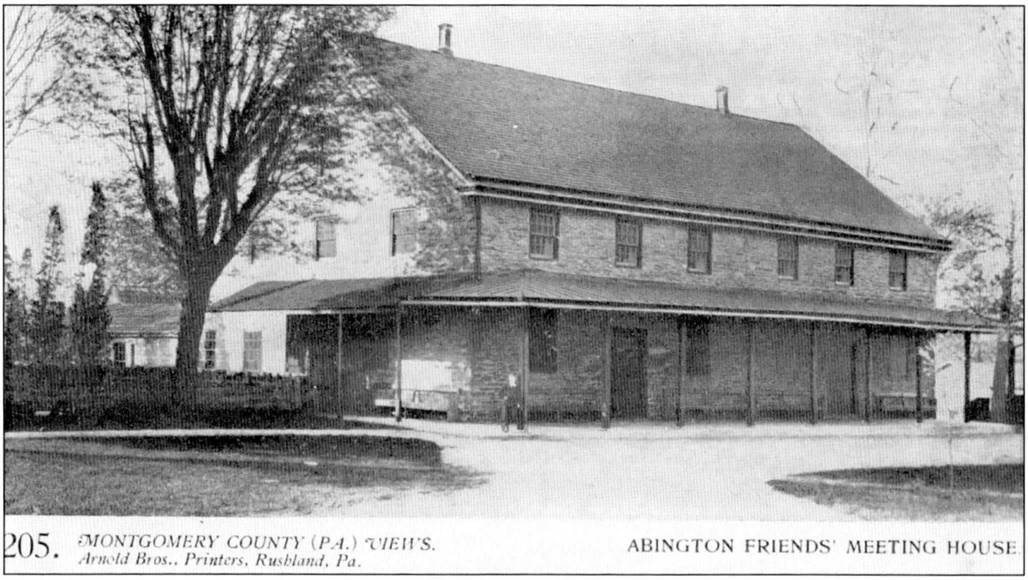

ABINGTON FRIENDS MEETINGHOUSE. Abington Quakers can trace their roots back to 1683. The meetinghouse was built in 1702, making it the oldest religious structure in the area. Additions and changes to the building along Meetinghouse Road have occurred throughout the years. Abington Quakers are still quite active and their private school is very well known. (Postcard published by the Arnold Brothers of Bucks County, one of only eight different views published by them for Montgomery County.)

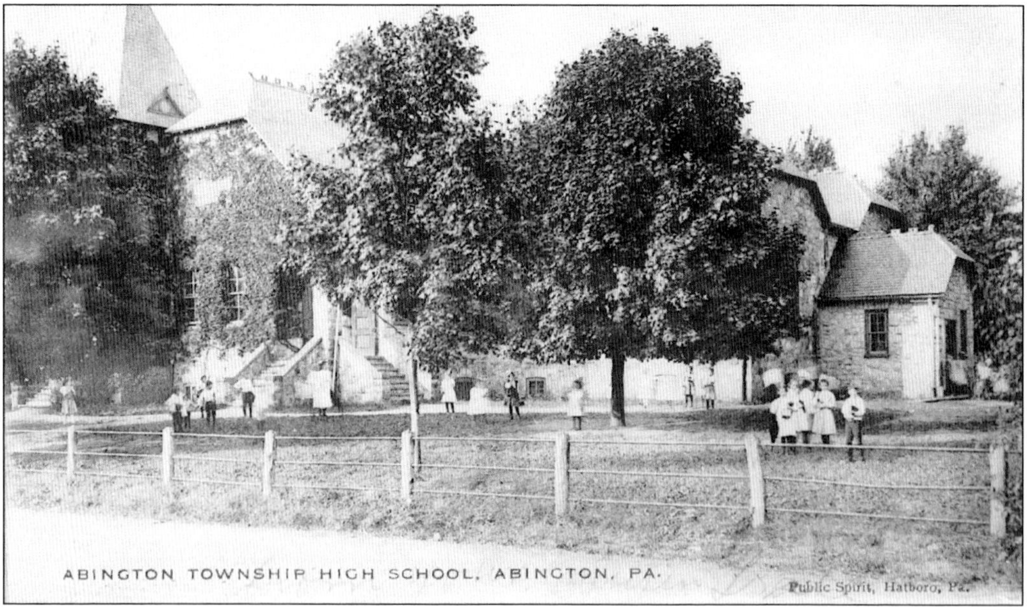

ABINGTON TOWNSHIP HIGH SCHOOL. The school was built in 1888 and is on Susquehanna Road, east of Old York Road. Later, when bigger schools were built, this building was used for township administrative offices. Originally, it contained only three rooms and combined elementary through high school curriculums. Although it has not been used as a school for many years, amazingly, the building is in perfect condition and is a good example of early schoolhouse architecture. (Postcard published by *The Public Spirit of Hatboro*.)

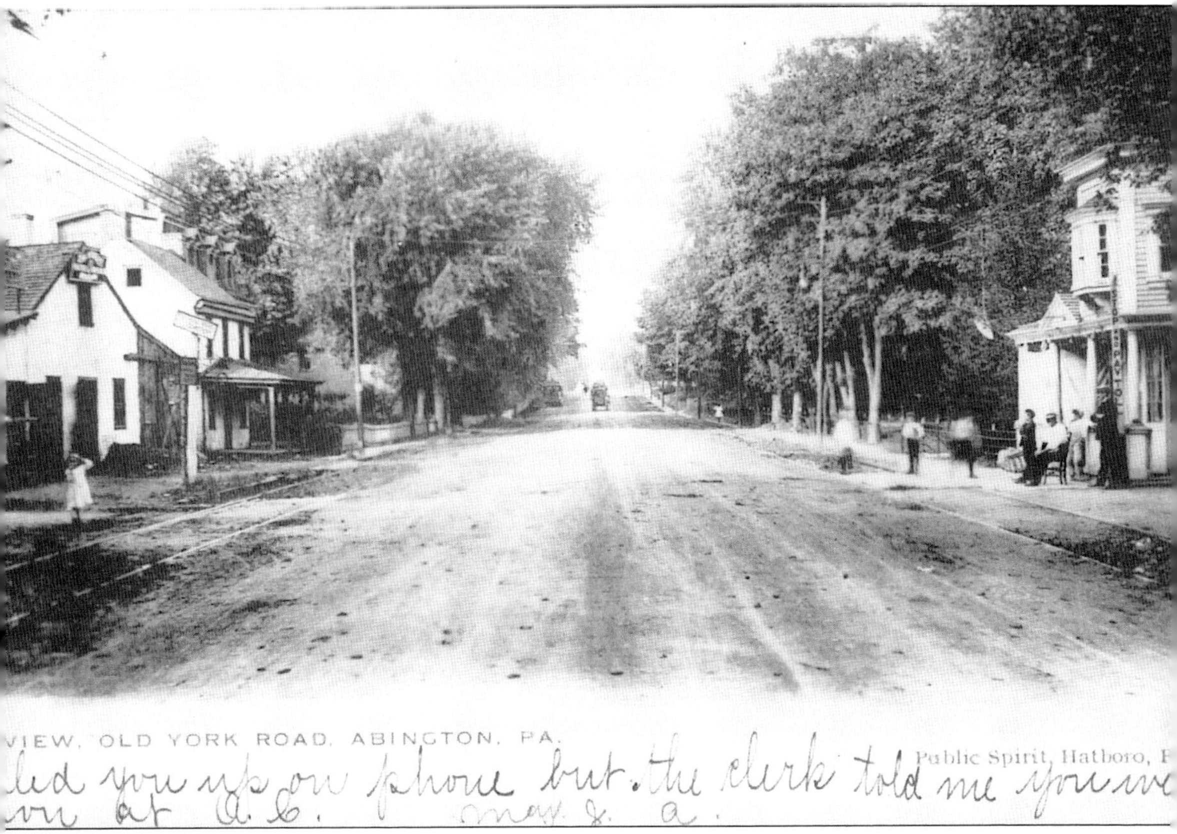

OLD YORK ROAD IN ABINGTON. This *Public Spirit of Hatboro* view shows Abington Village in 1906, looking north on York Road from Susquehanna Road. The tollhouse is on the right and trolley tracks line both sides of York Road.

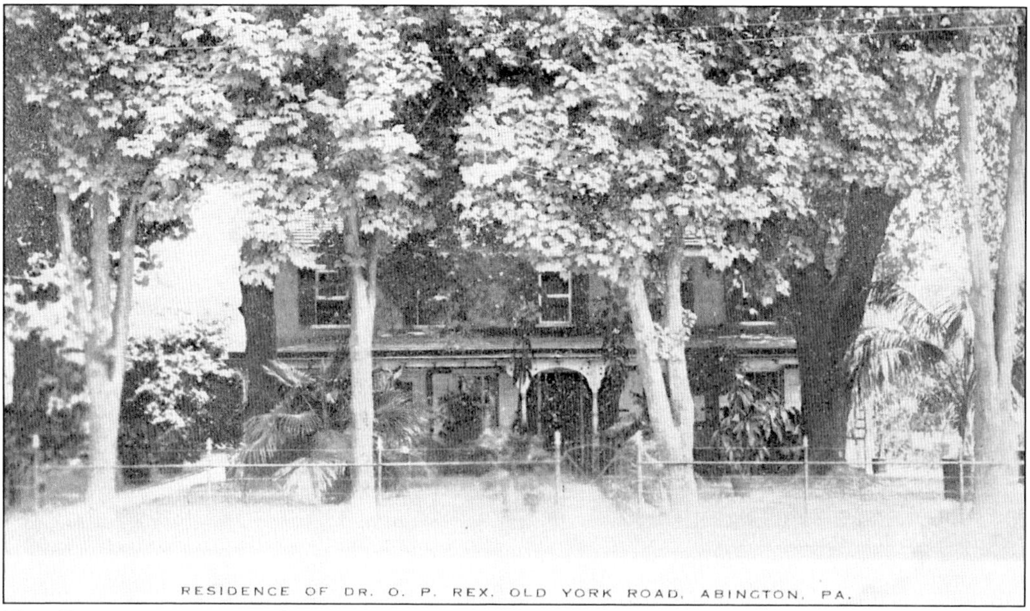

THE RESIDENCE OF DR. O.P. REX ON OLD YORK ROAD. The Rex house is typical of the old Colonial buildings that lined Old York Road throughout Montgomery County early in the 20th century. It stood north of Susquehanna Road in Abington Village and was deliberately burned down by the fire company years ago when the structure became unsafe. At one time this was a common practice in the demolition of old buildings. (Postcard published by *The Public Spirit of Hatboro.*)

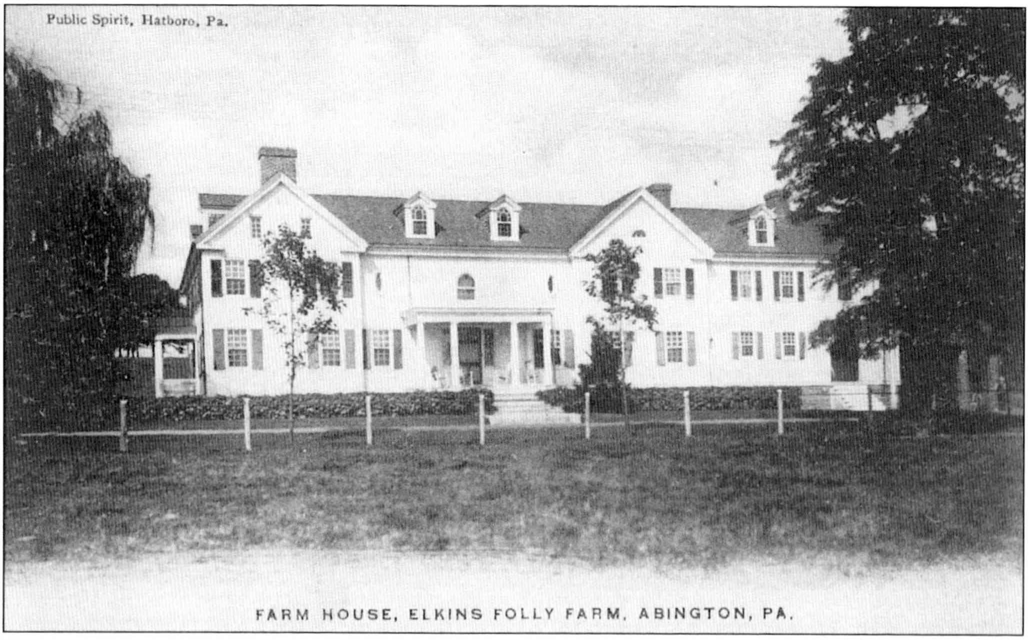

FARMHOUSE, ELKINS FOLLY FARM. Abington still had a few farms early in the 20th century as seen in this view of Folly Farms, then owned by George Elkins. The Atrium Mall/Abington Shopping Center on Old York Road now occupies this site. (Postcard published by *The Public Spirit of Hatboro.*)

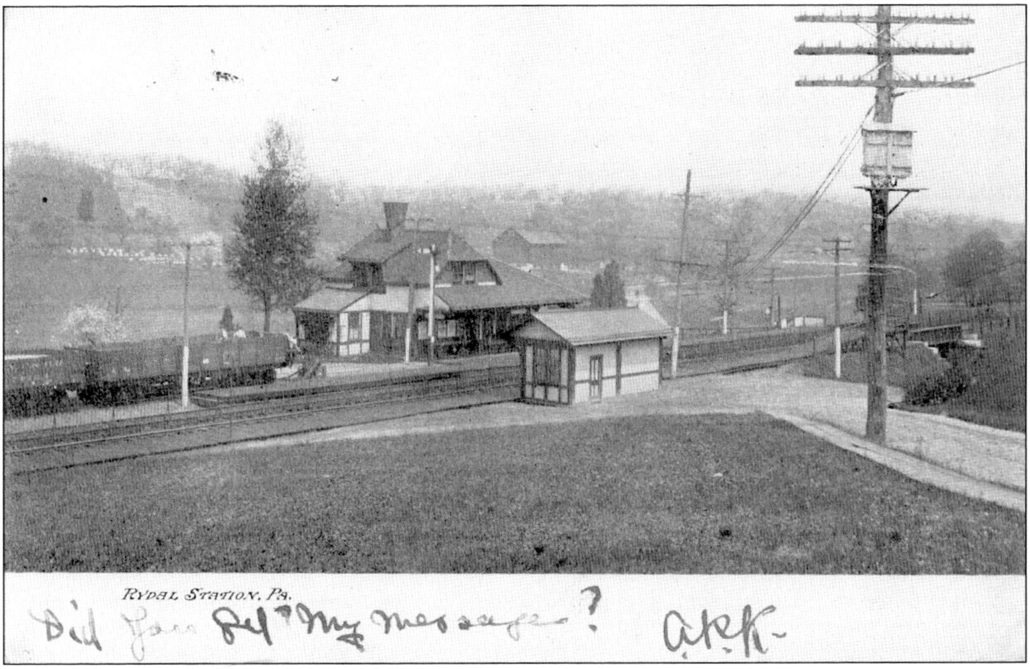

RYDAL STATION. Rydal Station was built in 1883 along Washington Lane near Susquehanna and Rydal Roads in Abington Township. It is still in use today. (World Post Card Company postcard.)

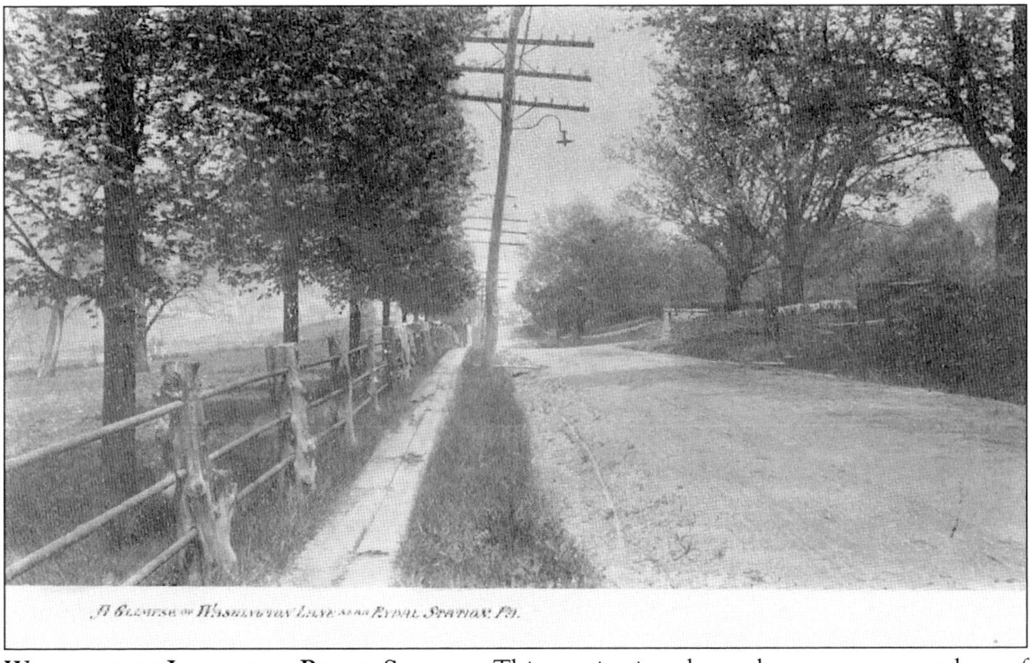

WASHINGTON LANE NEAR RYDAL STATION. This scenic view shows the country atmosphere of Washington Lane near Rydal Station c. 1908. In Colonial times, Washington Lane was known as Abington Road; it began at Germantown and extended into Abington Township. (World Post Card Company postcard.)

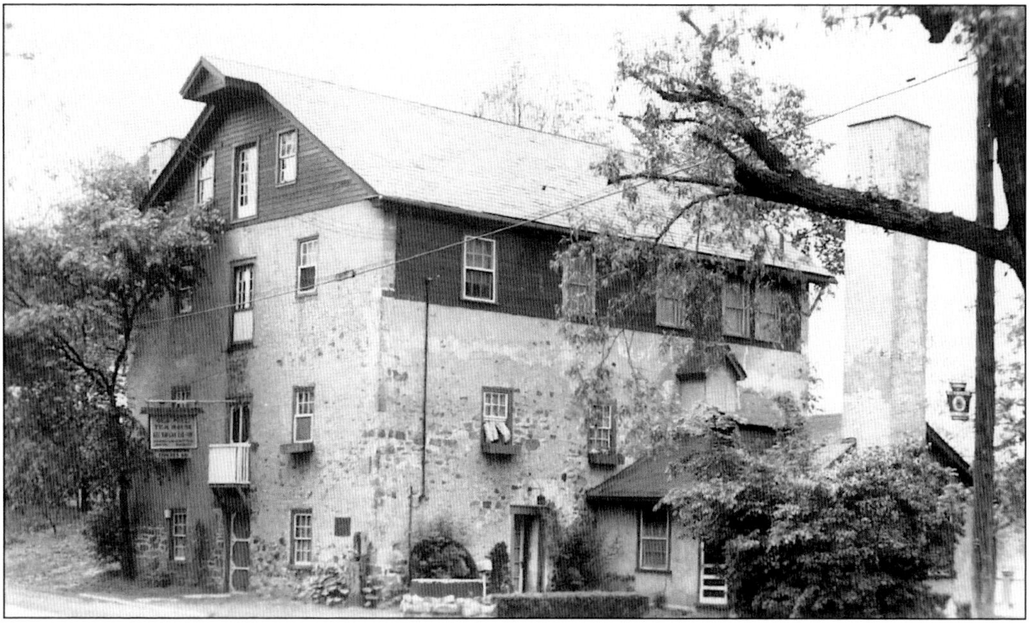

THE OLD MILL IN HATBORO. This building was originally built in 1724 by Emanuel Dungworth as a gristmill on Pennypack Creek at the corner of York and Horsham Roads in Hatboro. The mill ceased to operate *c.* 1910, and when the picture was taken *c.* 1950, it was the Old Mill Tea House. Today, it is the Old Mill Inn, and it still retains its Colonial appearance.

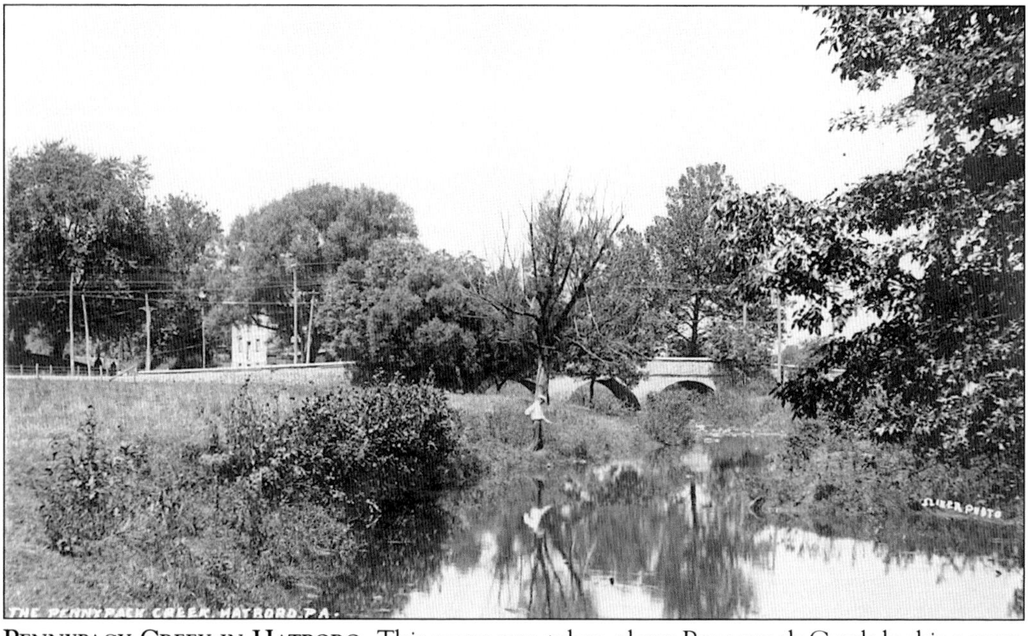

PENNYPACK CREEK IN HATBORO. This scene was taken along Pennypack Creek looking west. The old stone arch bridge is York Road and has since been replaced. In the middle left is the old mill at the corner of Horsham Road. (Sliker postcard.)

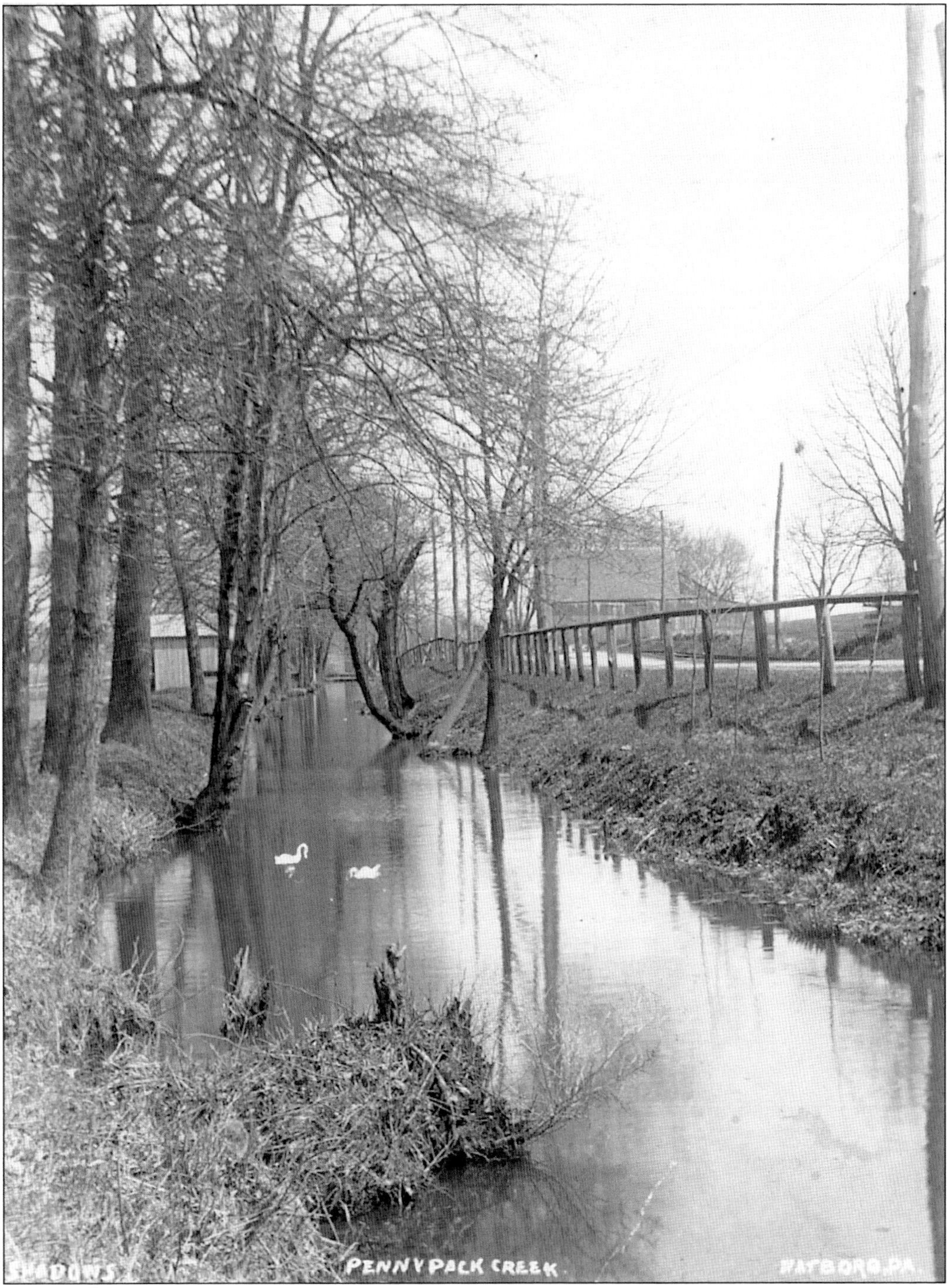

SHADOWS, PENNYPACK CREEK. William Sliker incorrectly labeled this waterway Pennypack Creek. It is actually the millrace, or a diversion of the Pennypack, which helped to power Dungworth's Mill. The photo was taken looking east and the cartway to the right is Horsham Road as it approaches York Road. Pennypack Creek is 100 yards to the left of this scene. The mill race at this location no longer exists.

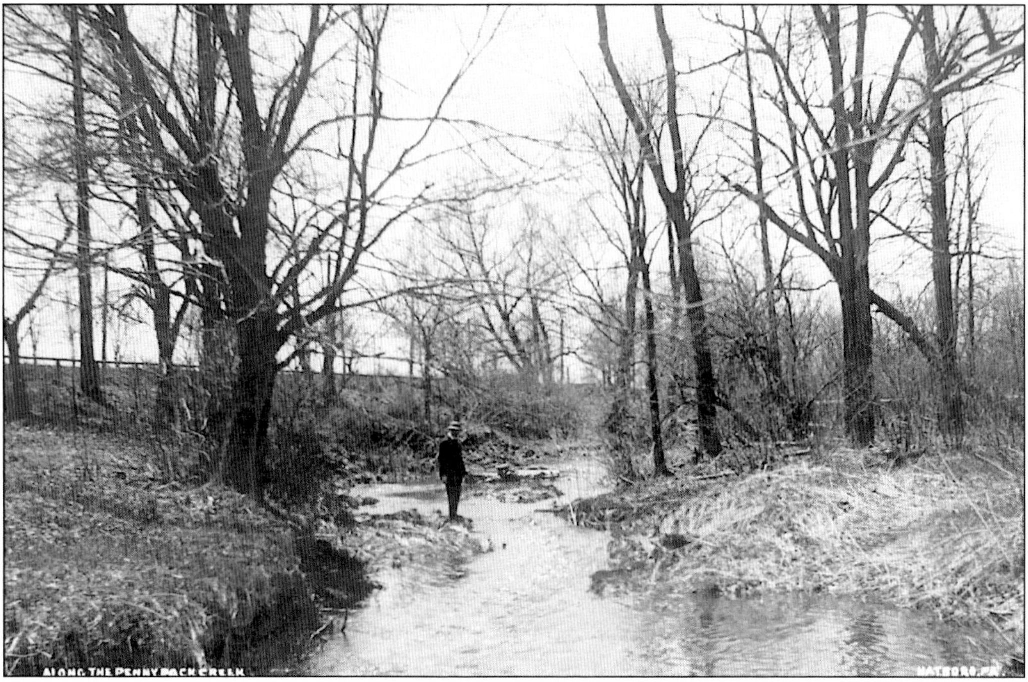

ALONG THE PENNYPACK. This is Pennypack Creek in Hatboro west of Old York Road. The fence at the top of the hill is along Horsham Road. (Sliker postcard.)

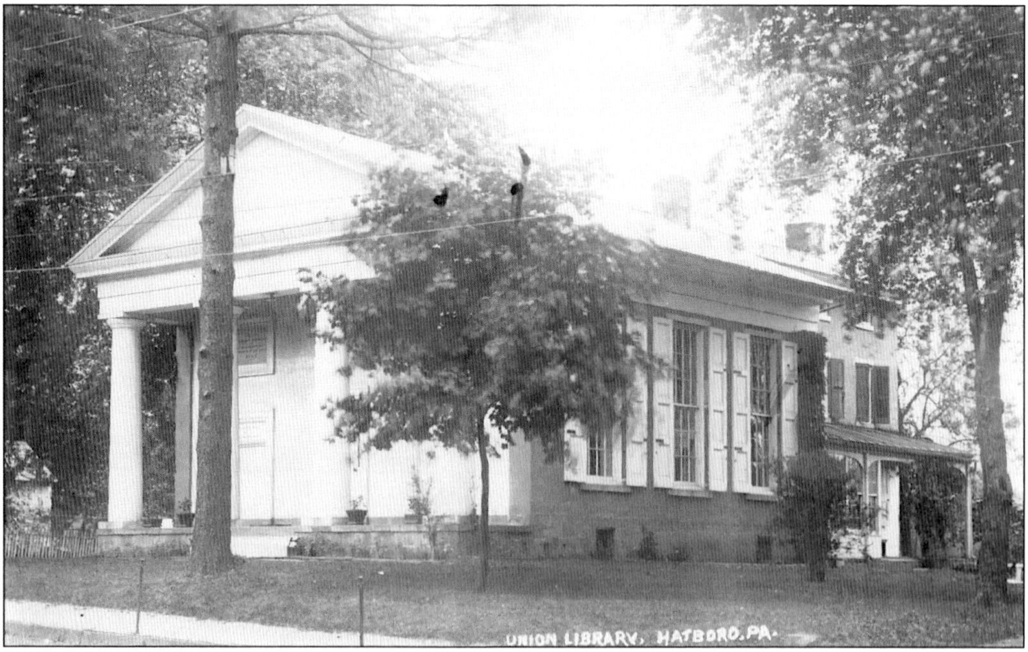

THE UNION LIBRARY IN HATBORO. The Union Library Company of Hatboro was founded in 1755, making it one of the oldest institutions of its kind in the state. After having several homes, this Greek Revival-style building was built and still serves the community today. Located on York Road, it remains virtually unchanged since this William Sliker postcard was made *c.* 1910.

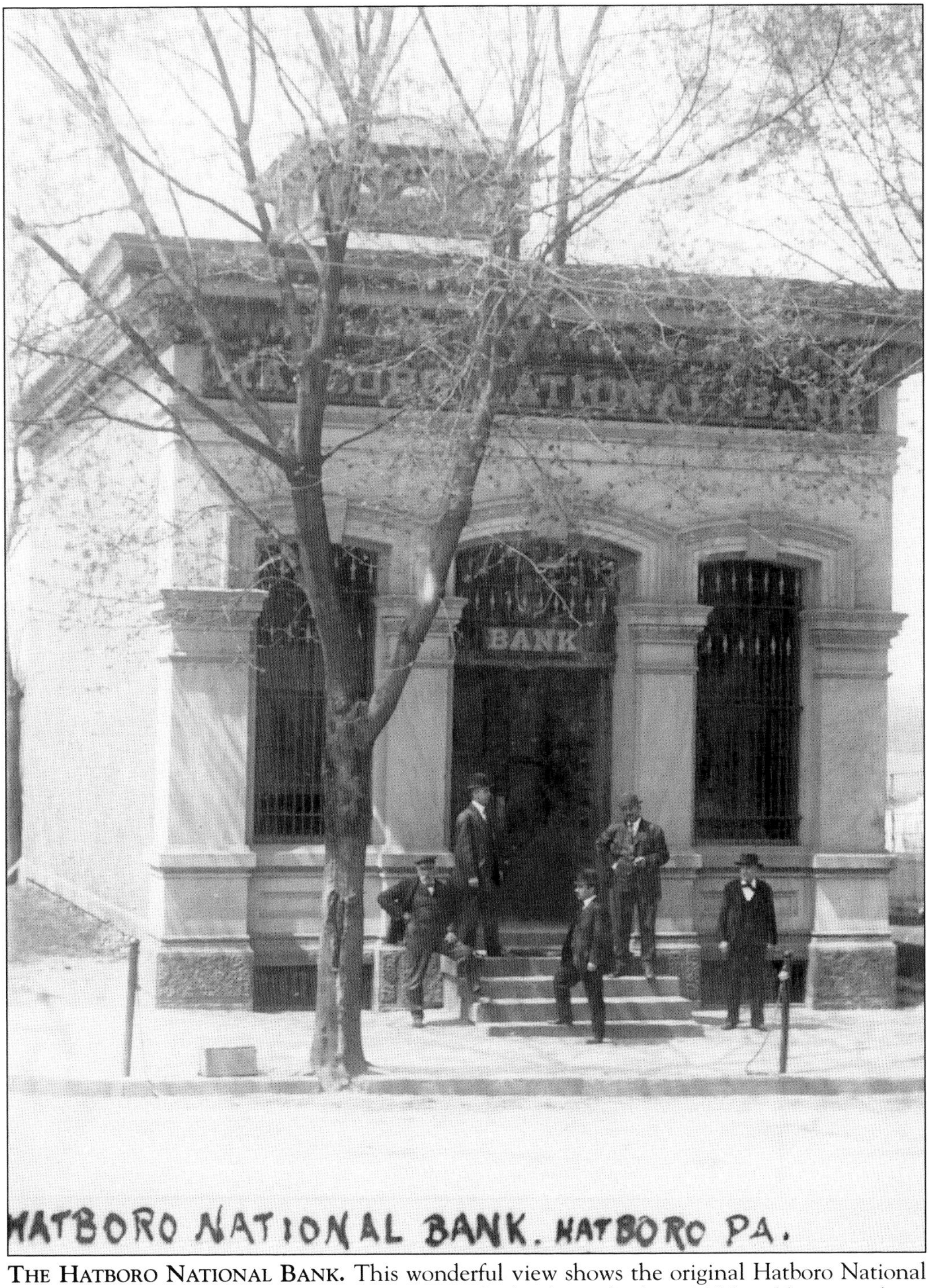

THE HATBORO NATIONAL BANK. This wonderful view shows the original Hatboro National Bank on York Road opposite Byberry Avenue. The bank was built in 1875 and has since been enlarged. It still stands today, though the Hatboro National Bank is no longer in business; another bank now operates in this building. Notice the bankers or businessmen shown in this view. (Sliker postcard.)

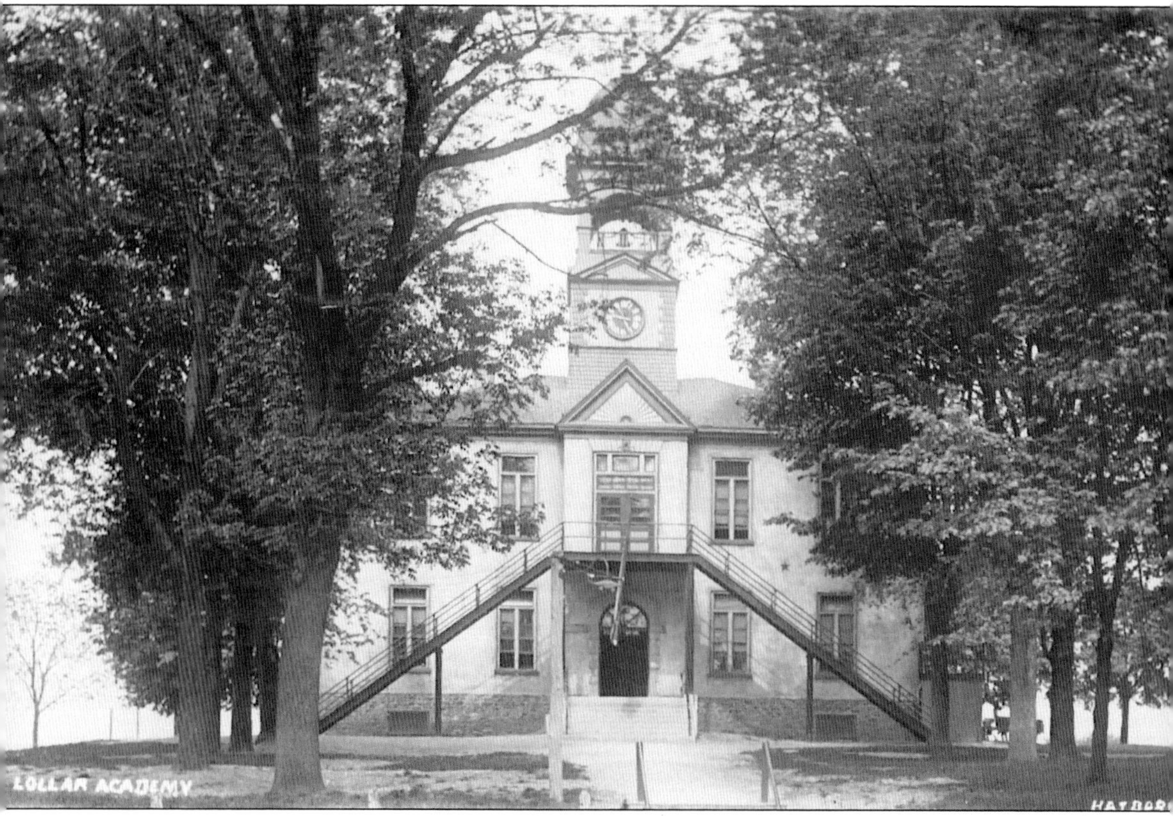

LOLLER ACADEMY IN HATBORO. Founded in 1811 by Colonel Robert Loller as a private school, its striking architecture has been a landmark on York Road for many years. Of particular interest is the fine bell tower and clock. The building has changed very little; it served for a time as a public school, and is now the Hatboro Borough Hall. (Sliker postcard.)

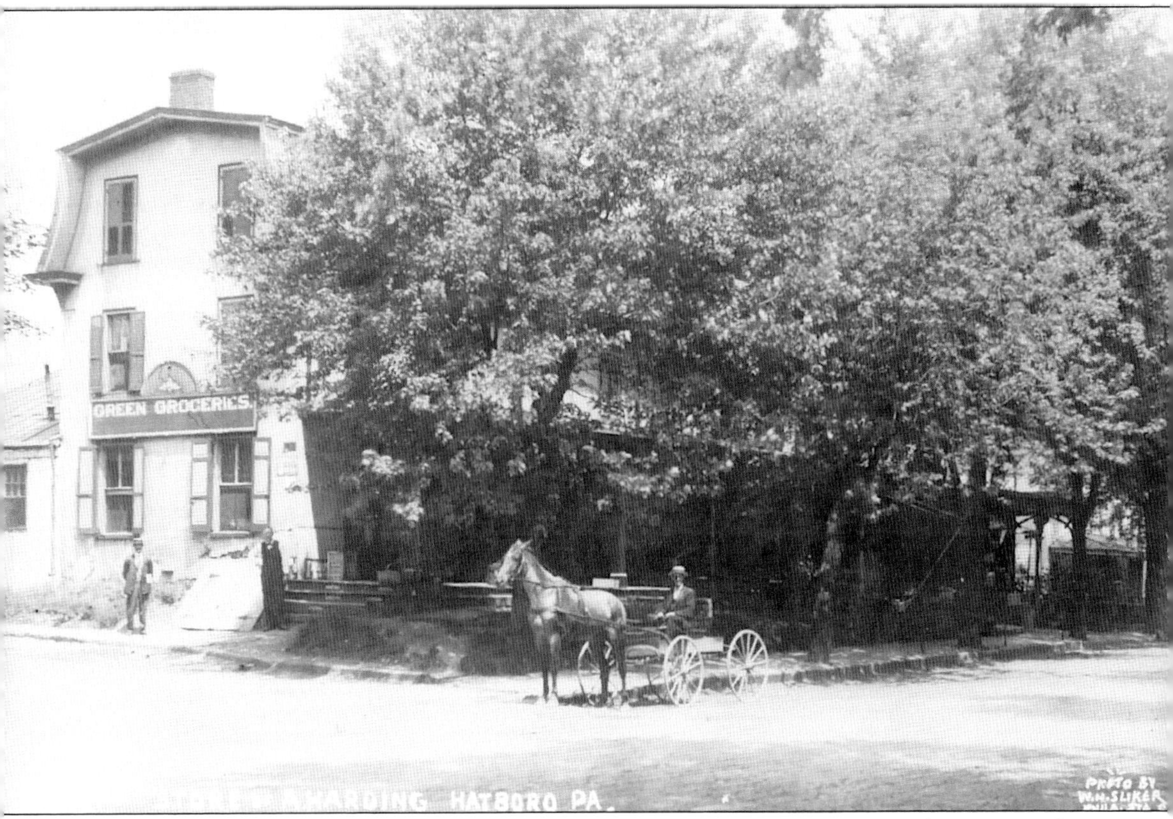

The Store of A. Harding in Hatboro. Stores, in many respects, represent the center of activity in a small town. This view shows a building constructed *c.* 1801 at the northwest corner of York Road and Moreland Avenue. It was first used as a house; in 1806 it became a general store, and after many additions, it was known as the Fisher Building. When this William Sliker view was taken it was the store of A. Harding. It is no longer standing.

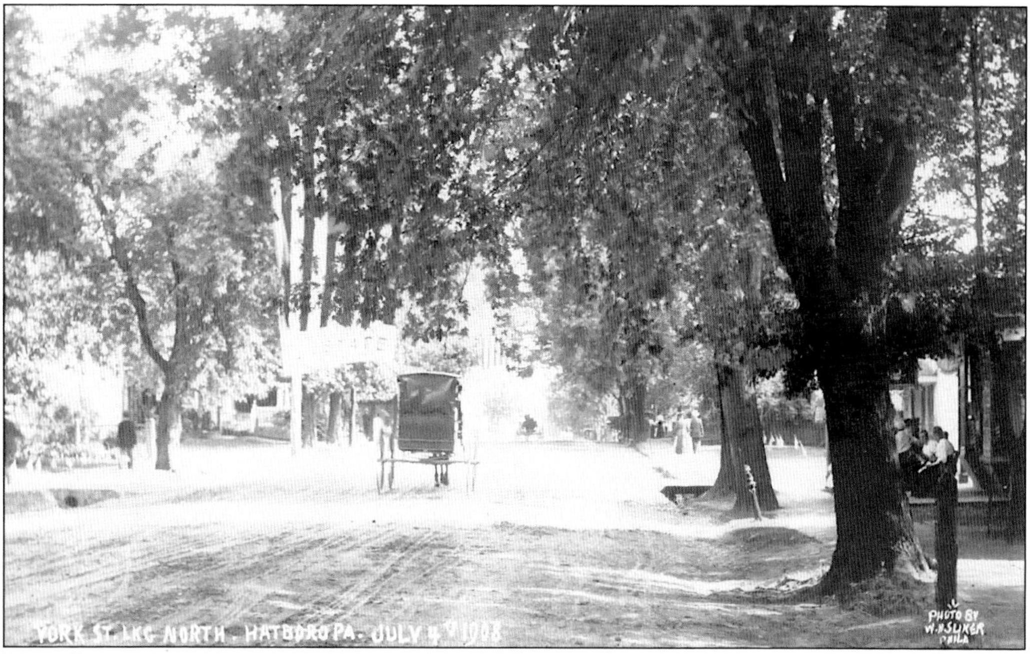

YORK ROAD, LOOKING NORTH. Here Sliker shows a view looking north on July 4, 1908. Notice the large flags above York Road indicating a parade was to occur.

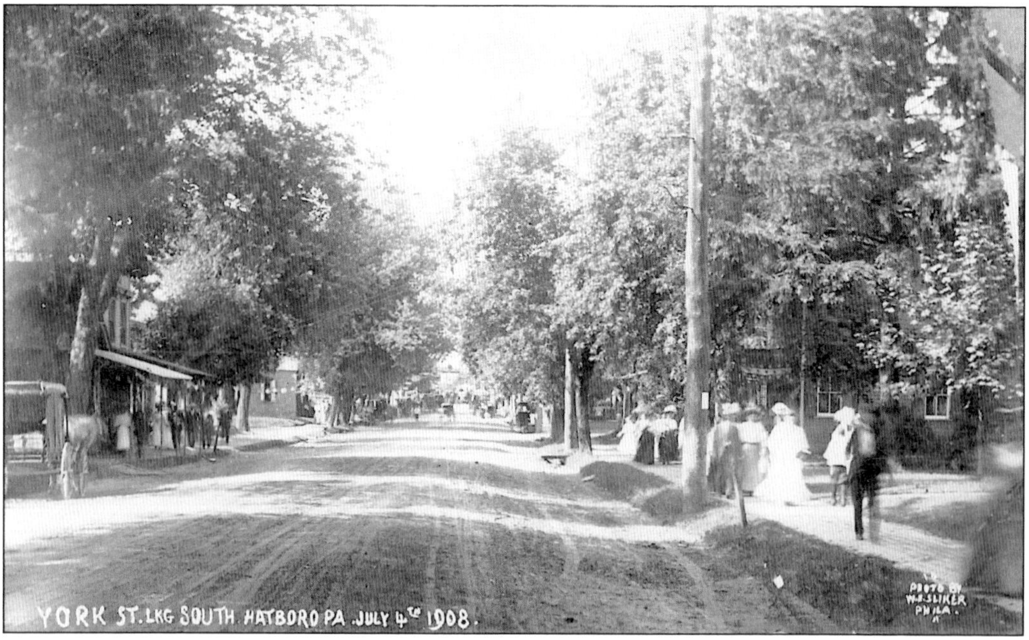

YORK ROAD, LOOKING SOUTH. July Fourth was a very patriotic time for small towns like Hatboro. This scene shows York Road in 1908 when there were more pedestrians than vehicles. (Sliker postcard.)

Three

EASTON ROAD

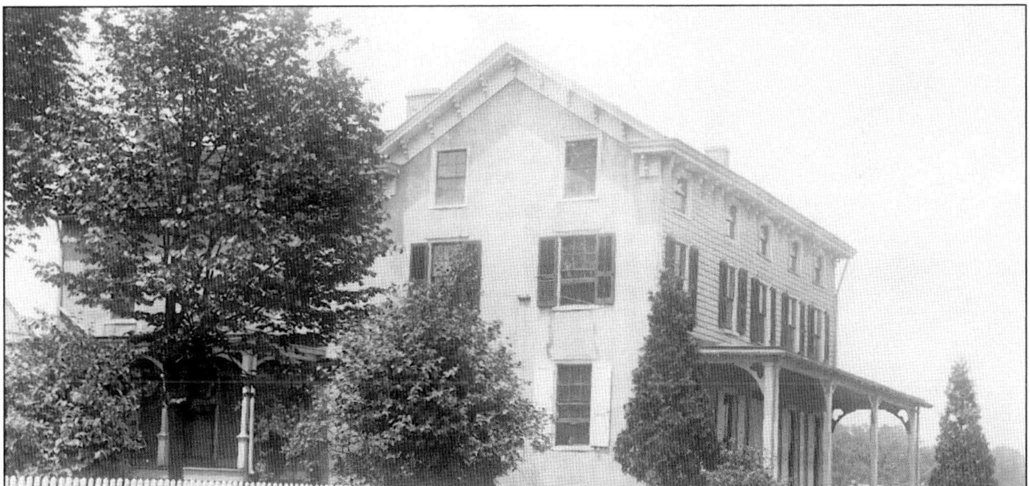

THE RESIDENCE OF JOS. WILDE ON WILLOW GROVE ROAD. This is a typical farmhouse setting that once dominated Montgomery County. Easton Road was sometimes referred to as Willow Grove Road. (Sliker postcard.)

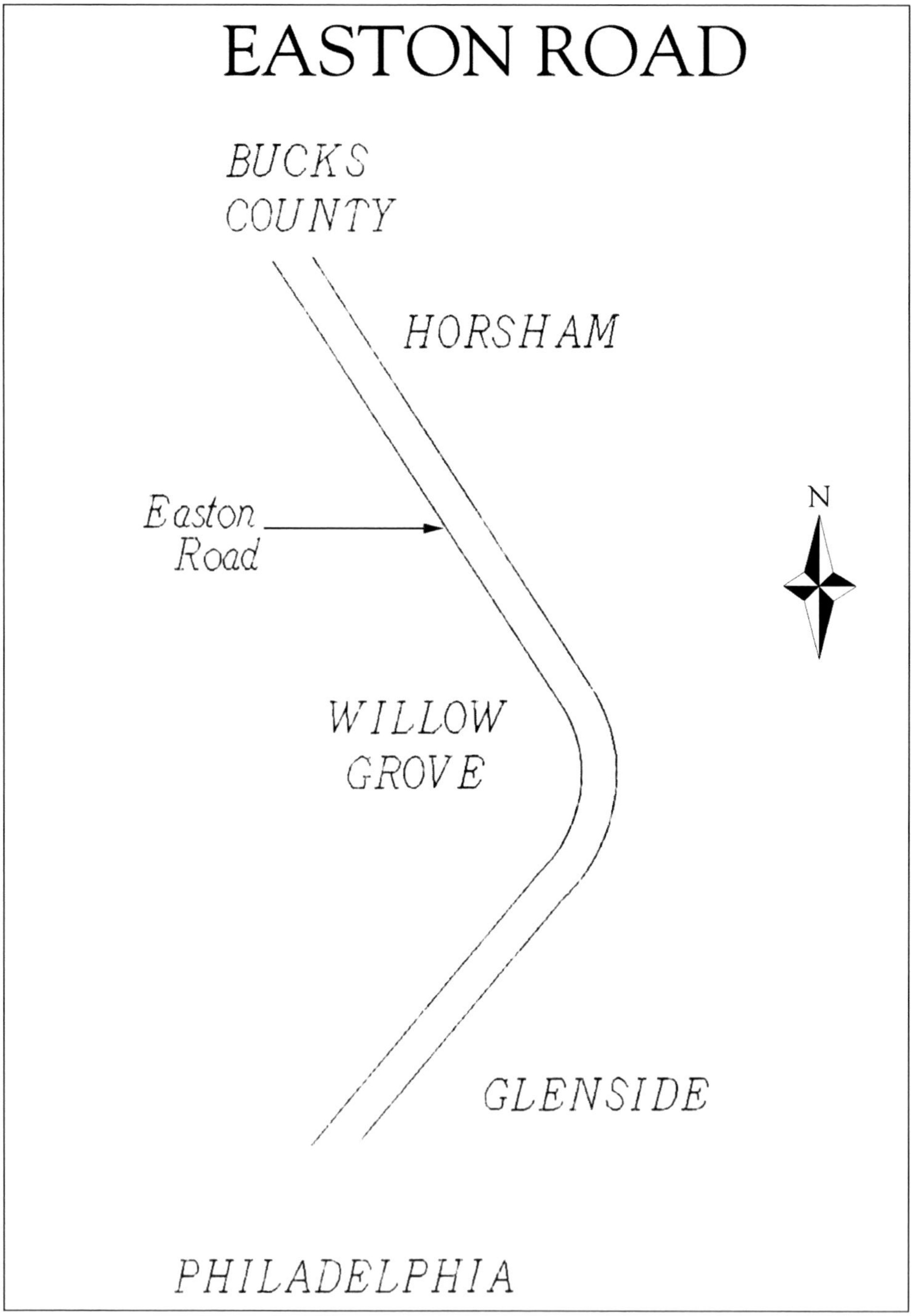

EASTON ROAD. Easton Road originally linked Willow Grove to Doylestown. It began at York Road in Willow Grove and was extended to Gov. Sir William Keith's mansion, Graeme Park, in 1722. It appears that much later the road from Willow Grove was extended southward to Glenside and Philadelphia. This section was called the Germantown and Willow Grove Plank Road in 1853. Today, Easton Road connects northwest Philadelphia with Easton.

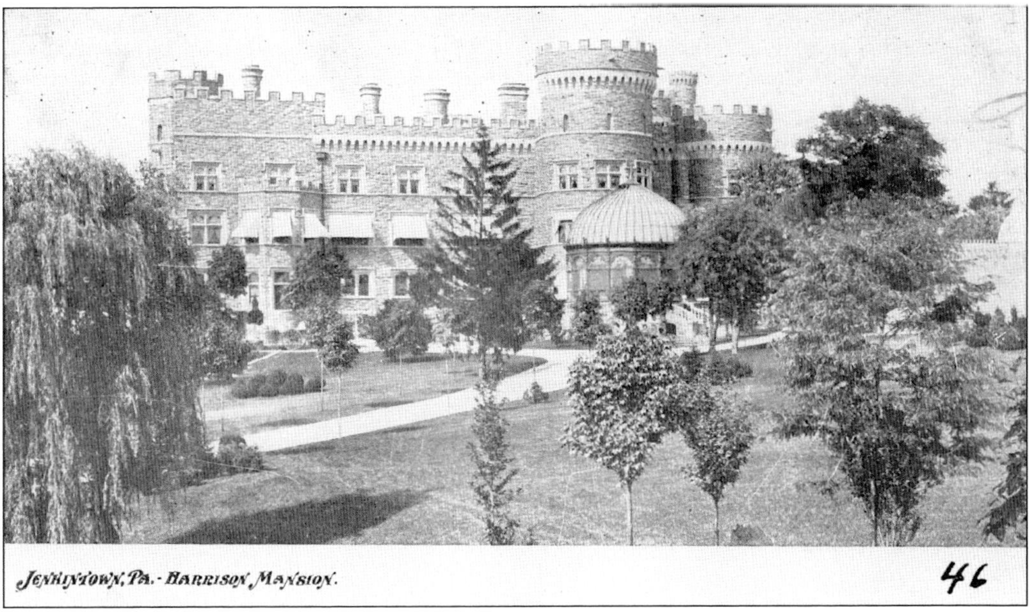

The Harrison Mansion in Glenside. At the intersections of Limekiln Pike, Church, and Easton Roads stands Grey Towers, the one-time castle estate of William Welsh Harrison. He was a millionaire who made fortunes in the sugar refinery business. Designed by noted Philadelphia architect Horace Trumbauer, Grey Towers, built in 1892, is said to have been modeled after a 14th-century castle in England. Harrison died in 1927 and his estate was bought by Beaver College the following year. (World Post Card Company postcard.)

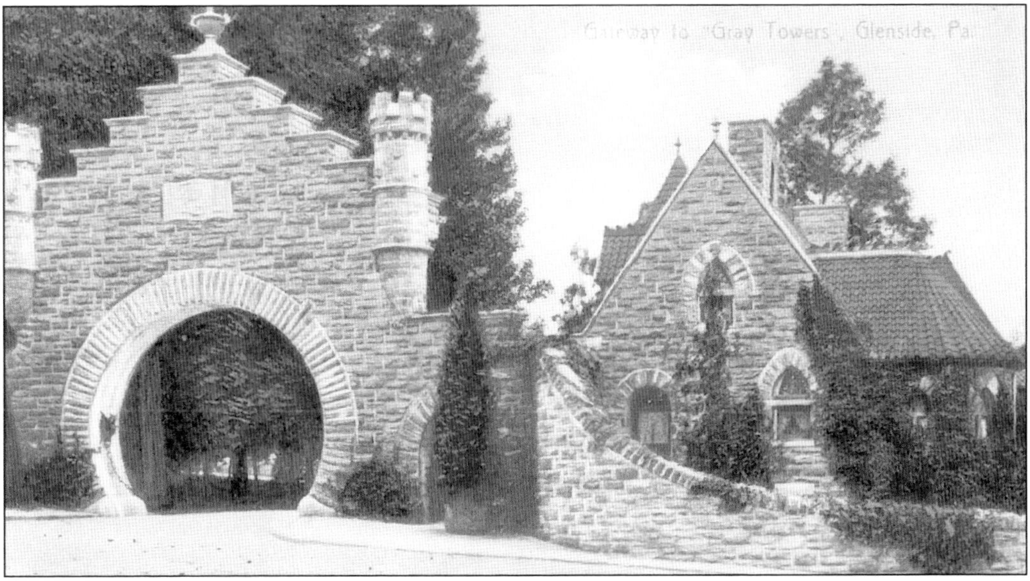

The Gateway to Grey Towers. The architecture of Grey Towers was not just limited to the main house. Many outbuildings, gateways, and walls contained the similar castle-like appearance, complete with heavy stone walls and circular towers. This entrance is along Easton Road and gave visitors a hint of what was inside the property walls. The Grey Towers complex represents a creative approach to high-style living that was unique to the surrounding countryside. (Moore postcard, 1910.)

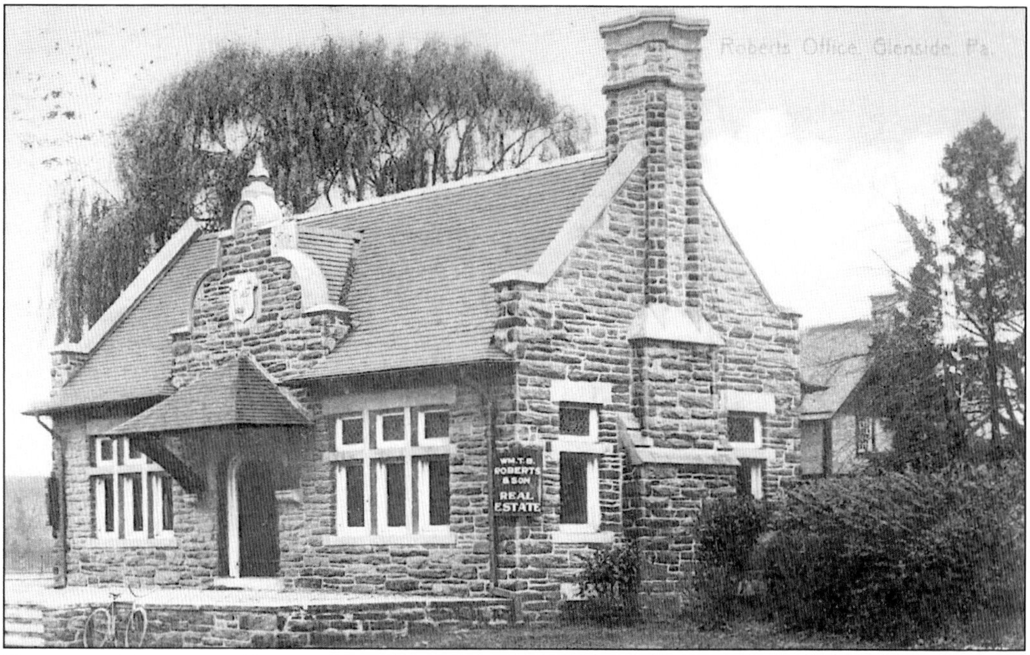

ROBERTS OFFICE IN GLENSIDE. This view shows the William Roberts Real Estate Office. Roberts was responsible for much of the housing in the Glenside area. He died in 1936 and his son continued the business into the 1950s. The building is still standing next to the railroad station off Mount Carmel Avenue. (Moore postcard.)

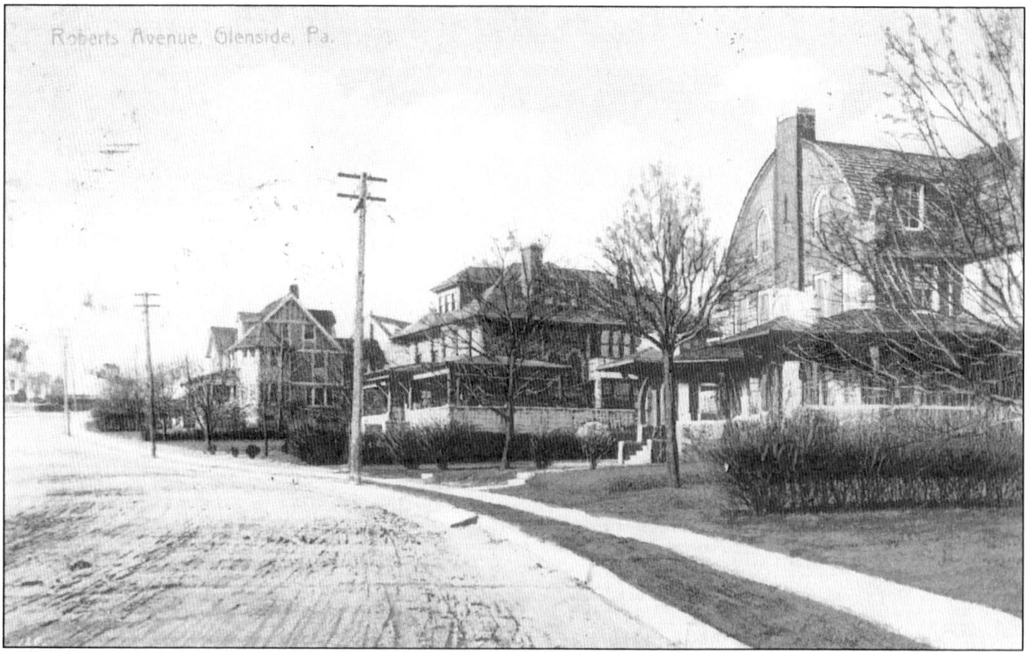

ROBERTS AVENUE IN GLENSIDE. This scene is typical of the beautiful suburban development that William Roberts created. Each home is distinctive and different, complete with a sidewalk and trees. The winding road pattern adds a pleasing dimension to the area. This 1910 view shows Roberts Avenue north of Mount Carmel Avenue. (Moore postcard.)

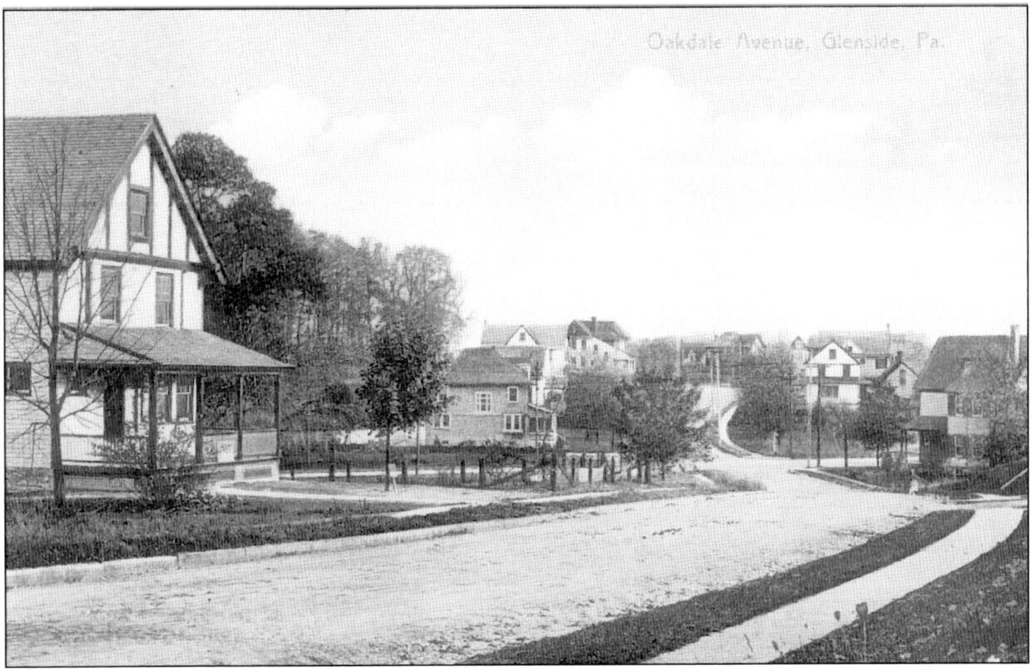

Oakdale Avenue. Oakdale Avenue is another beautiful street in Glenside. Large homes on spacious grounds helped define early suburban life in Montgomery County. Shown here is Oakdale, looking east from Easton Road toward Keswick Avenue in 1910. (Moore postcard.)

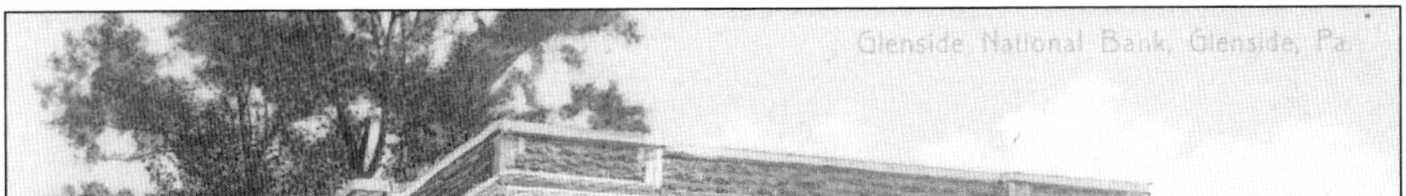

The Glenside National Bank in Glenside. Organized in 1909, the name was later changed to the Glenside Bank and Trust Company. This was their first structure at the southeast corner of Easton Road and Glenside Avenue. In 1930, the building was completely rebuilt to its present appearance. Presently, in 1999, it is a branch of PNC Bank.

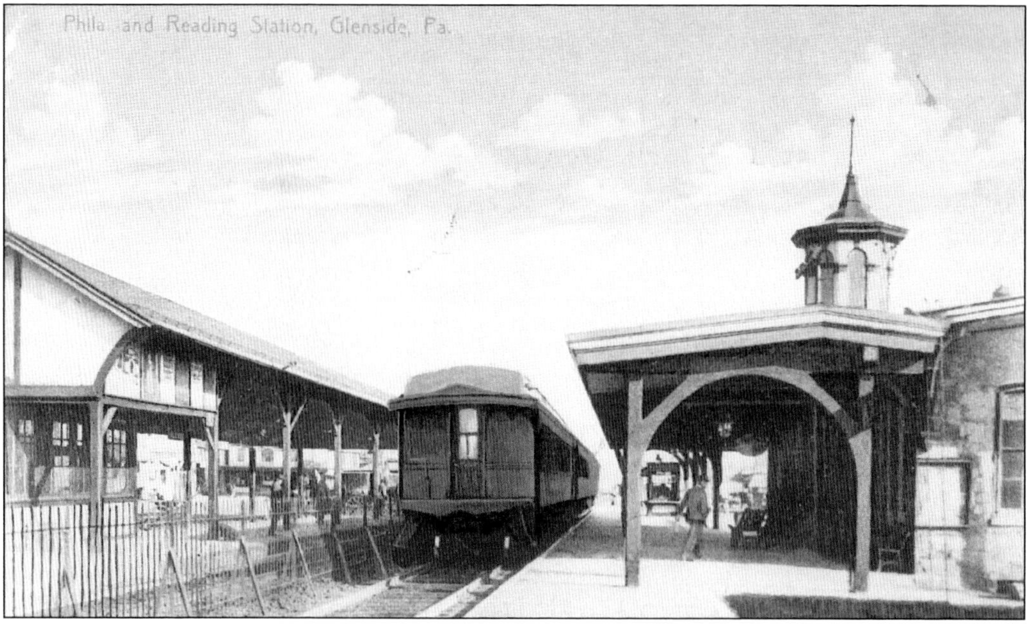

THE PHILADELPHIA AND READING STATION IN GLENSIDE. Originally called Tacony Station, Glenside Station was built in 1855. A few years later, it came to be called Abington Station. In 1888, when the Glenside Post Office was established, the station name was changed to Glenside. It is still in use and is located off Easton Road between Glenside and Mount Carmel Avenues. (Moore postcard, *c.* 1912.)

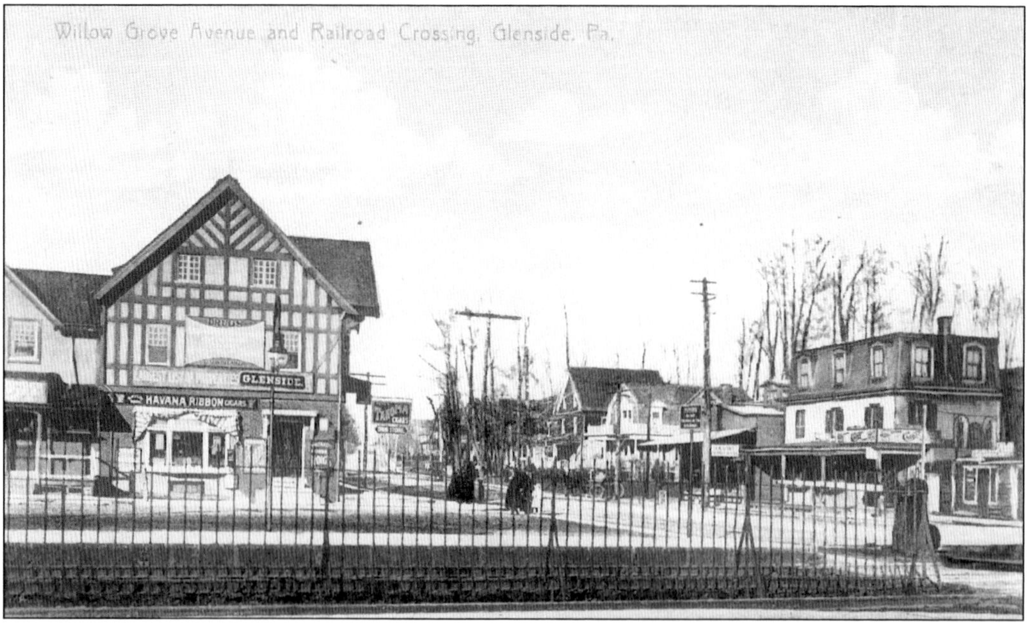

WILLOW GROVE AVENUE AND RAILROAD CROSSING. Willow Grove Avenue is now known as Easton Road. This Philip Moore postcard, mailed in 1911, shows central Glenside at the railroad crossing looking north from Glenside Avenue. Radical changes occurred here in the 1920s when Easton was lowered and a railroad bridge was erected to avoid train crossings. Many buildings shown here were taken down for the project.

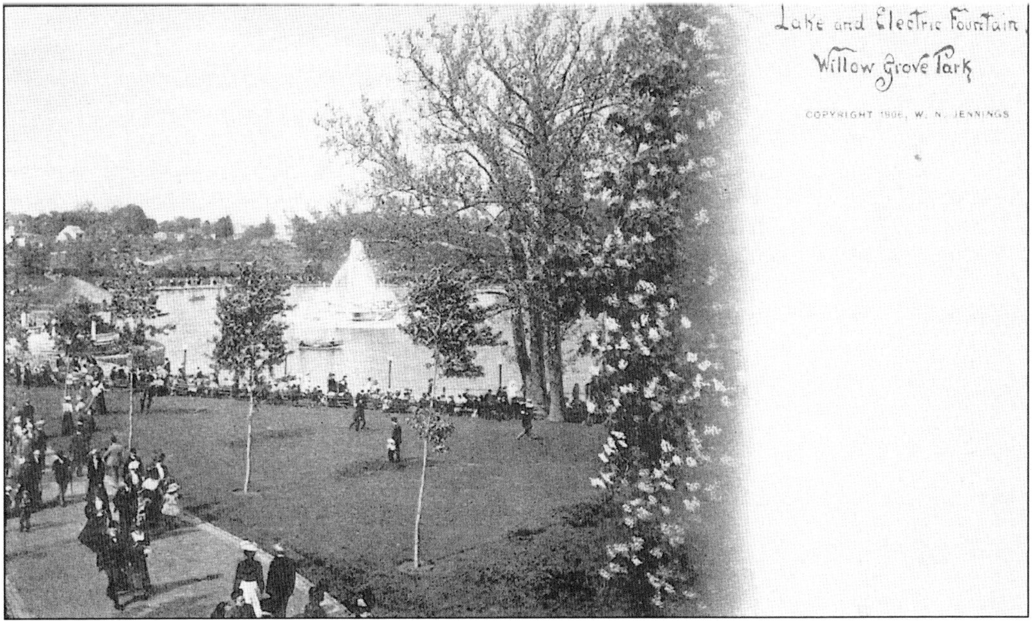

The Lake and Electric Fountain in Willow Grove Park. Willow Grove Park was an amusement and picnic park on Easton and Moreland Roads near Old York Road. It opened in May 1896 and was developed through the interest of the Philadelphia Rapid Transit Company, which ran trolleys to the park. The electric fountain shown here was very expensive, costing $100,000. (W.H. Jennings postcard, 1906.)

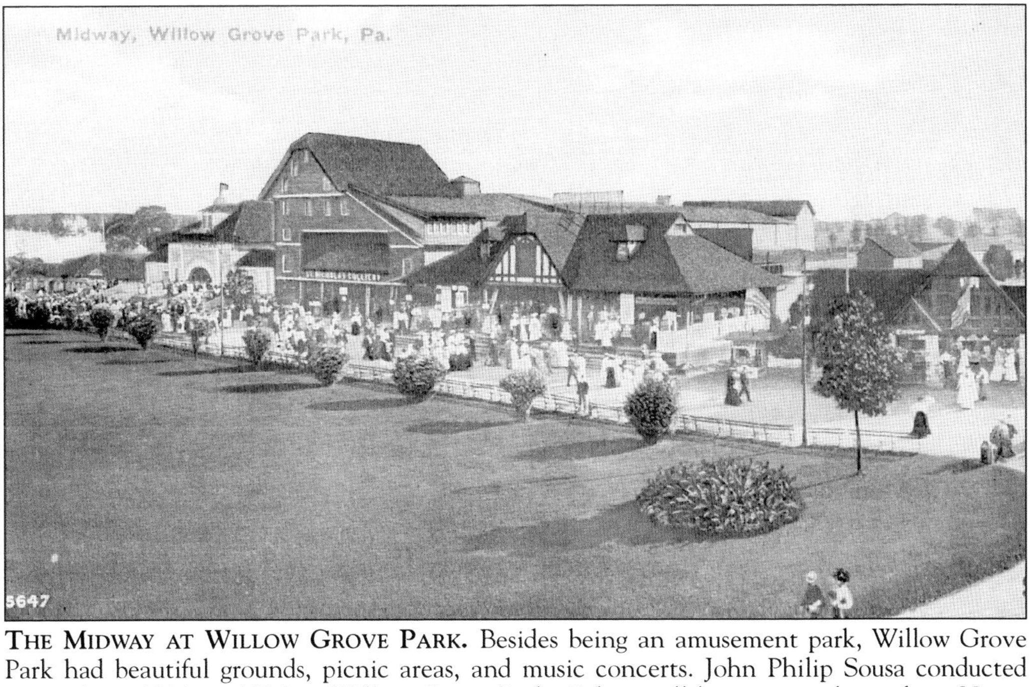

The Midway at Willow Grove Park. Besides being an amusement park, Willow Grove Park had beautiful grounds, picnic areas, and music concerts. John Philip Sousa conducted music from 1901 to 1926 at Willow Grove Park. Other well-known people, such as Victor Herbert, were also at Willow Grove Park. This view shows the immense midway and grounds at the park, *c.* 1910.

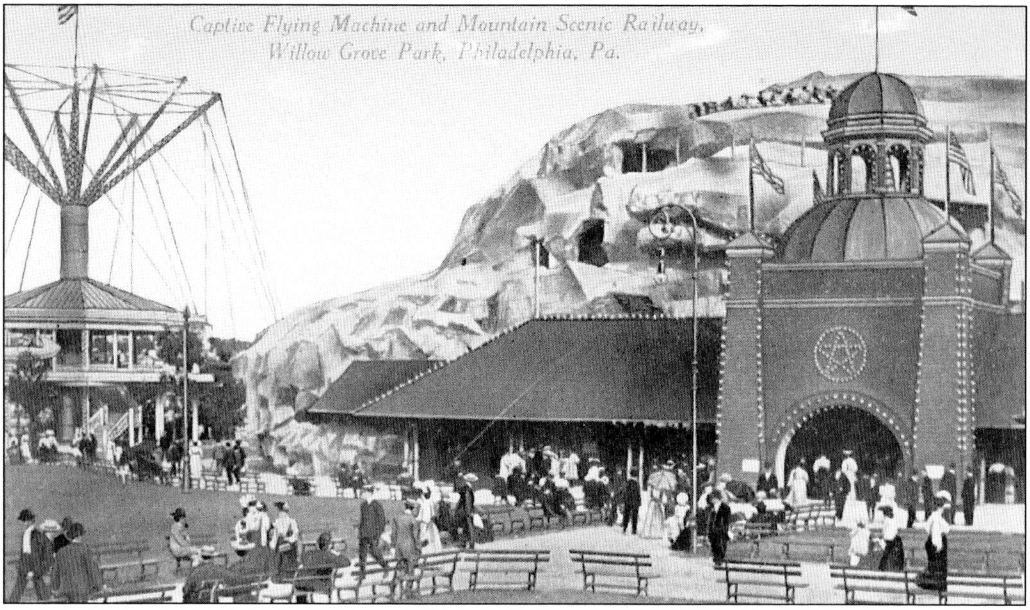

THE CAPTIVE FLYING MACHINE AND MOUNTAIN SCENIC RAILWAY AT WILLOW GROVE PARK. These were two of the more popular attractions at Willow Grove Park early inthe 20th century. On the reverse side of the c. 1915 postcard, the Mountain Scenic Railway is described as "affording a most unique and delightful ride by gravity over an elevated course nearly a mile long."

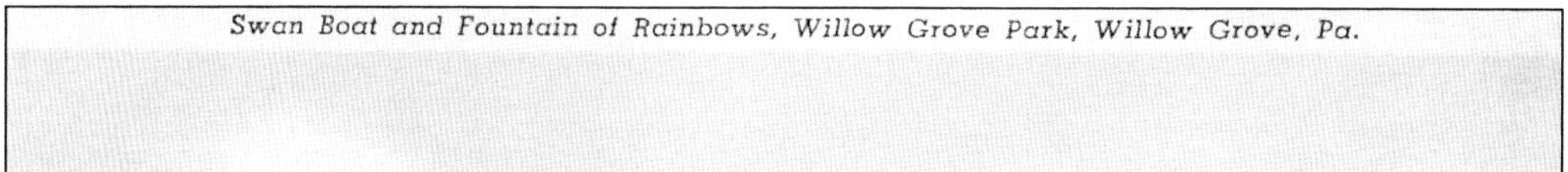

THE SWAN BOAT AND FOUNTAIN OF RAINBOWS AT WILLOW GROVE PARK. This linen postcard from c. 1940 shows the swan boat in the lake at Willow Grove Park. In 1927, the park changed ownership and its decline began. In the late 1960s it became "Six Gun Territory" and on April 14, 1976, the park closed. Nothing remains of Willow Grove Park today, though on its site rose the Willow Grove Park Mall in 1982.

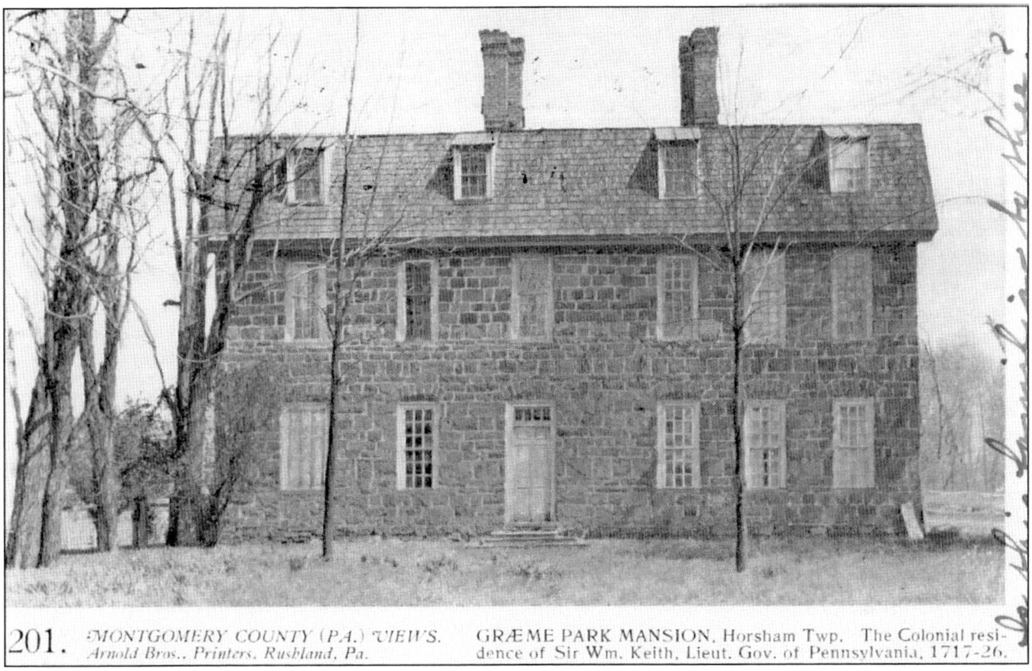

GRAEME PARK MANSION. In Horsham Township, on County Line Road and west of Easton Road, stands Graeme Park Mansion. Built *c.* 1720, it was the residence of Sir William Keith, governor of Pennsylvania. He was Horsham's most important individual in his day and his mansion reflected this in its size and design. (Arnold Brothers postcard, Rushland PA,from 1907.)

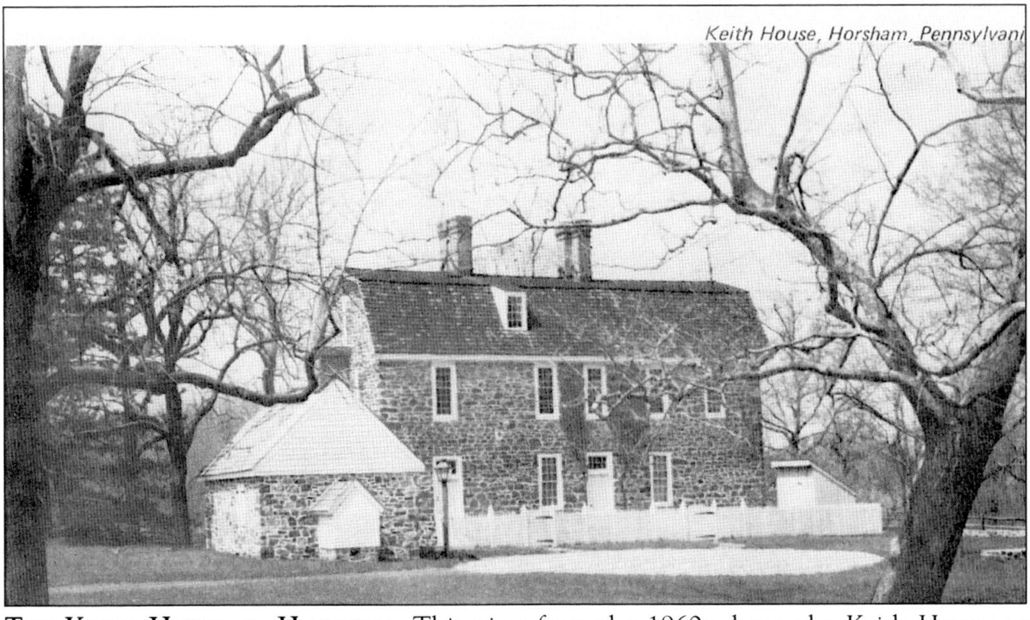

THE KEITH HOUSE IN HORSHAM. This view from the 1960s shows the Keith House, or Graeme Park Mansion. Today it is owned by the state of Pennsylvania and is a historic housemuseum open to the public. Graeme Park is truly one of Montgomery County's most important historic sites.

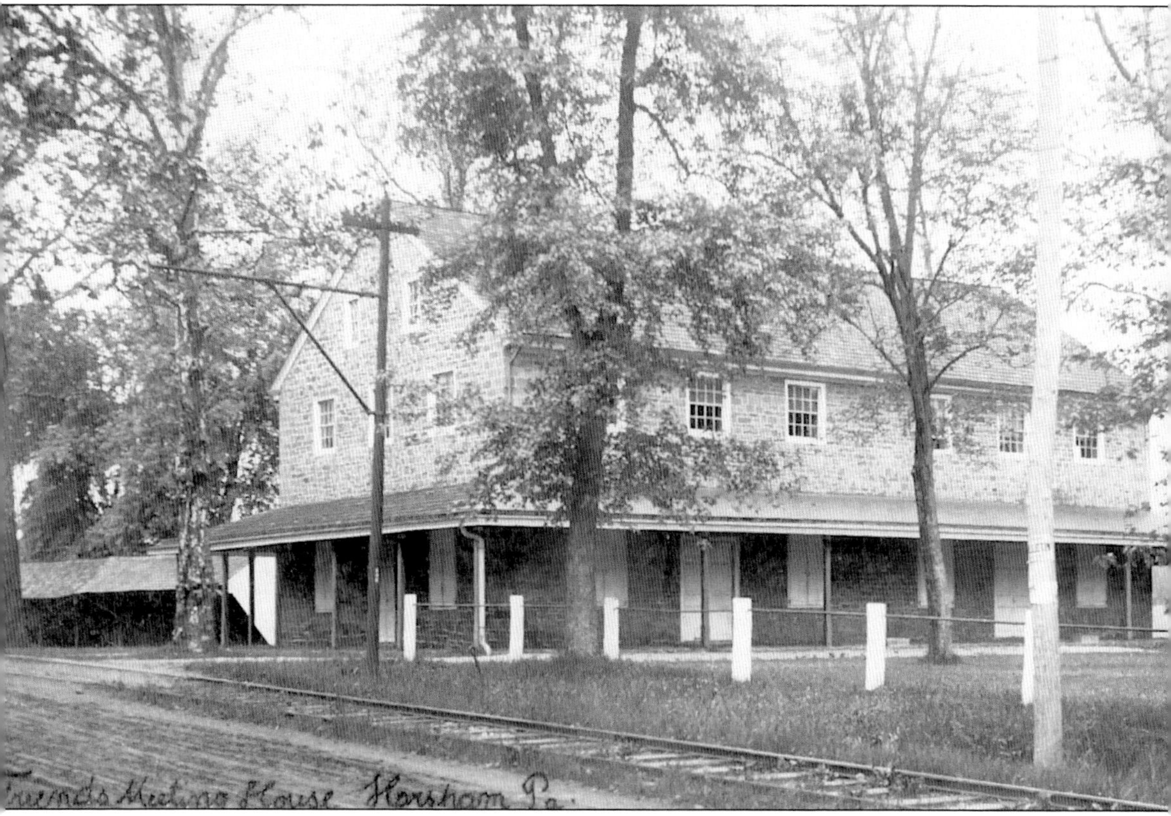

THE HORSHAM FRIENDS MEETING. The Horsham Friends Meeting dates from early 1700s. The present meetinghouse was built *c.* 1803 and is located on Easton Road north of Meetinghouse Road. The meetinghouse is virtually unchanged from this 1910 view, which shows the Willow Grove-Doylestown Trolley tracks.

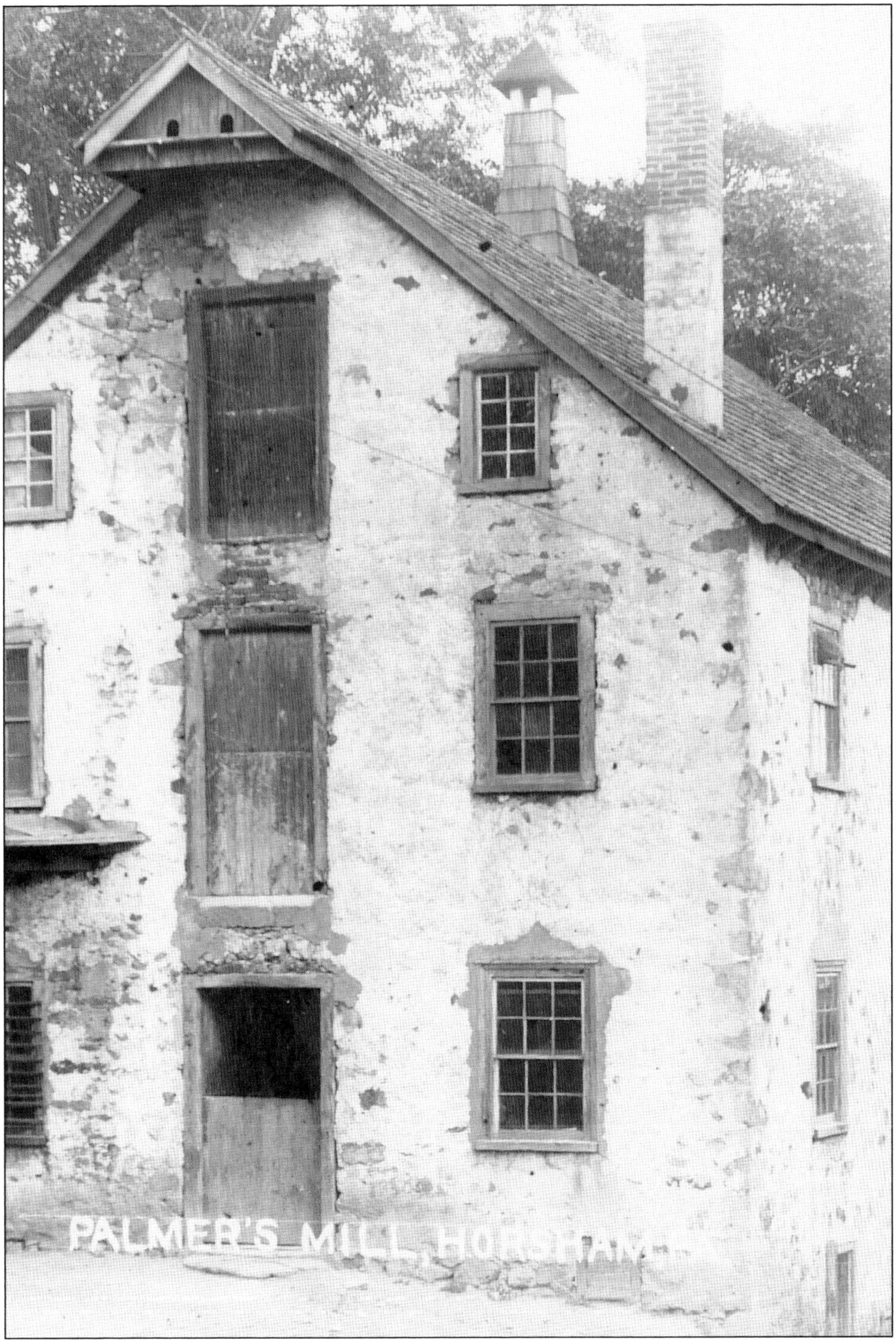

THE PALMERS MILL IN HORSHAM. The Palmer name can be traced back to a land grant from William Penn in 1682. Palmer did not arrive in the Horsham area until *c.* 1710. This is a typical Colonial mill that was part of the large Palmer tract. It still stands on Dresher Road, west of Horsham Road, at Pennypack Creek.

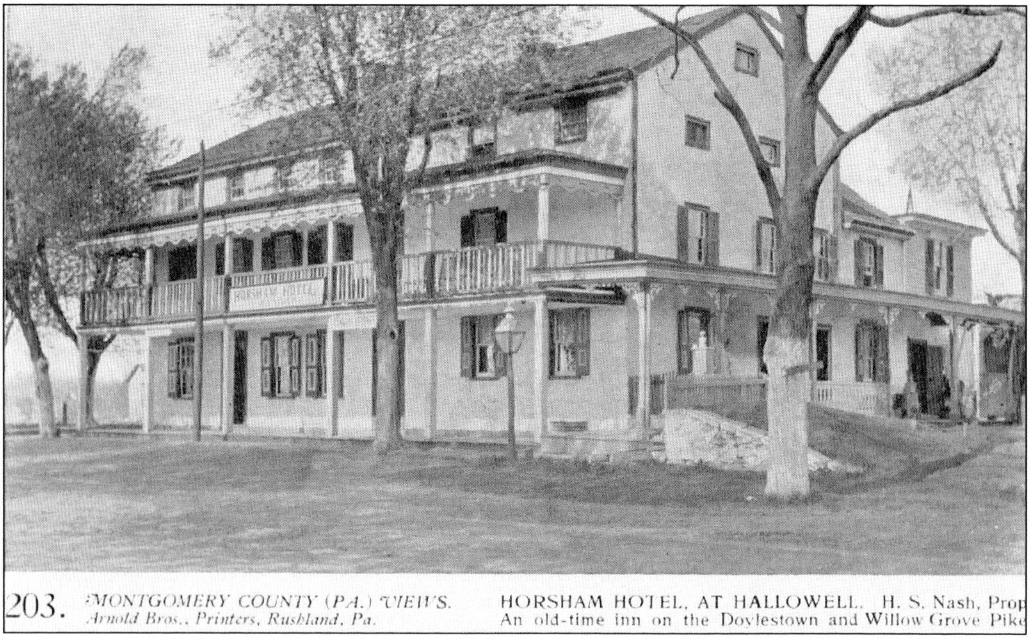

THE HORSHAM HOTEL AT HALLOWELL. A tavern on Easton or Doylestown Road in the early 1800s, this building still stands at Easton Road and Moreland Avenue. Presently known as the Horsham Inn, it appears today much as it does in this 1907 view. (Arnold Brothers postcard.)

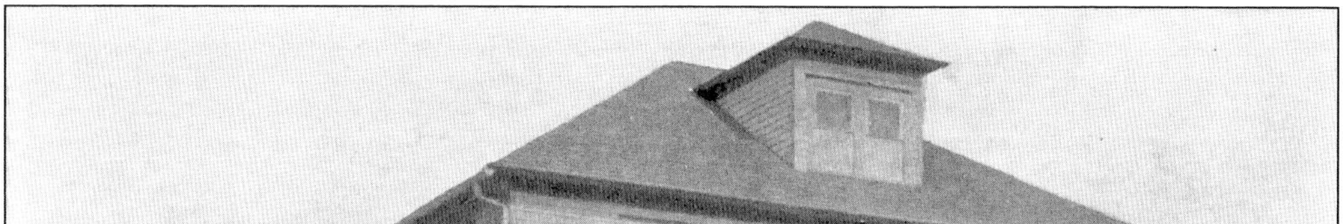

THE HALLOWELL STORE AND POST OFFICE. It stands directly across Moreland Avenue from the Horsham Hotel on Easton Road. Hallowell was a small village in Horsham Township and this was its primary commercial building. The store is still standing and has been home to a number of different establishments throughout the years. (Arnold Brothers postcard.)

Four

BETHLEHEM PIKE

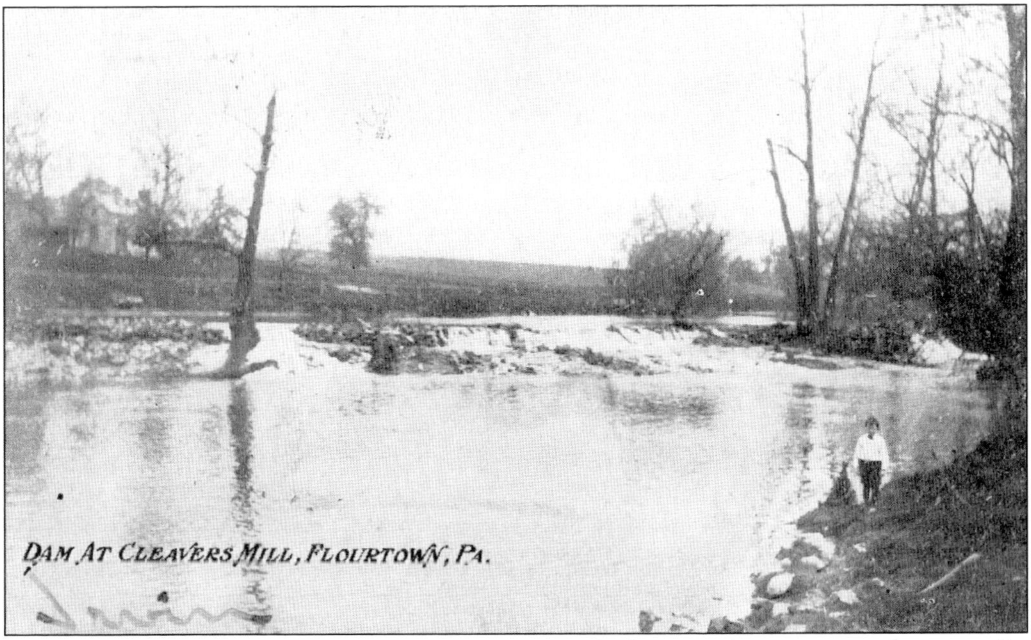

THE DAM AT CLEAVER'S MILL IN FLOURTOWN. Wissahickon Creek once powered many mills, one of which was the Cleaver's Mill near Flourtown. Mill dams were created to power the mills. Neither Cleaver's Mill nor its dam, once located near Stenton Avenue, survive today.

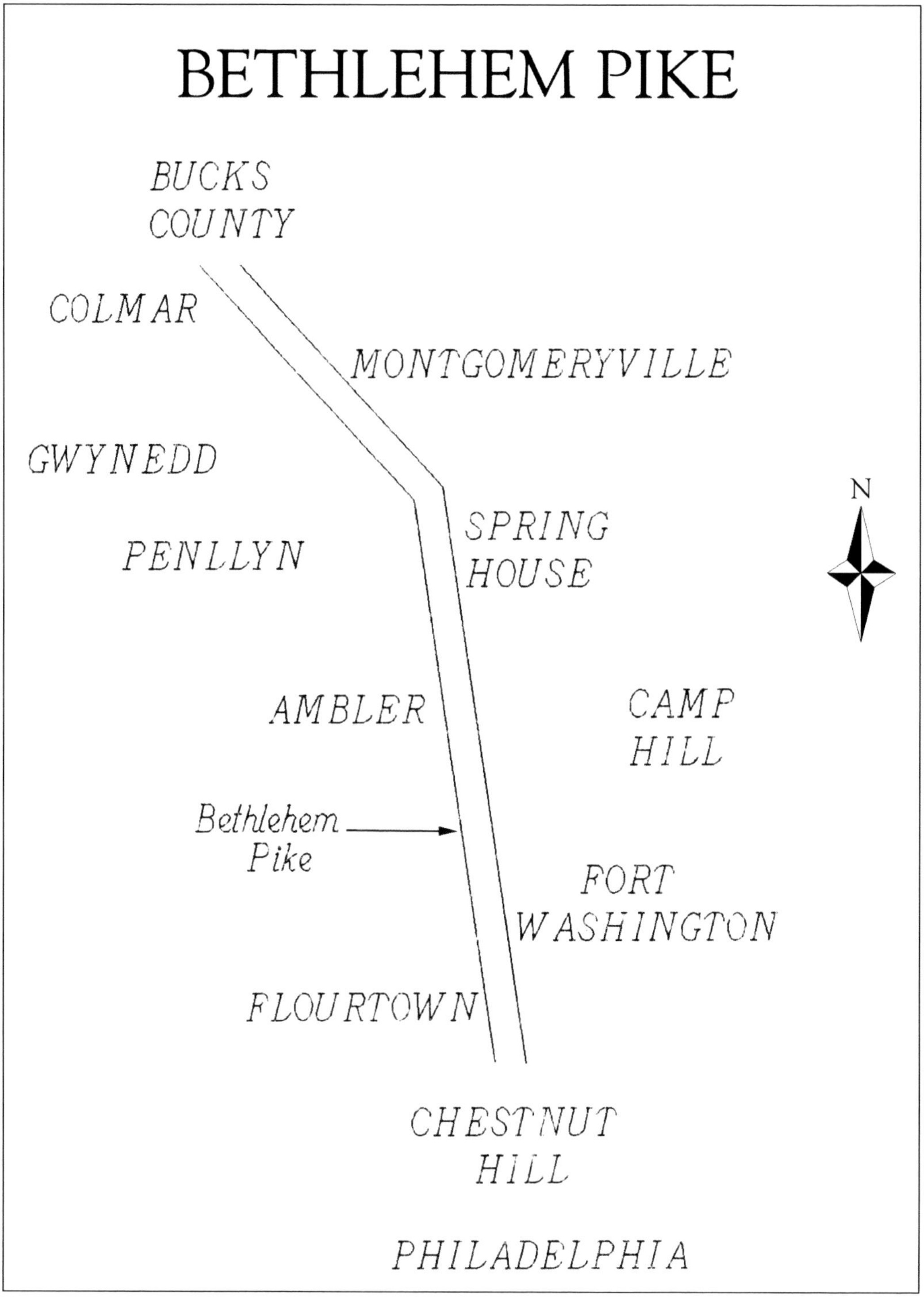

BETHLEHEM PIKE. It begins at Germantown Pike in Chestnut Hill and continues north to the city of Bethlehem. A section of this road, leading to Whitemarsh, opened in 1703. The road was later extended to Spring House and eventually to Bucks County.

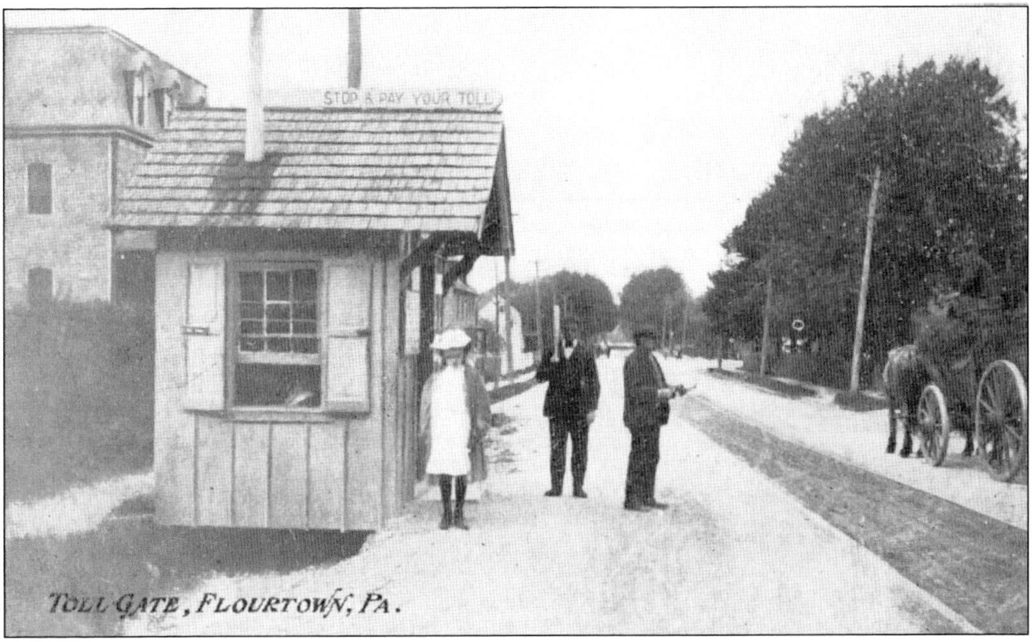

THE TOLLGATE IN FLOURTOWN. This postcard of Bethlehem Pike shows several modes of transportation that were used around the turn of the 20th century. The trolley tracks are from Lehigh Valley Transit Company, which operated on the pike from 1902 to 1926. In 1804, the Chestnut Hill and Spring House Turnpike was established along the pike. (Douglass Post Card Company postcard, Philadelphia, PA.)

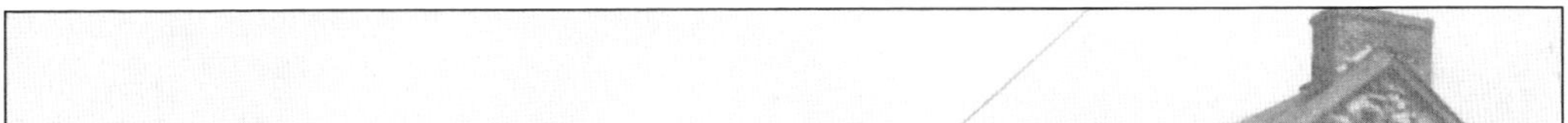

THE SPRINGFIELD HOTEL IN FLOURTOWN. Flourtown is a heavily commercialized area, especially along Bethlehem Pike. Fortunately, it retains many older historic buildings like the Springfield Hotel. Built in 1811, it has been serving travelers along the pike for almost two centuries. It was still in operation up until a few years ago. Presently, it is empty and for sale. (Douglass Post Card Company postcard, Philadelphia, PA.)

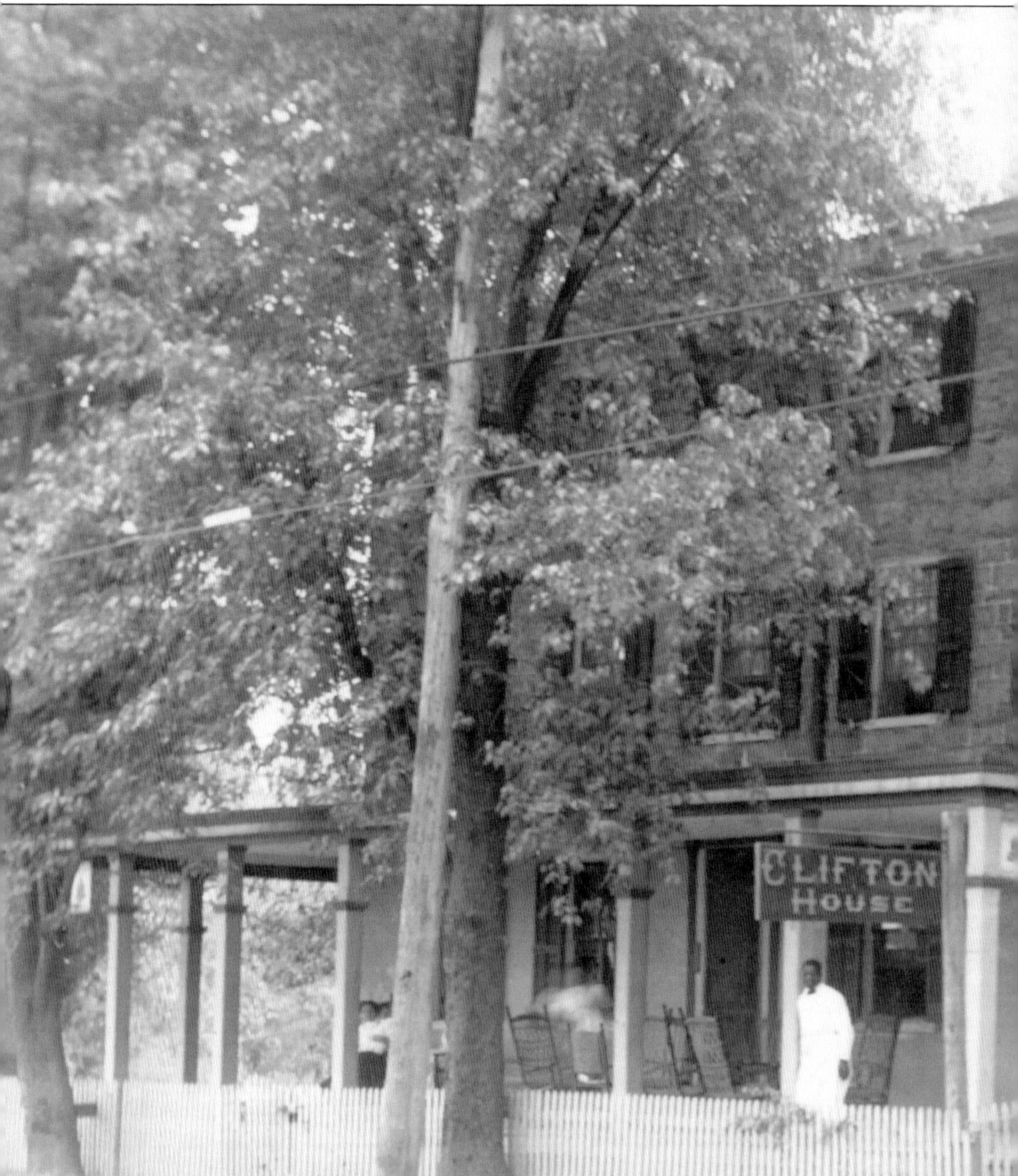

THE CLIFTON HOUSE IN FORT WASHINGTON. The Clifton House still stands on Bethlehem Pike in Fort Washington. General Washington's fort, during the Whitemarsh Encampment, stood on a hill behind this building in 1777 during the Revolutionary War. Several hills in this vicinity, including Fort Hill, Militia Hill, and Camp Hill, helped Washington's troops keep a

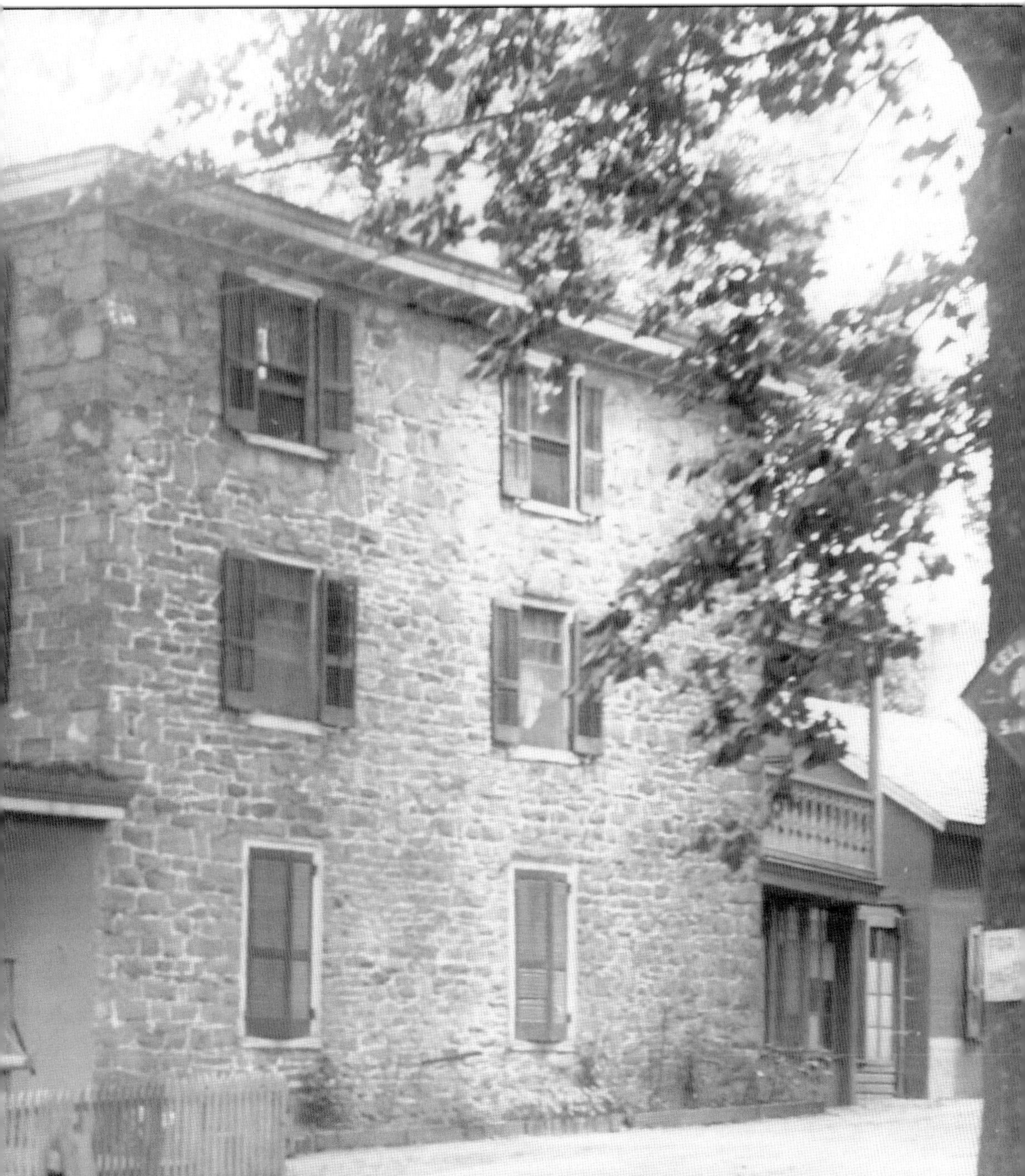

watchful eye on the British Army. Some of these hills have been incorporated into Fort Washington State Park. The Clifton House in 1777 was known as the Sandy Run Tavern and was rebuilt several times. Today it is a museum devoted to local history and is operated by the Fort Washington Historical Society.

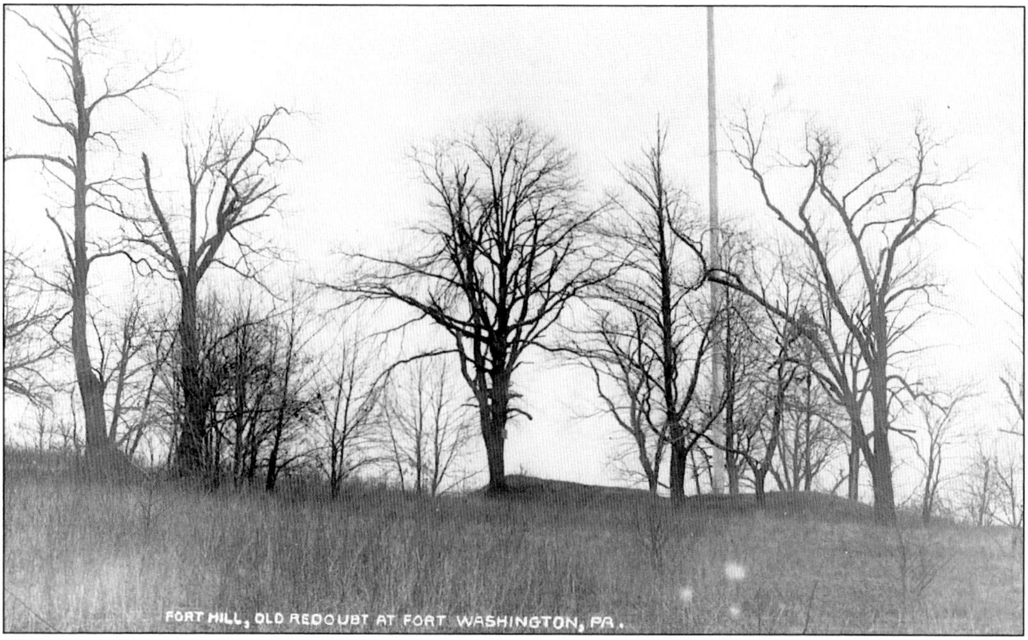

THE OLD REDOUBT AT FORT WASHINGTON. Washington's army could safely watch the activities of the British during the Revolutionary War from the forts atop Fort Hill. In the 1930s, workers accidentally destroyed the forts. The area is now the Fort Hill section of Fort Washington State Park where markers commemorate the fortification of Washington' s army.

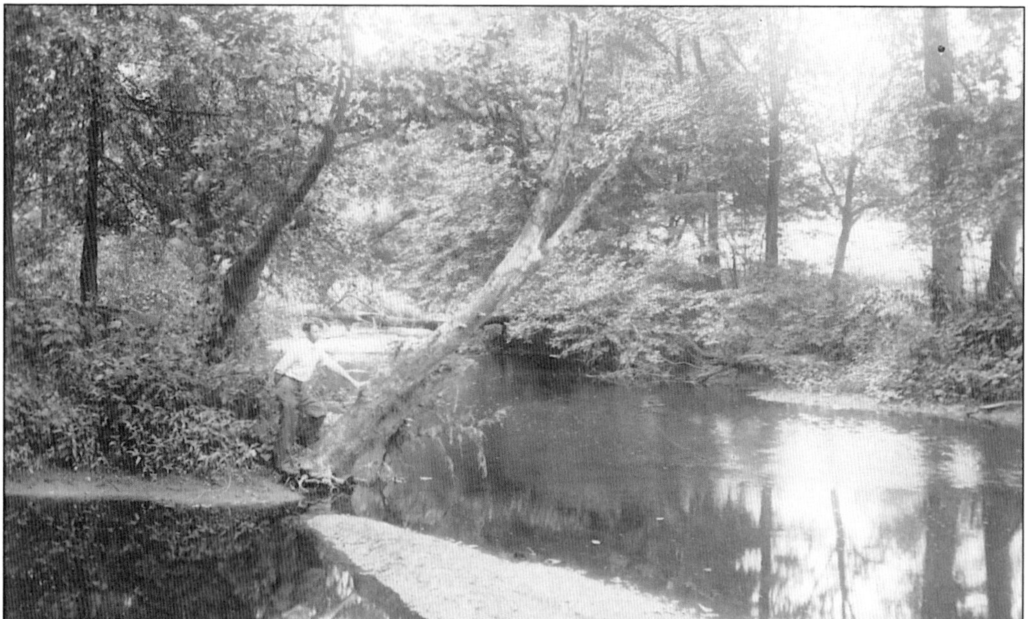

WISSAHICKON CREEK AT FORT WASHINGTON. Beautiful Wissahickon Creek has been the source of many postcard views. Its natural beauty and historic significance have long been of interest to many local residents. Much of it has been preserved either in parks, land trusts, or by watershed associations. (Sliker postcard.)

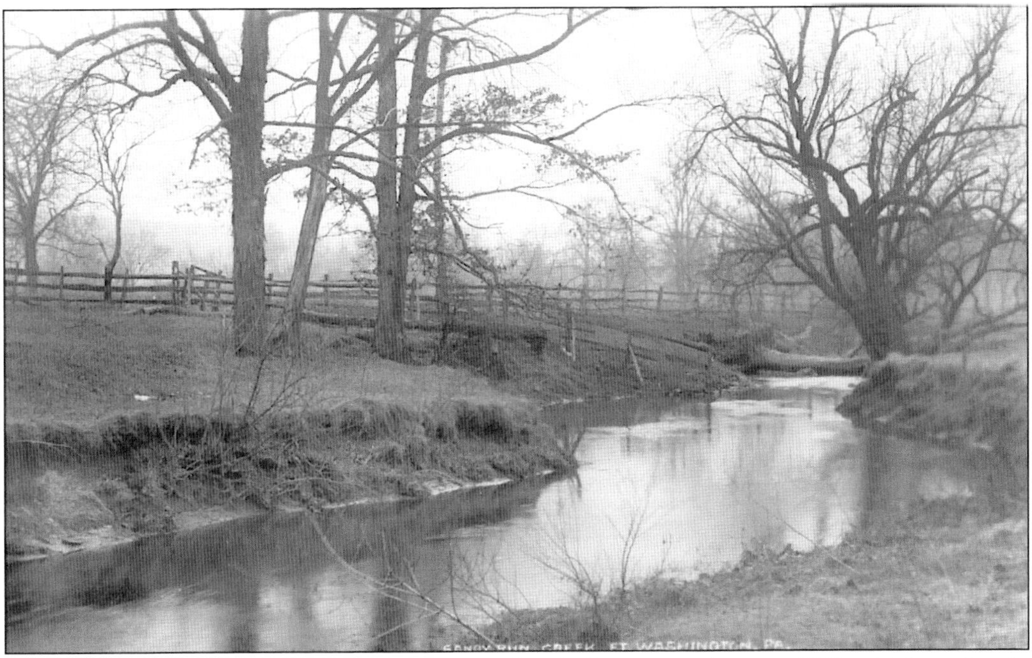

SANDY RUN CREEK AT FORT WASHINGTON. Sandy Run is a tributary of Wissahickon Creek. Some of the area around this stream is preserved in Fort Washington State Park. (Postcard published by William W. Miller of North Wales, PA.)

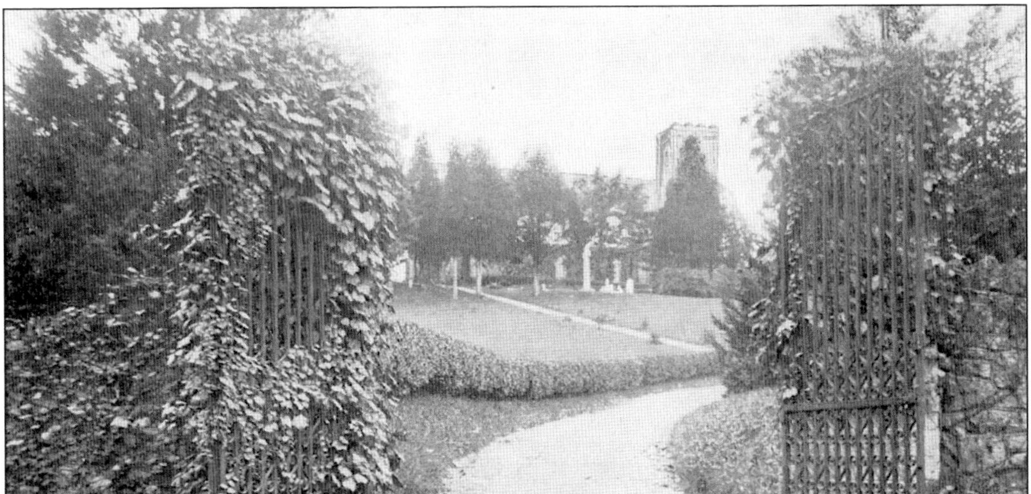

ST. THOMAS P.E. CHURCH IN WHITEMARSH. St. Thomas Church is an old landmark on Bethlehem Pike at Church Road. Founded in 1710, it witnessed some of the fighting during the Whitemarsh Encampment. The church sits on a rather conspicuous hill, referred to as Church Hill. At the time of the Revolution, there was a smaller church on the site. The St. Thomas Church and cemetery have expanded over the years. (World Post Card Company postcard.)

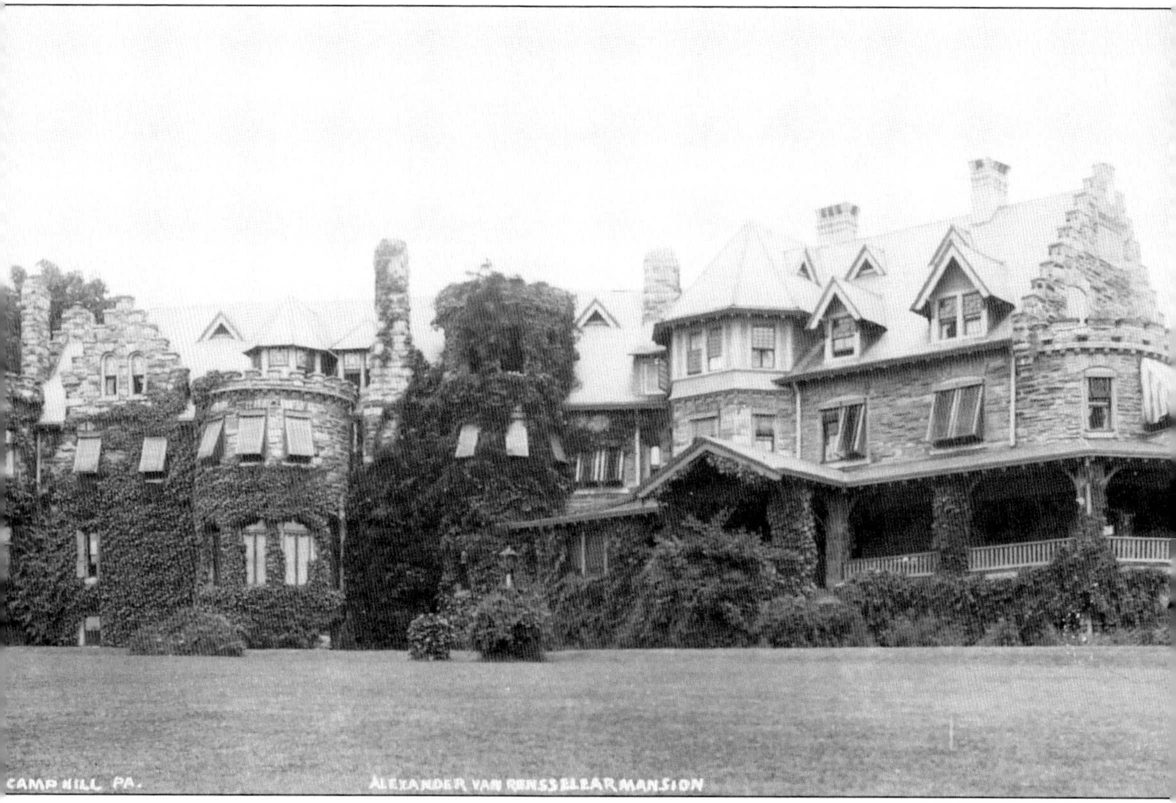

THE ALEXANDER VAN RENSSELAER MANSION. Perhaps one of the lesser-known mansions in Montgomery County is the beautiful, late-Victorian estate once occupied by Alexander Van Rensselaer. Known as Camp Hill Hall, it was built in 1882 and enlarged a decade later. Originally, the house was built for a daughter of the Drexel banking family whose second husband was Van Rensselaer. The estate occupies the summit of Camp Hill, an imposing hill rising above the Whitemarsh Valley. Camp Hill was occupied by Washington's troops in 1777 as a lookout point for the British Army during the Revolutionary War. Oddly, the enormous mansion and spacious grounds were home to only the couple; they had no children, and when they died the Van Rensselaer name vanished from this area. The property was vacant for a while until it was sold to a missionary group of evangelists for their headquarters in the early 1950s. Today, the mansion is in good condition and is located off a long steep drive off of Pennsylvania Avenue near Route 309. (Sliker postcard.)

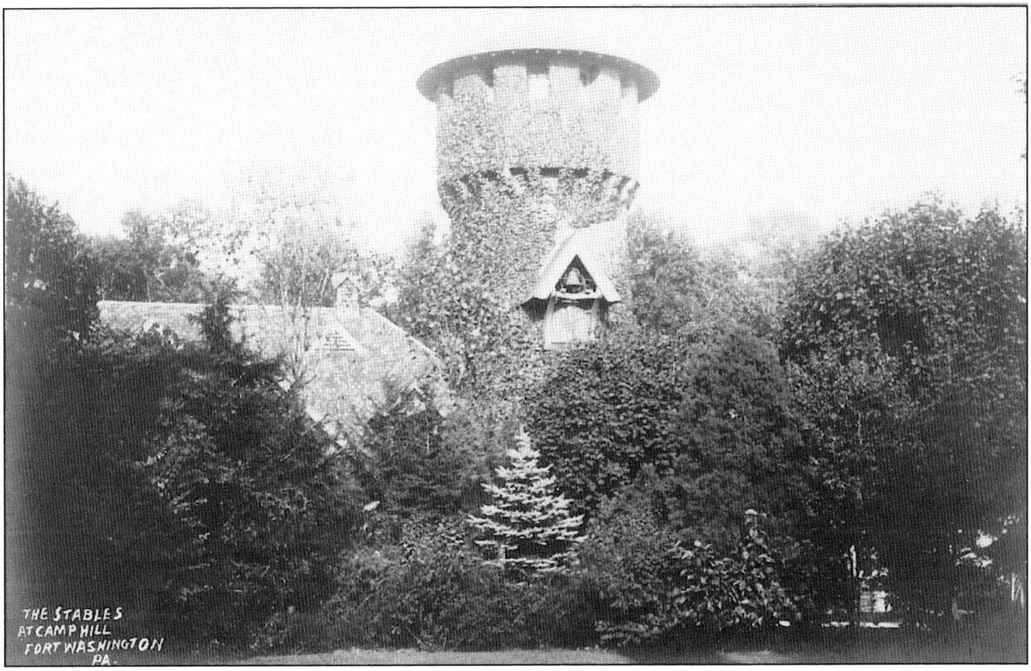

THE STABLES AT CAMP HILL. Camp Hill Hall had a number of interesting features and buildings on the property, including an in-ground swimming pool and stables, both of which remain there today. The stable tower, constructed entirely of stone, has a clock and bell along with a spiral staircase to the top. (Sliker postcard.)

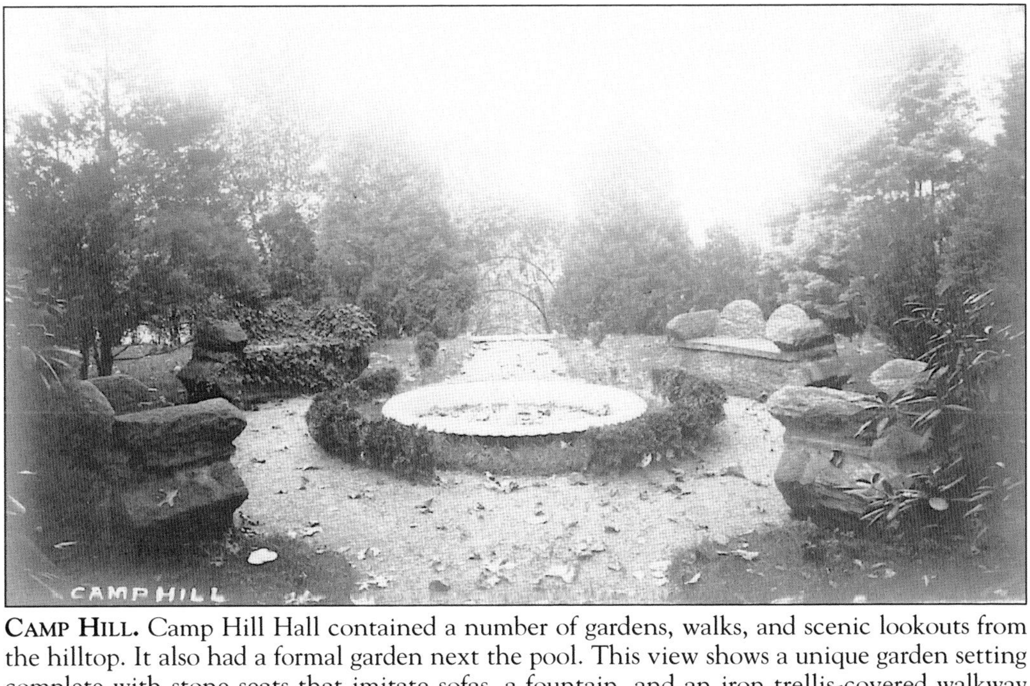

CAMP HILL. Camp Hill Hall contained a number of gardens, walks, and scenic lookouts from the hilltop. It also had a formal garden next the pool. This view shows a unique garden setting complete with stone seats that imitate sofas, a fountain, and an iron trellis-covered walkway leading down the hillside. Amazingly, this spot, though somewhat overgrown, is still intact. (Sliker postcard.)

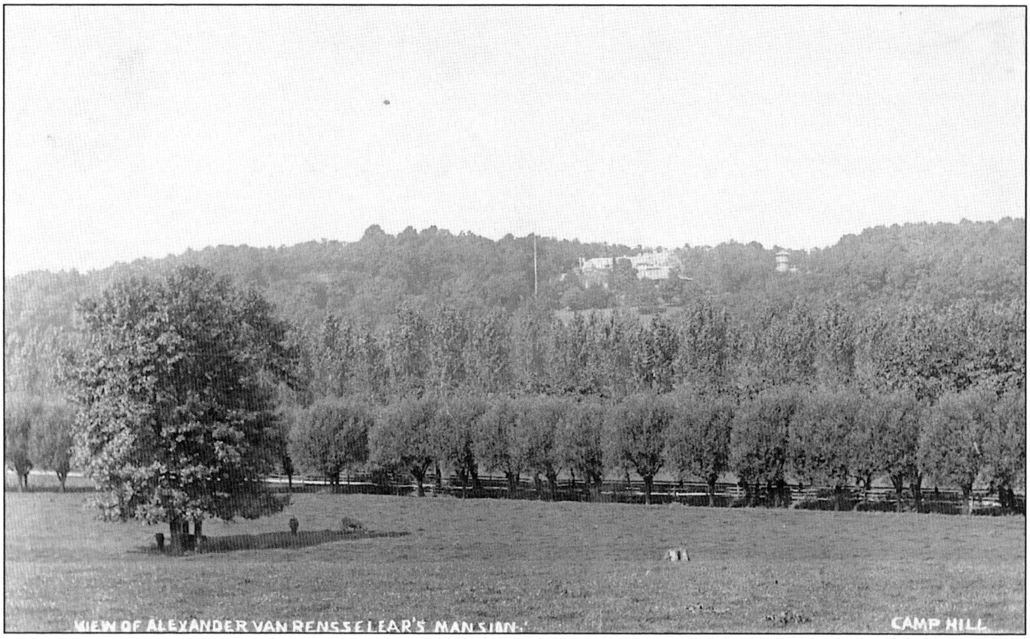

A VIEW OF THE ALEXANDER VAN RENSSELAER MANSION. The Van Rensselaer mansion and stable are shown at the top of Camp Hill. The hill rises several hundred feet above the surrounding farmland. (Sliker postcard.)

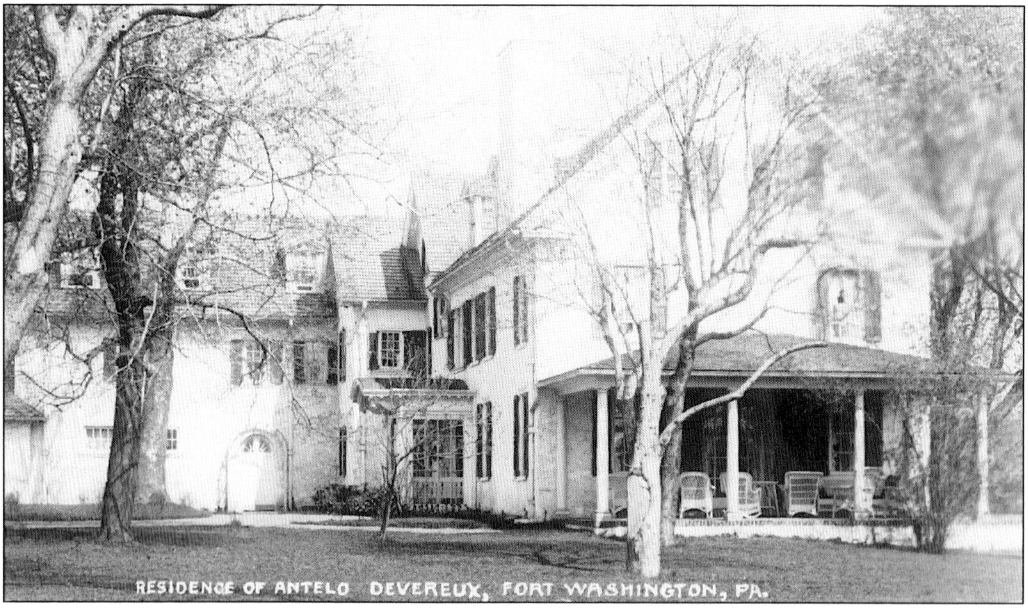

THE RESIDENCE OF ANTELO DEVEREUX IN FORT WASHINGTON. Commonly referred to as the Emlen House and named for its first owner, George Emlen, the home was the headquarters of George Washington during the Whitemarsh Encampment. Marquis de Lafayette and other generals are known to have stayed here. Built in 1720, the house has been added to several times. Today, state historical markers along the property on Pennsylvania Avenue inform the passersby of its importance during the Revolutionary War. (Herkness and Miller postcard, North Wales, PA.)

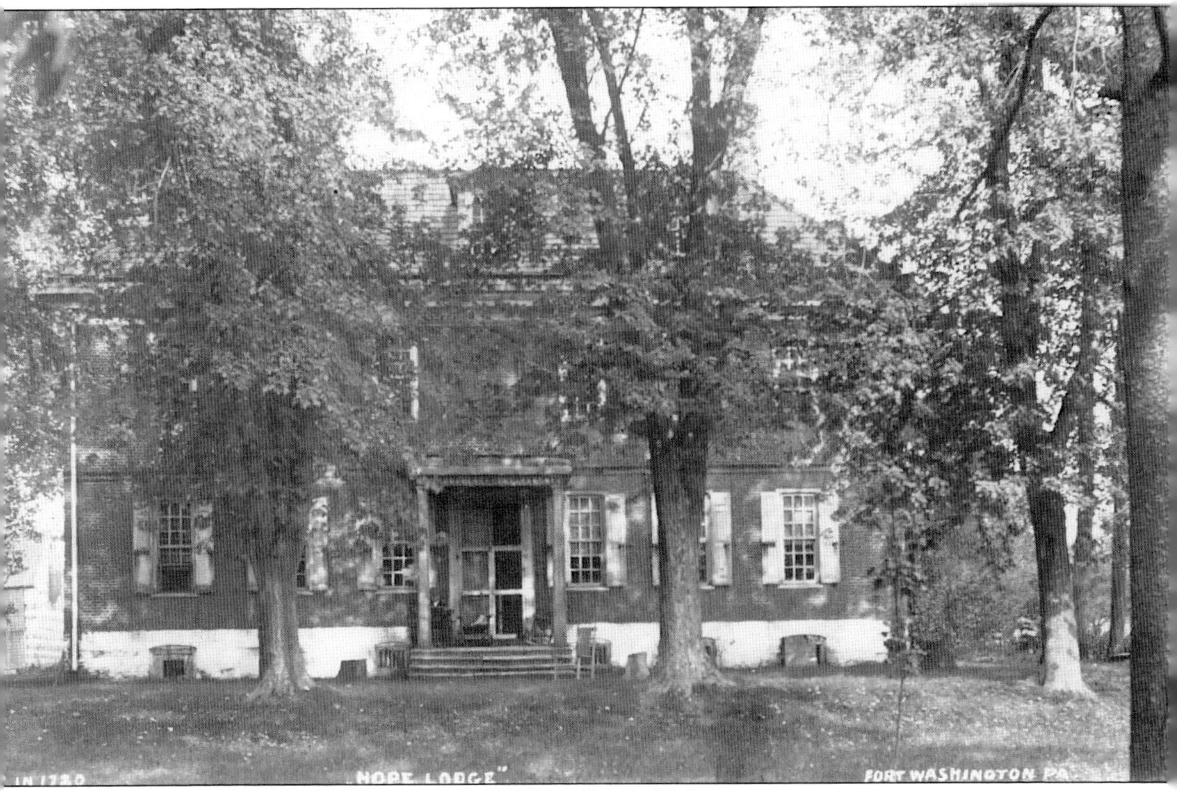

HOPE LODGE IN FORT WASHINGTON, 1910. Hope Lodge is a very unique mansion in Montgomery County. Built in the 1720s, it is a classic example of Colonial Georgian architecture. Its brick symmetrical front represents wealth and prosperity rarely seen outside of Philadelphia. Brick was mainly used for city buildings, whereas stone was found in the country. Hope Lodge, facing Bethlehem Pike north of Skippack Pike, was privately owned until the 1950s, when its owner bequeathed the property to the state of Pennsylvania. Today, the glorious mansion is a historic house museum open to the public and operated by the Pennsylvania Museum and Historic Commission. (Sliker postcard.)

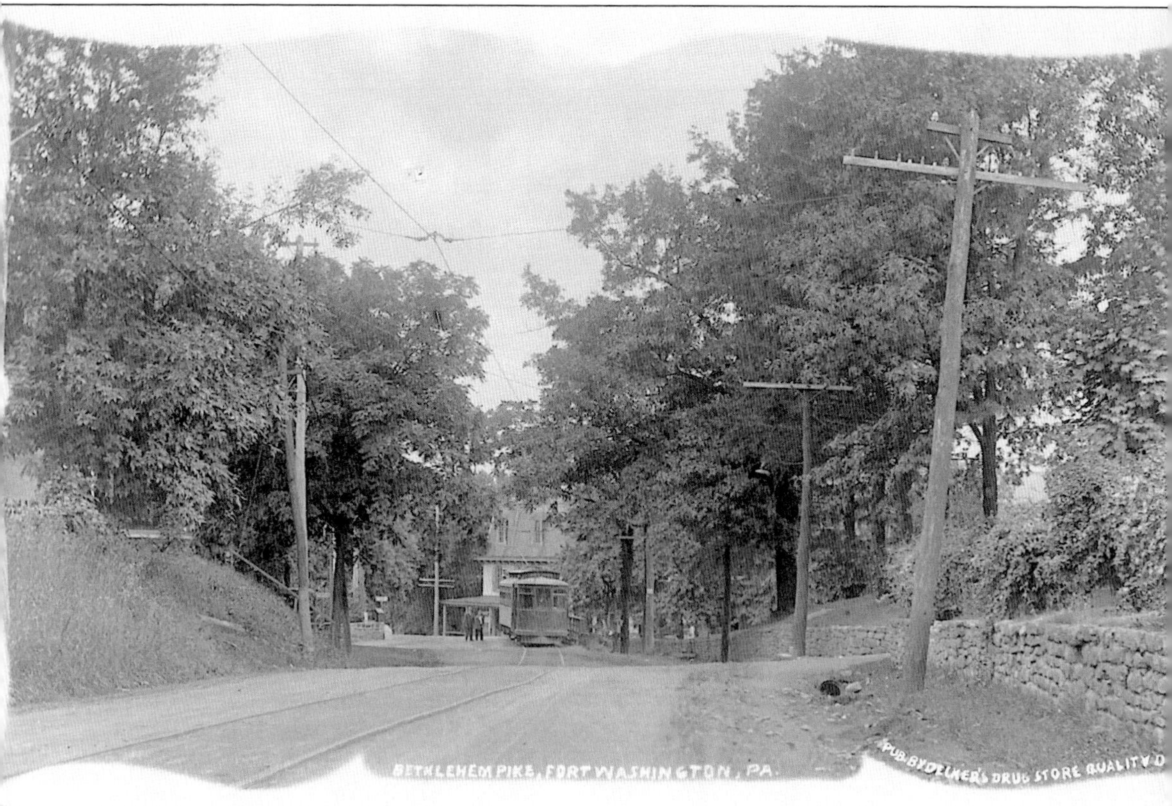

BETHLEHEM PIKE IN FORT WASHINGTON. Looking south on Bethlehem Pike where Morris Road, Lafayette Avenue, and the railroad meet, the trolley is heading to North Wales. Trolley lines on the Bethlehem Pike were established *c.* 1900. (Sliker postcard.)

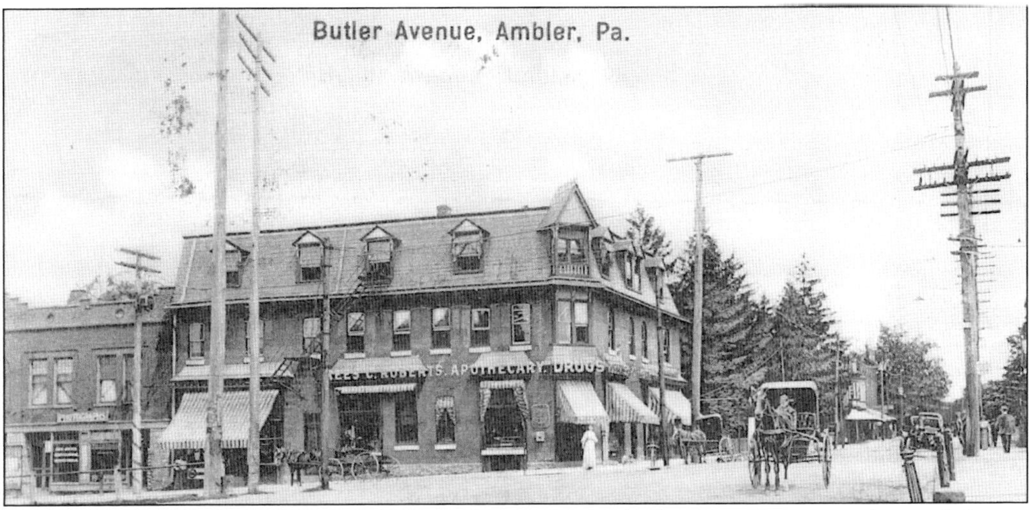

BUTLER AVENUE IN AMBLER. Butler Avenue or Butler Pike has been the main thoroughfare in Ambler since its founding. Stores, banks, hotels, and even an opera house once lined the street. This view shows the intersection of Main Street and Butler Avenue with the Rees C. Roberts Apothecary Drug Store on the corner looking east. Many views of the Ambler area, including several in this book, were published by Roberts and sold in this store. This building still stands and, as late as the 1980s, was a drugstore. (Rees C. Roberts postcard.)

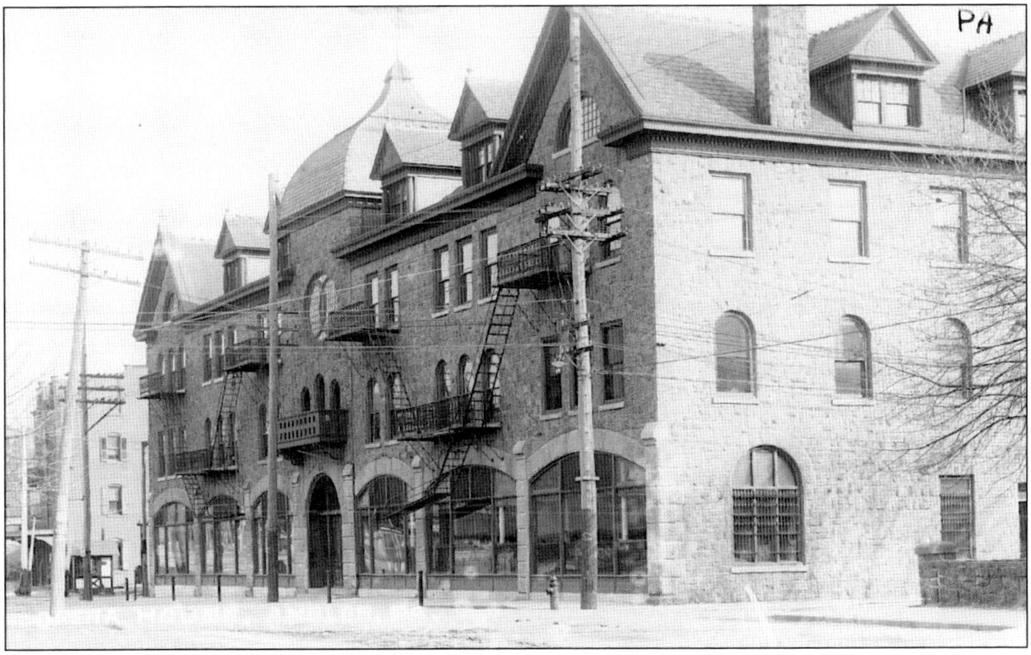

THE OPERA HOUSE IN AMBLER. Certainly a unique structure for small Ambler Borough, the opera house was an imposing building on Butler Avenue across from the railroad station. Built in 1890, it was a major cultural attraction that also contained a library, offices, and stores. Dr. Richard Mattison, who made a fortune in his asbestos textile plant in Ambler, built the opera house and office building. Operas flourished until moving pictures became popular. In the 1930s, Keasbey converted the opera house to a movie theater, which was demolished in 1967. A gas station now occupies the site. (W.W. Miller postcard.)

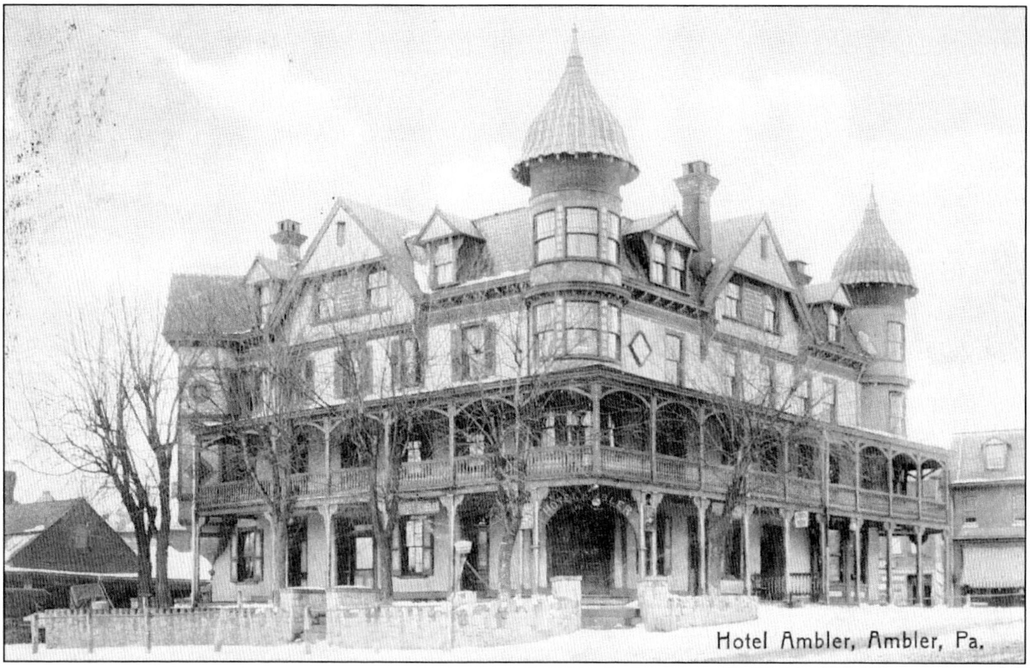

HOTEL AMBLER. Built in 1870–71, this was Ambler's first hotel. It stood on the north side of Butler Pike and east of the railroad station. Notice the wonderful second-floor balcony and turrets at each end of the building on the front facade that faced Butler Pike. The hotel burned down in 1944. (Rees C. Roberts postcard, 1908.)

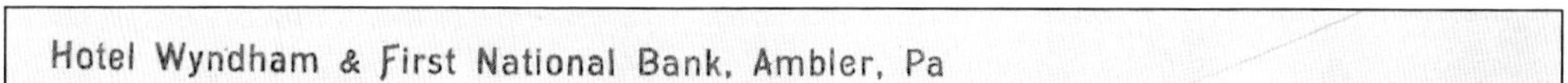

HOTEL WYNDHAM AND THE FIRST NATIONAL BANK IN AMBLER, 1906. The Wyndham Hotel was built in 1893 at the corner of Butler Pike and Spring Garden Street. The First National Bank was built in 1894, and in 1923 it was moved behind a larger bank building on Butler Pike. It would later be torn down to make way for a drive-through window for the larger building. The Wyndham is still standing and is a unique example of Ambler's Victorian past. (Rees C. Roberts postcard.)

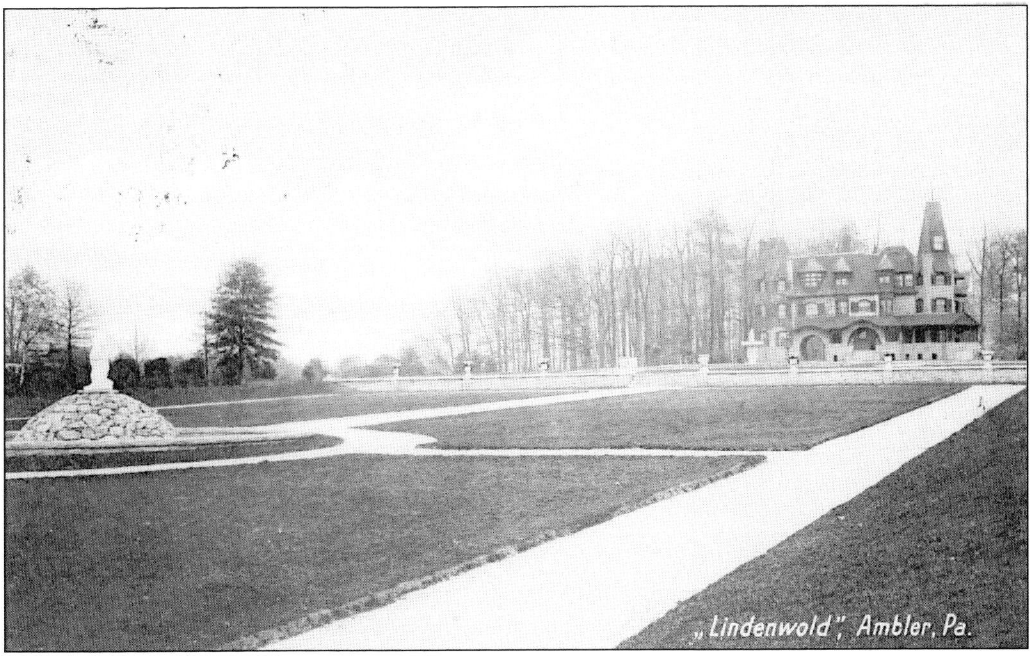

LINDENWOLD IN AMBLER. Dr. Richard Mattison's mansion was called Lindenwold and was located in Upper Dublin Township on Bethlehem Pike at Highland Avenue. Construction began in 1901 on the 13-room, 400-acre estate. In 1912, the building was drastically changed—the entire exterior was encompassed in stone and was remodeled after Windsor Castle in England. In 1936, the property was bought by Sisters of The Holy Family and the stone castle still stands on the property. (Rees C. Roberts postcard.)

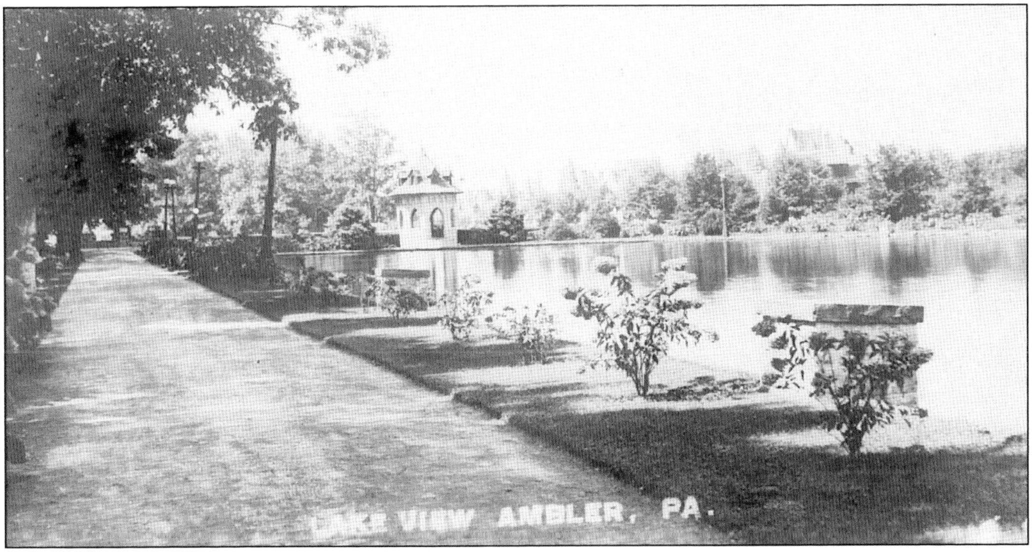

A LAKE VIEW, LINDENWOLD. Lindenwold boasted beautiful grounds, statuary, and this 6-acre lake called Loch Linden. The mansion and formal gardens were enclosed by beautiful stone walls and contained several majestic iron-gated entrances. Some of this property has been developed for housing, but there is still a large area of open space where much of the once-elegant estate can still be seen. (John Bartholomew postcard.)

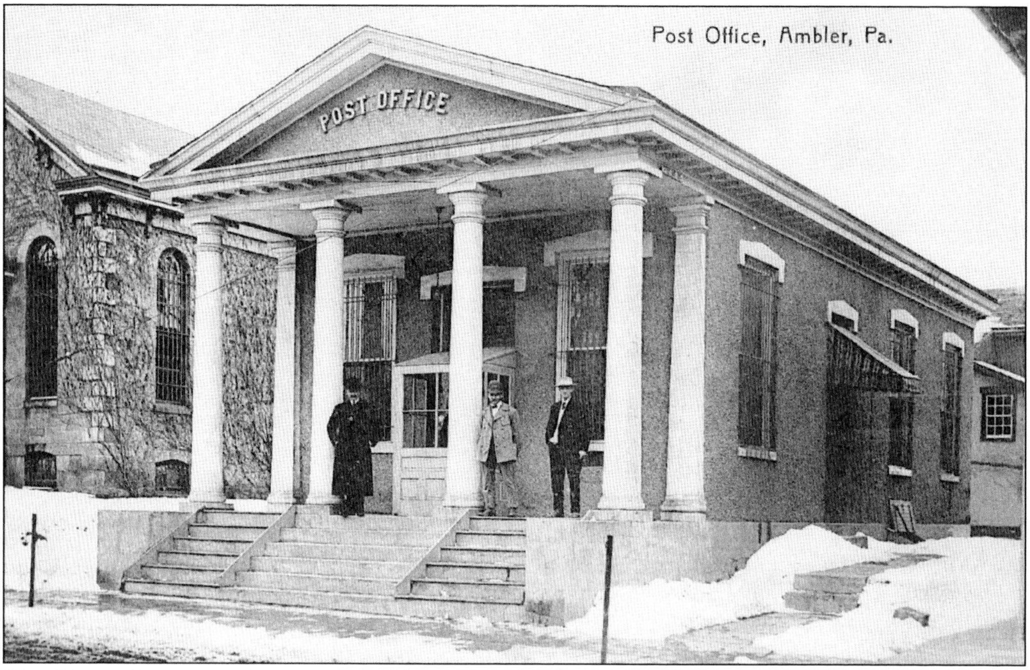

THE POST OFFICE IN AMBLER. Ambler Borough's first post office building was located on the south side of Butler Pike, next to the old First National Bank (visible to the left in this 1908 view). The Greek Revival architecture that encompassed this building's front indicated a rather fashionable style for a post office. Built in 1898, the building, or at least a portion of it, still exists, though it has been incorporated into another structure. The beautiful columns are now gone. (Rees C. Roberts postcard.)

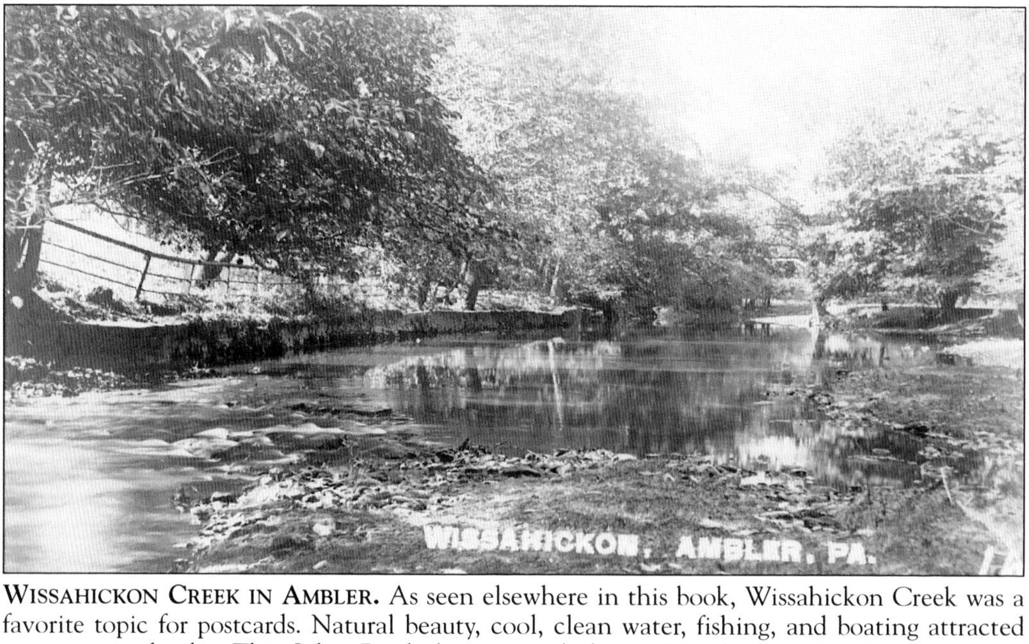

WISSAHICKON CREEK IN AMBLER. As seen elsewhere in this book, Wissahickon Creek was a favorite topic for postcards. Natural beauty, cool, clean water, fishing, and boating attracted many to its banks. This John Bartholomew card shows Wissahickon Creek on a sunny summer day c. 1910.

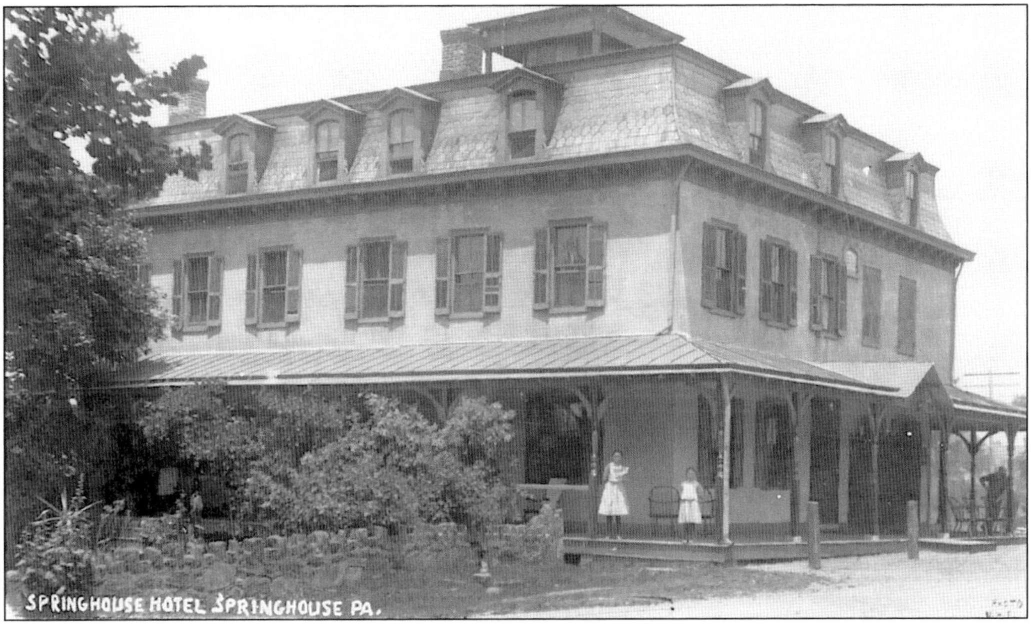

THE SPRING HOUSE HOTEL. The Spring House Hotel, located on Bethlehem Pike, near Norristown Road, Sumneytown Pike, and Penllyn-Blue Bell Pike, has been in existence since the 18th century. In 1888, the building burned down, but it was later rebuilt. Today, it is a tavern and a landmark in Spring House, as it has been for over 200 years. (Sliker postcard.)

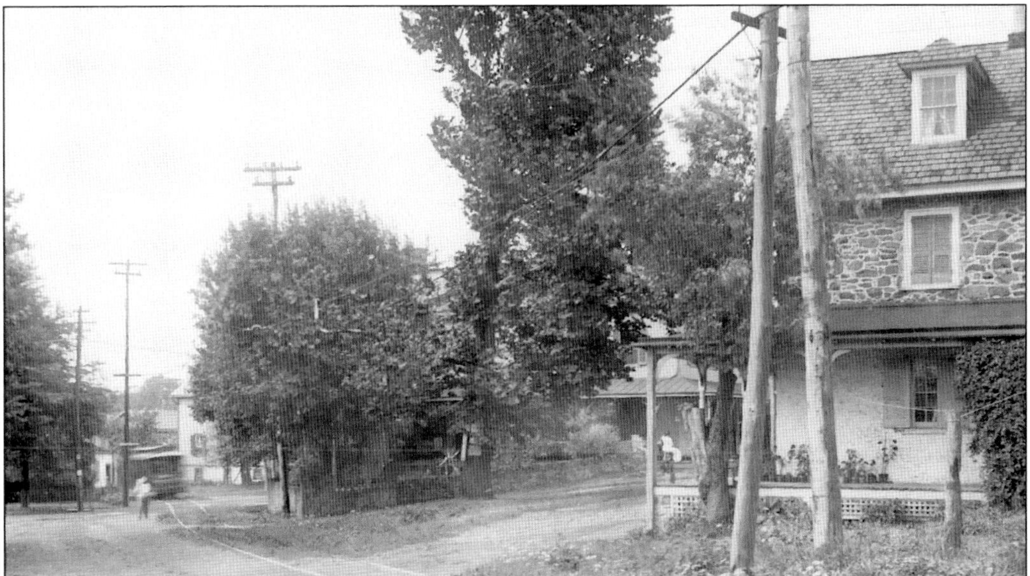

TROLLEY ROAD IN SPRING HOUSE. This 1910 view shows the Bethlehem Pike looking north toward Sumneytown Pike. Bethlehem Pike would take a sharp right near where the trolley is seen. The trolley itself is on Sumneytown Pike. The stone building on the right is no longer standing, but the building behind it is the Spring House Hotel. This is an outstanding view of what Bethlehem Pike and Spring House looked almost 100 years ago. (Sliker postcard.)

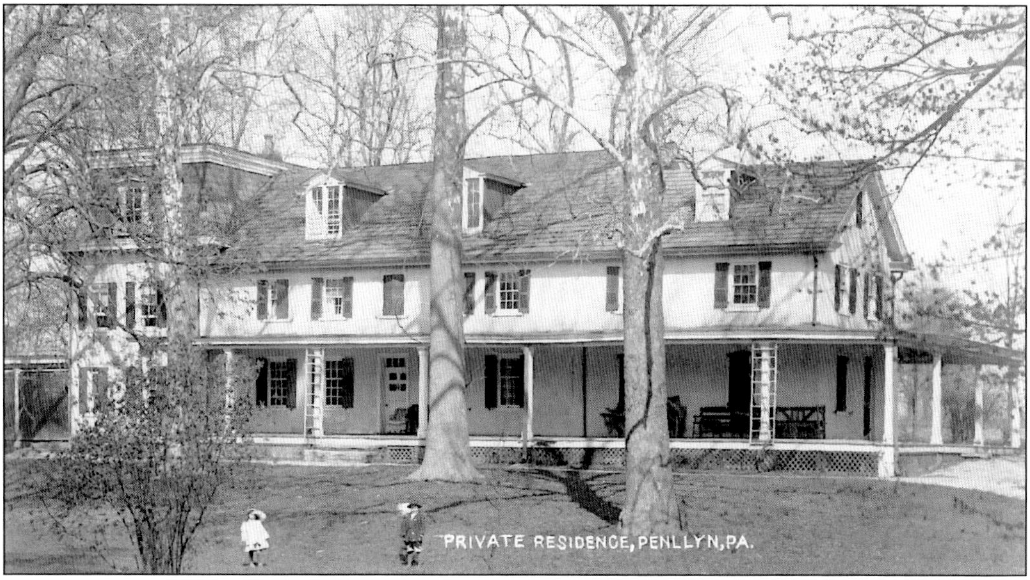

A Private Residence in Penllyn. The Foulke Mansion was one of the earliest built in the Penllyn area, dating back to the early 1700s. Members of the Foulke family were well-known Quakers in the area. During the Revolution, Sally Wister, then living in the house, documented events of the time in a journal, which was later published and became rather well known. Unfortunately, the home on Penllyn-Blue Bell Pike was torn down in the 1980s. (W.W. Miller postcard.)

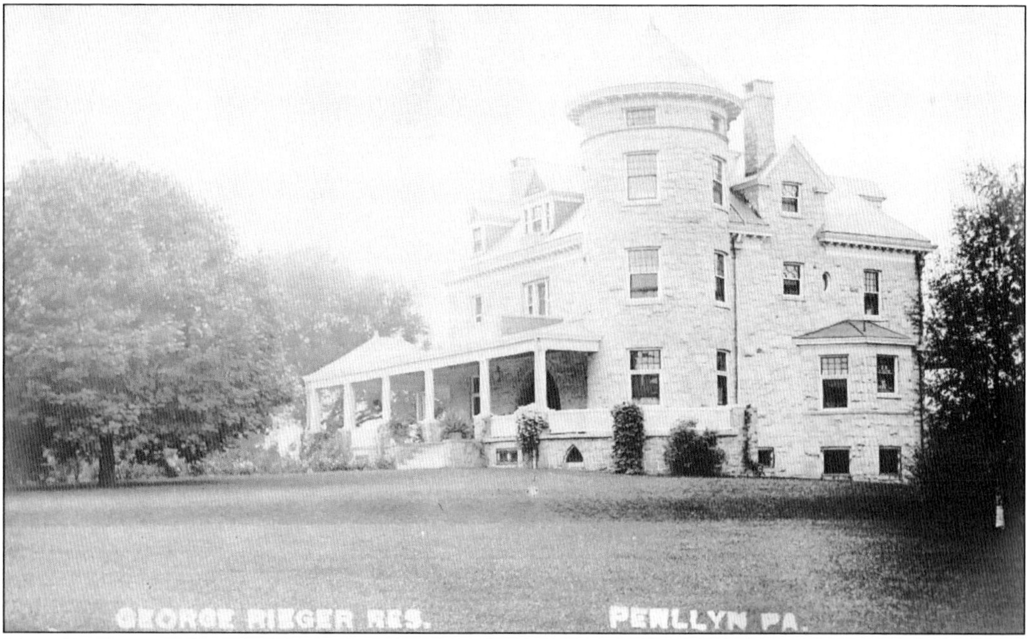

The George Rieger Residence in Penllyn. The magnificent mansion built by George Rieger is an example of the wealth of many residents in the Penllyn area. Built between 1896 and 1899, the handsome stone mansion still stands on Penllyn-Blue Bell Pike. Today, along with other building additions, it is a nursing home. Rieger was the Bergdoll Beer brewmaster. (John Bartholomew postcard.)

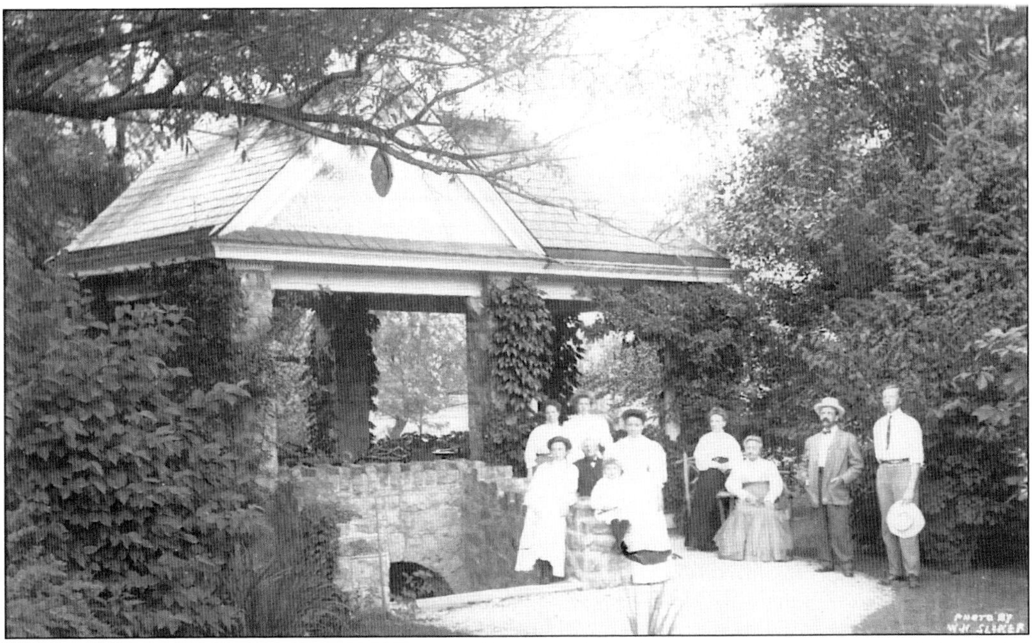

A House on the Property of George Rieger. The Rieger property contained beautiful grounds, including a lovely garden pavilion. This Sliker postcard from c. 1908 shows a gathering of people. Many mansions in the Penllyn area were used as summer homes for the wealthy folks from Philadelphia.

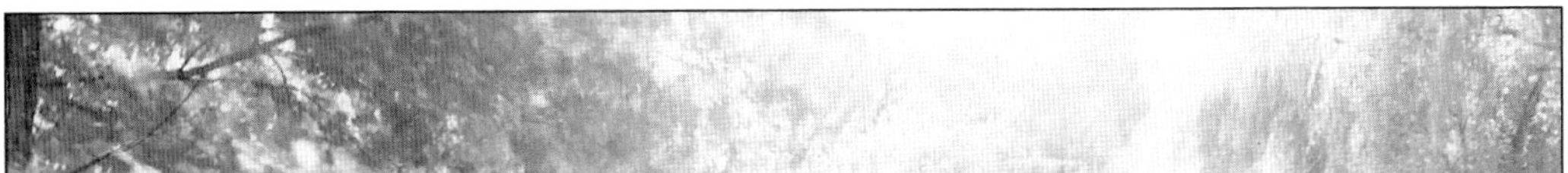

A Lake and Rustic Bridges, the Property of George Rieger. Willow Run, a tributary of Wissahickon Creek, ran through the Rieger property. Obviously a small lake was formed on this stream and provided a beautiful scene. The property also had a number of rustic wooded footbridges spanning the stream, which are visible in this view. Also, note the small log house to the left. (Sliker postcard.)

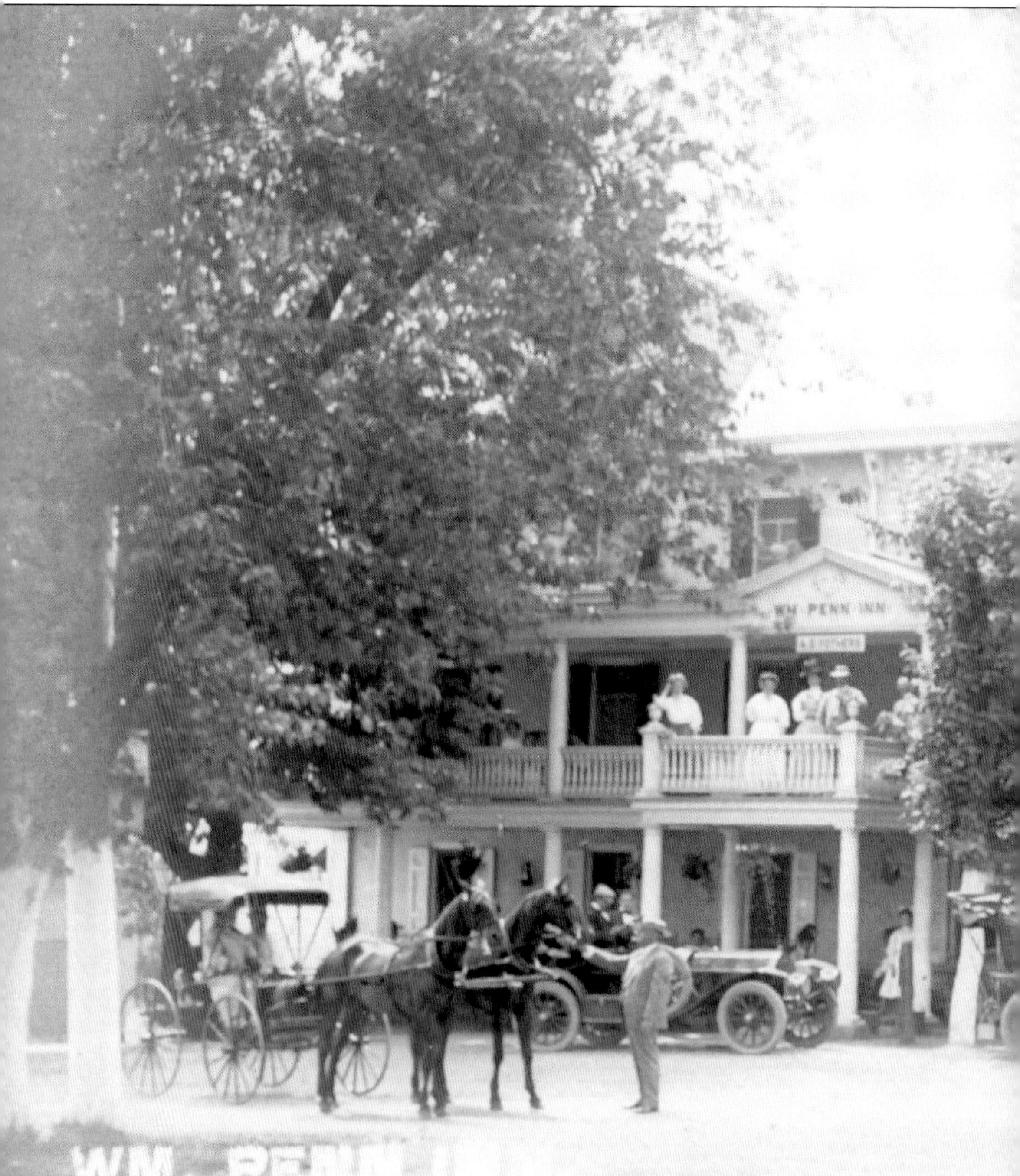

THE WILLIAM PENN INN. Along Dekalb and Sumneytown Pikes stands the majestic and historic William Penn Inn. Named in honor of the founder of Pennsylvania, legend has it that he stayed here while visiting some Welsh Quakers in Gwynedd *c.* 1700. It is possible that Penn did make it to Gwynedd, but it is rather unlikely that this building was standing at that early

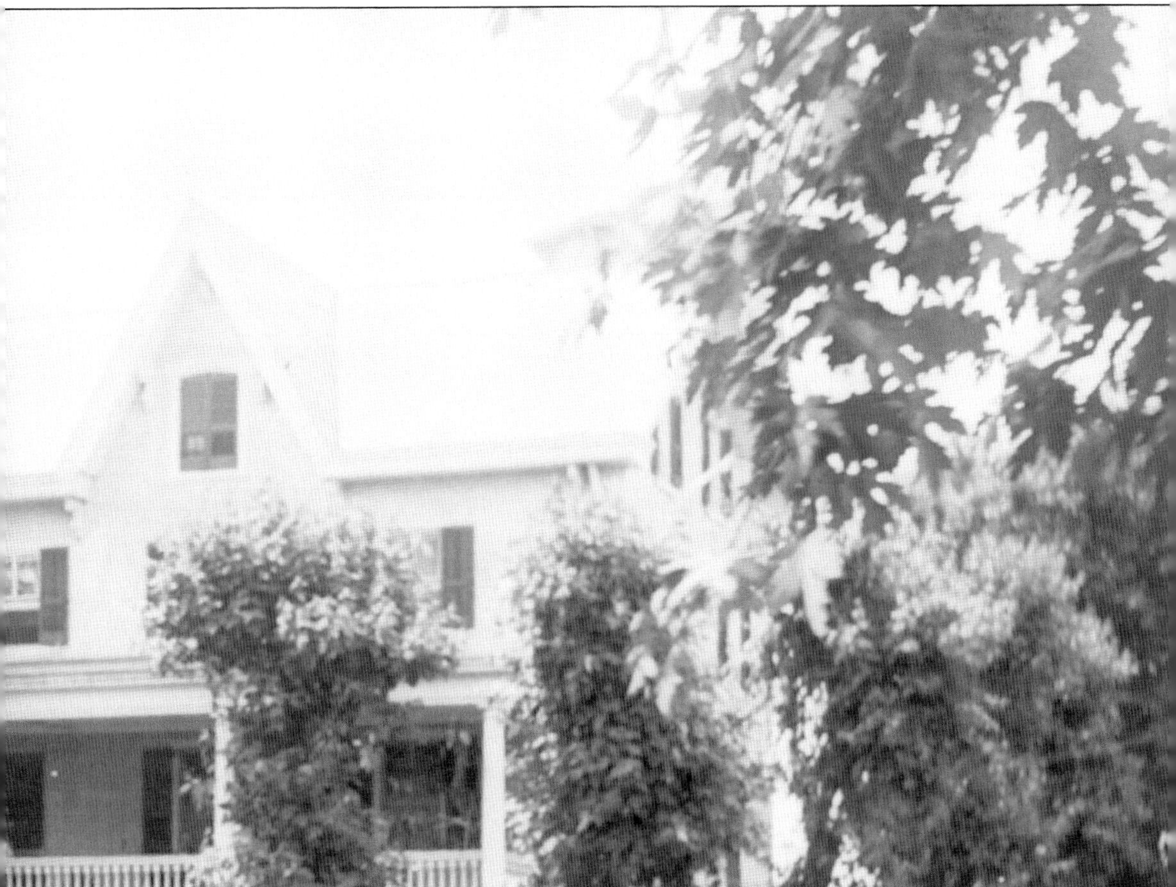

time period. Whatever its history may be, it does date from the early 1700s and has been serving the public food and drink for almost 300 years. This view shows busy activity at the inn. Of particular interest are the different modes of transportation, from horse-drawn wagons to "modern" automobiles. (John Bartholomew postcard.)

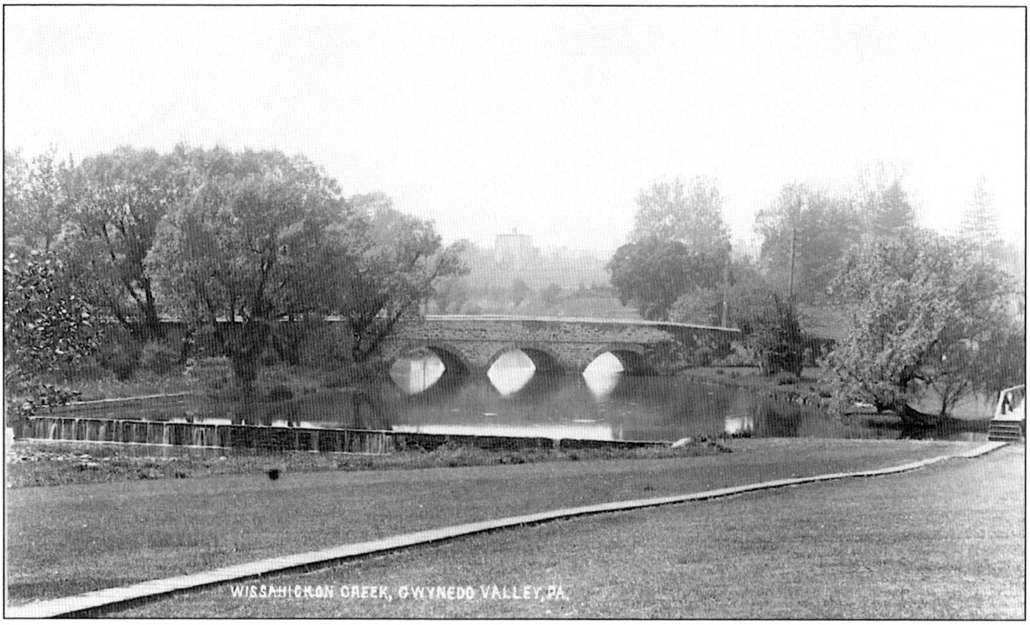

WISSAHICKON CREEK IN GWYNEDD VALLEY. This scenic view is of Wissahickon Creek, looking west toward the Plymouth Road Bridge in Lower Gwynedd Township. Plymouth Road is an old road and the bridge has three date stones on it, one from 1839, 1914, and 1977. (W.W. Miller postcard.)

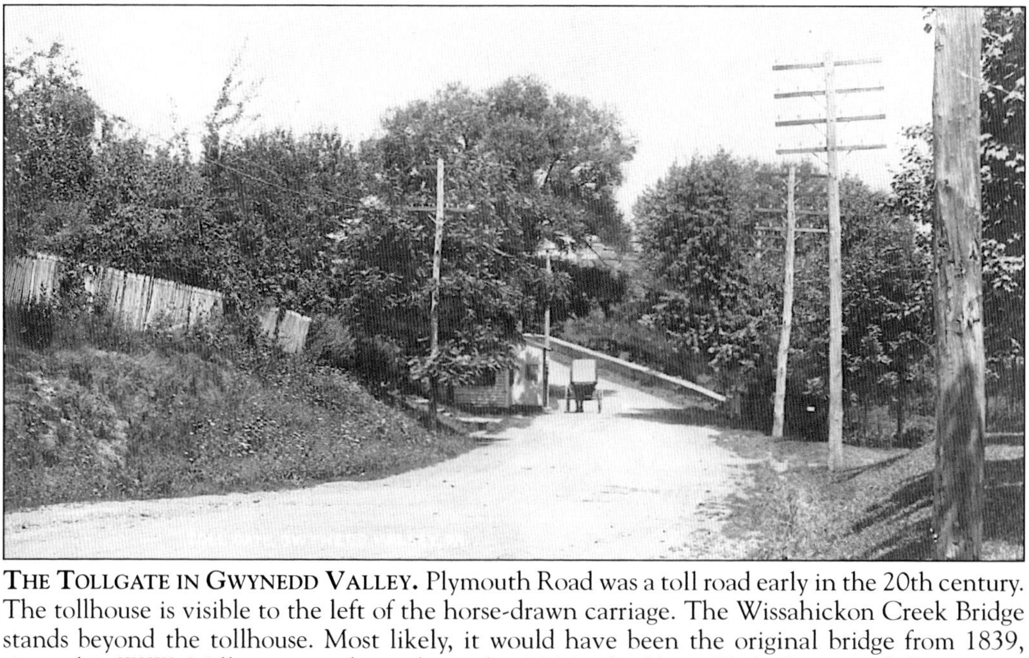

THE TOLLGATE IN GWYNEDD VALLEY. Plymouth Road was a toll road early in the 20th century. The tollhouse is visible to the left of the horse-drawn carriage. The Wissahickon Creek Bridge stands beyond the tollhouse. Most likely, it would have been the original bridge from 1839, since this W.W. Miller postcard pre-dates the 1914 rebuilding. Today's view of this spot is remarkably similar, except that the tollhouse is gone and the road is paved.

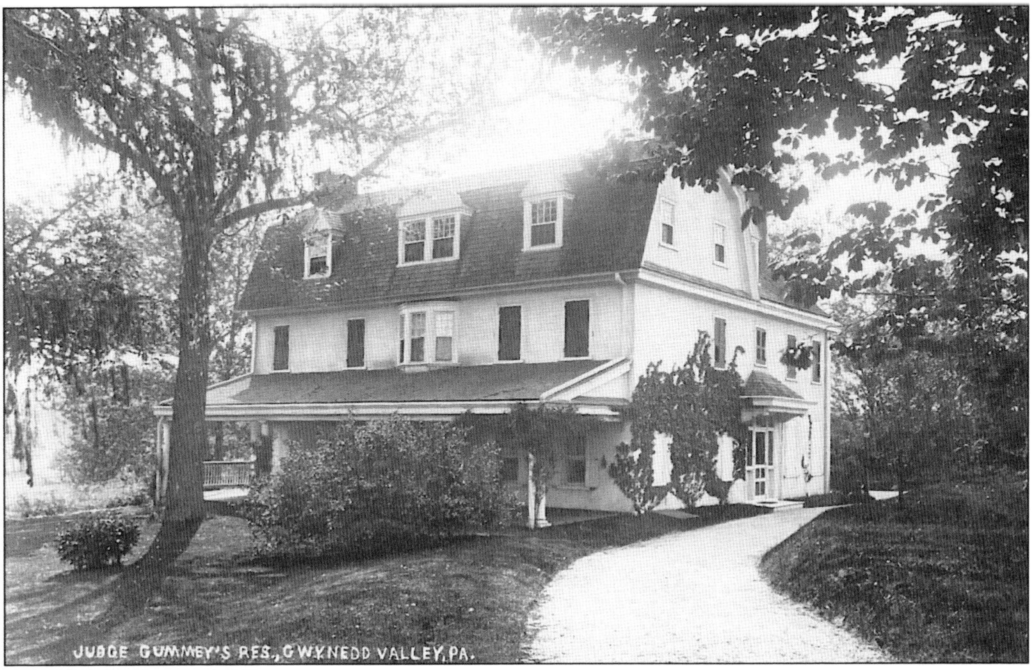

JUDGE GUMMEY'S RESIDENCE IN GWYNEDD VALLEY. The Gwynedd area has been a mecca for wealthy people since the 1700s. This attractive farmhouse dates back to the mid-1700s and is standing on Plymouth Road north of the Wissahickon Creek. (W.W. Miller postcard.)

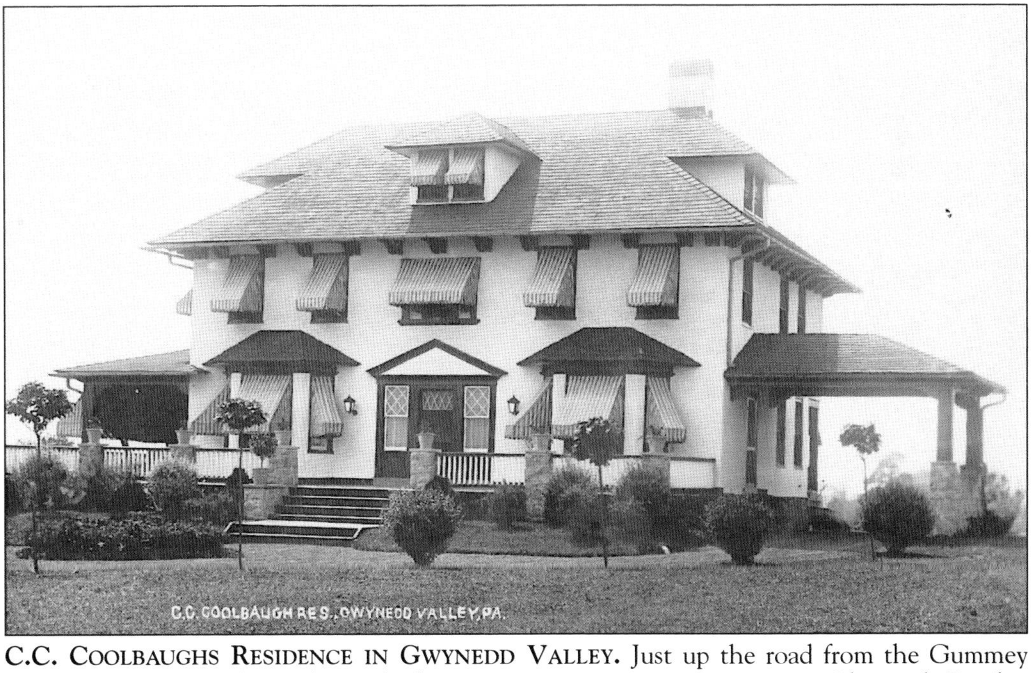

C.C. COOLBAUGHS RESIDENCE IN GWYNEDD VALLEY. Just up the road from the Gummey residence is this handsome house built *c.* 1908. Its current appearance on Plymouth Road is almost identical to this postcard mailed in 1913. (W.W. Miller postcard.)

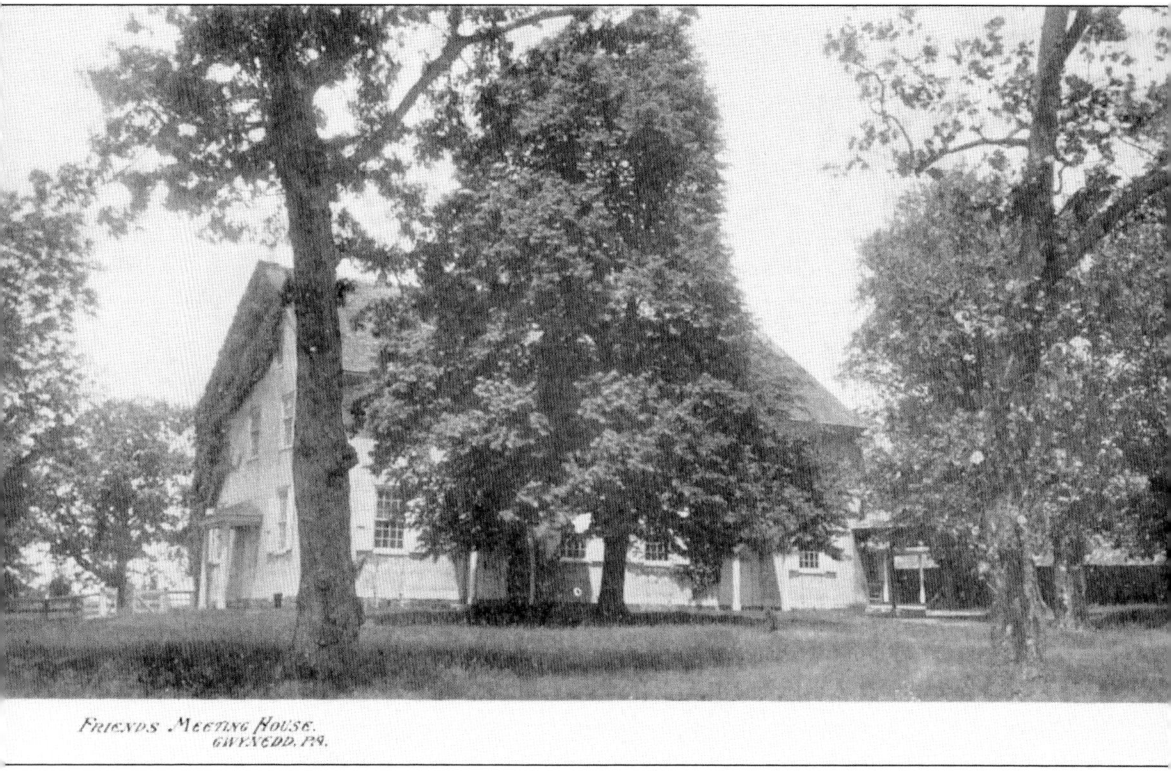

FRIENDS MEETINGHOUSE IN GWYNEDD. The Quaker community in Gwynedd goes back to the time of William Penn, *c.* 1700. Welsh Friends built their first meetinghouse around that time. As time went on, a bigger meetinghouse was needed, and in 1823, the present structure was erected. Gwynedd Friends is one of the most active in the area. In 1998, a new addition was added. It is located at DeKalb and Sumneytown Pikes. (World Post Card Company postcard.)

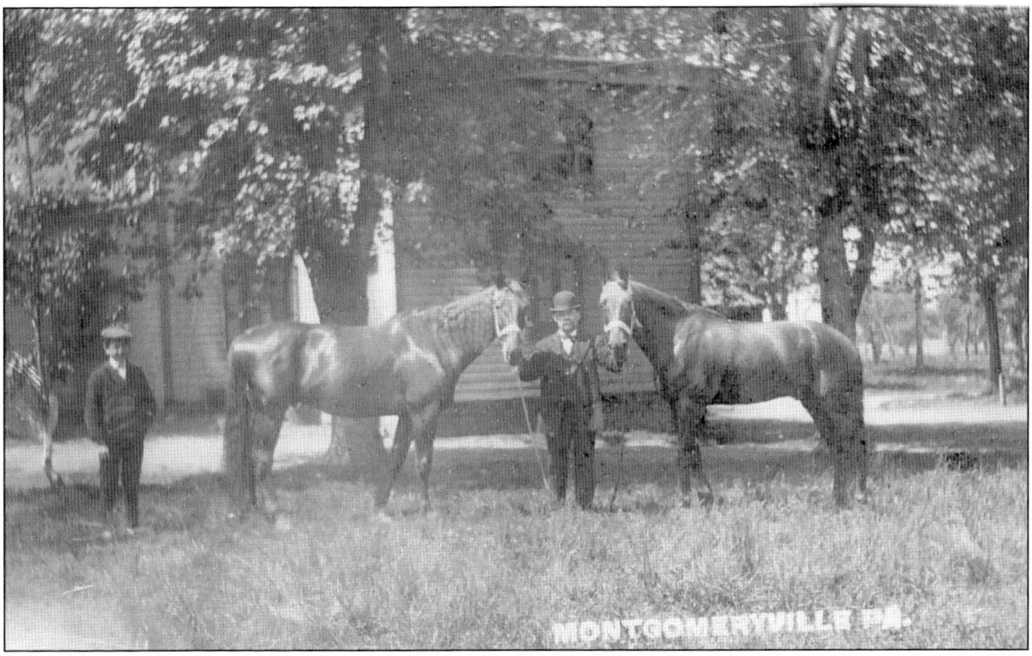

MONTGOMERYVILLE. This wonderfully posed picture shows a proud man showing off two of his prized horses. Farming, agriculture, and living close to nature were all part of the culture and landscape early in the 20th century, as illustrated by this unidentified location somewhere in Montgomeryville. (John Bartholomew postcard.)

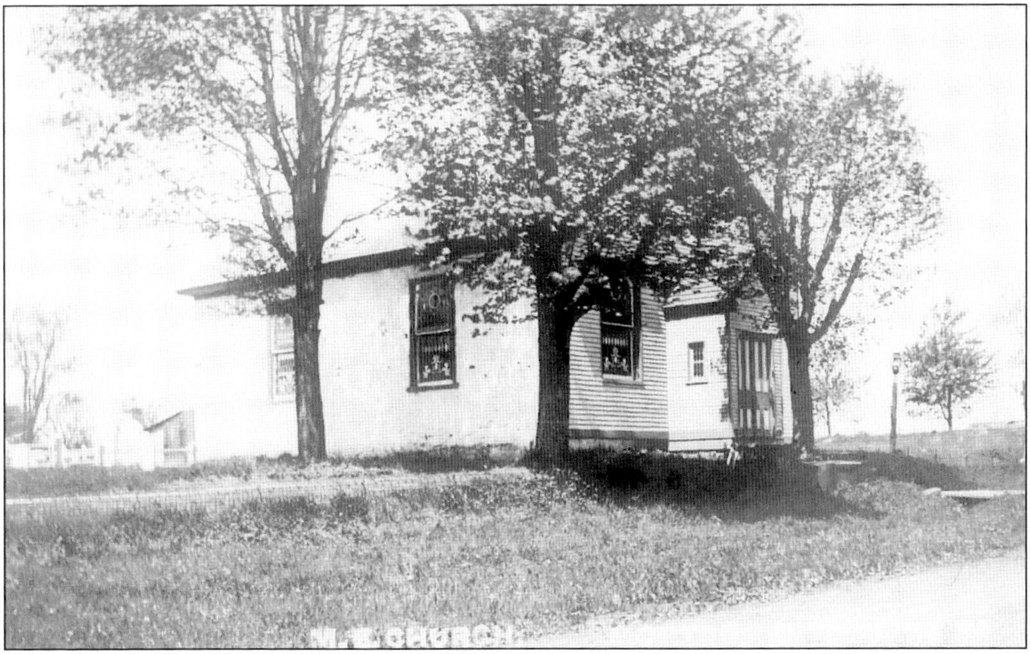

THE M.E. CHURCH IN MONTGOMERY SQUARE. Montgomery Square was a village at the intersection of DeKalb Pike, Upper State Road, and Bethlehem Pike. Built in 1842, this building still stands, with a few additions, on Bethlehem Pike, south of the Montgomery Mall. (John Bartholomew postcard.)

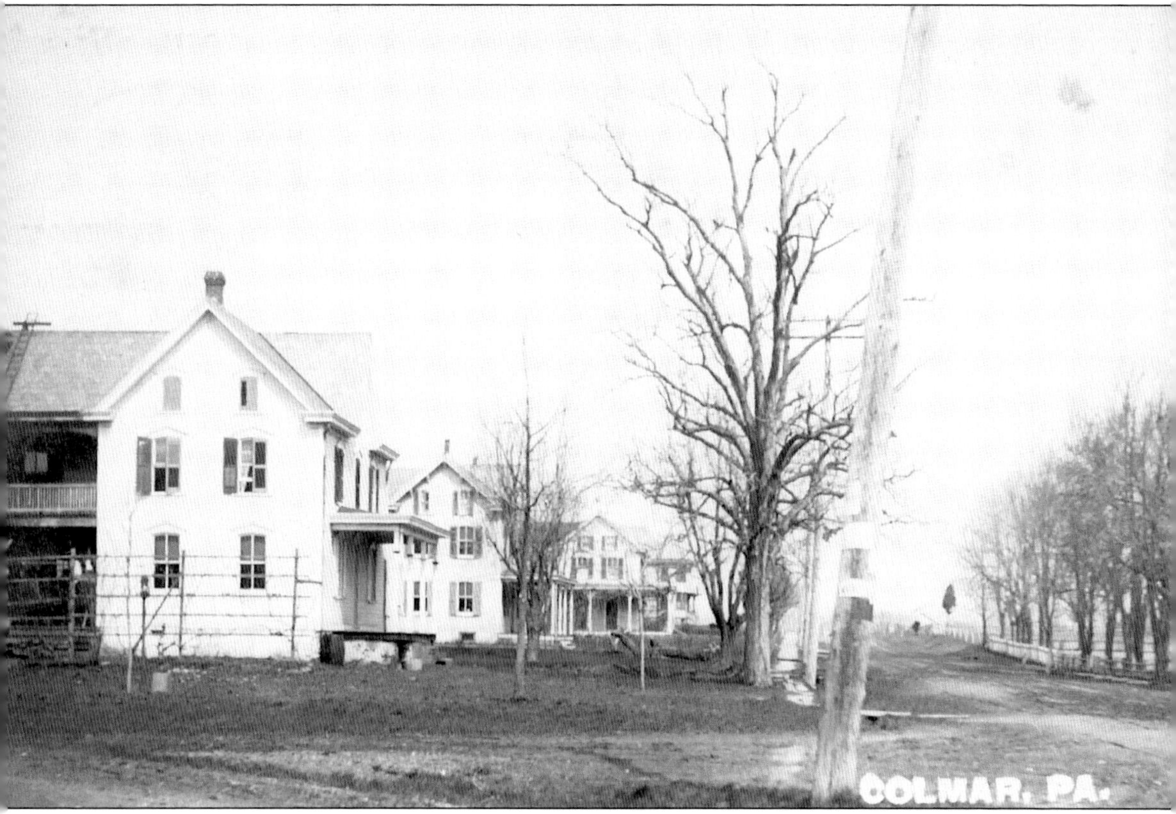

COLMAR. Bethlehem Pike was a dirt road when John Batholomew of Lansdale published this postcard. Most of the buildings pictured here, north of the railroad crossing, are still standing, but have been converted to business establishments. Colmar is the northernmost town on the Bethlehem Pike in Montgomery County. The Bucks County line is about one mile north of this view.

Five

Ridge Pike and Germantown Pike

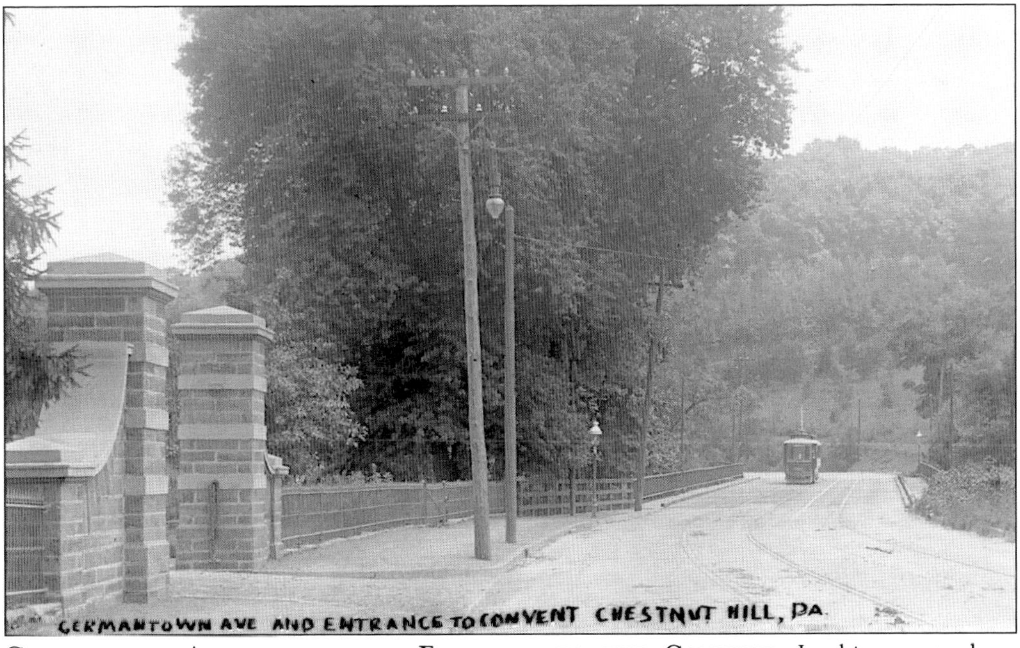

GERMANTOWN AVENUE AND THE ENTRANCE TO THE CONVENT. Looking east along Germantown Avenue in front of Chestnut Hill College in Philadelphia, the trolley is just about to cross Wissahickon Creek. This is a 1910 view of what Germantown Pike looked like as it approached the Montgomery County line. The trolley is part of the Chestnut Hill-Norristown Line established in 1895 and is heading for Norristown. (Sliker postcard.)

GERMANTOWN PIKE
RIDGE PIKE

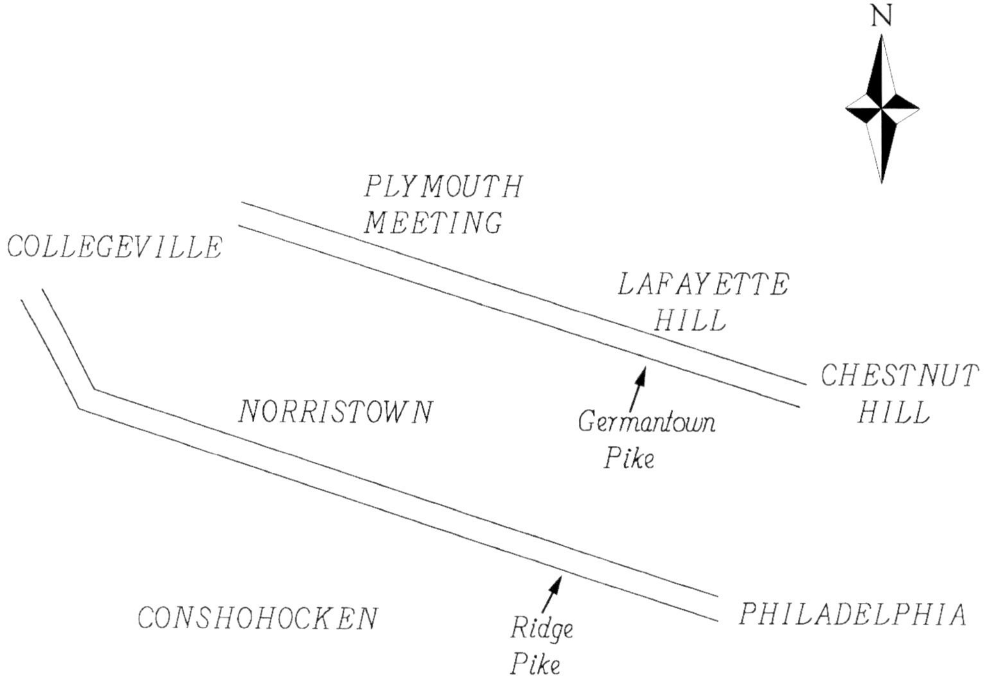

GERMANTOWN PIKE. Germantown was settled in 1683 with land grants from William Penn. It was then 6 miles northwest of Philadelphia. Today, of course, it is part of the city. During these early years a road was developed and like so many other Colonial roads, it followed an old Native-American trail. By 1710, a group of Quakers established the Plymouth Friends Meeting and the road was further extended to this point. It eventually became the Germantown and Perkiomen Turnpike. Its western terminus is at Perkiomen Creek in Collegeville.

RIDGE PIKE. It takes its name from its location on a ridge between the Schuylkill River and Wissahickon Creek in Philadelphia. Sections of the road, which begin near Vine Street in Center City, Philadelphia, date from *c.* 1700. As expansion moved westward, the road was extended into Montgomery County until it eventually linked Philadelphia with Reading.

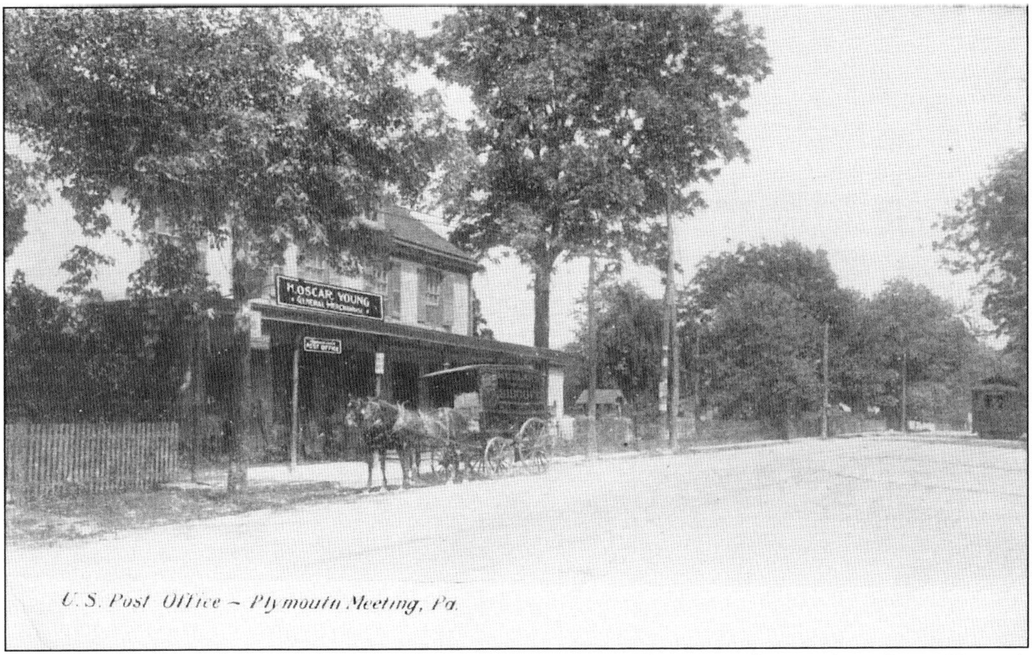

THE U.S. POST OFFICE IN PLYMOUTH MEETING, 1905. The post office and H. Oscar Young's general store in the village of Plymouth Meeting stood on the north side of Germantown Pike, at the corner of Butler Pike. The post office has been moved out of the building and the general store no long exists, but the old Colonial structure still stands.

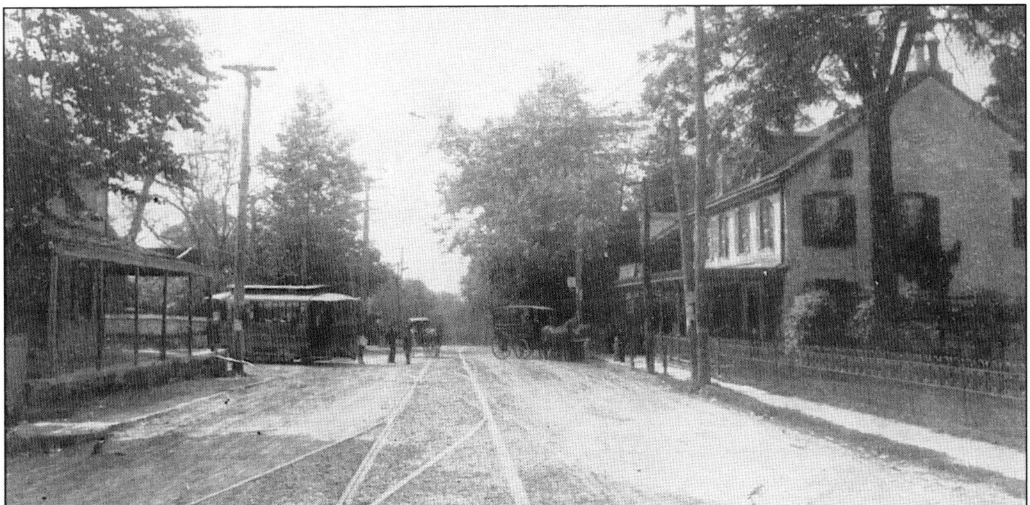

PLYMOUTH MEETING, 1905. Looking west on the Germantown Pike, the post office and general store are on the right. The trolley is turning onto Butler Pike, heading for Conshohocken. Amazingly, with all the traffic to the mall, turnpike, and Blue Route, Plymouth Meeting retains most of its older buildings, many of which date before the Revolutionary War.

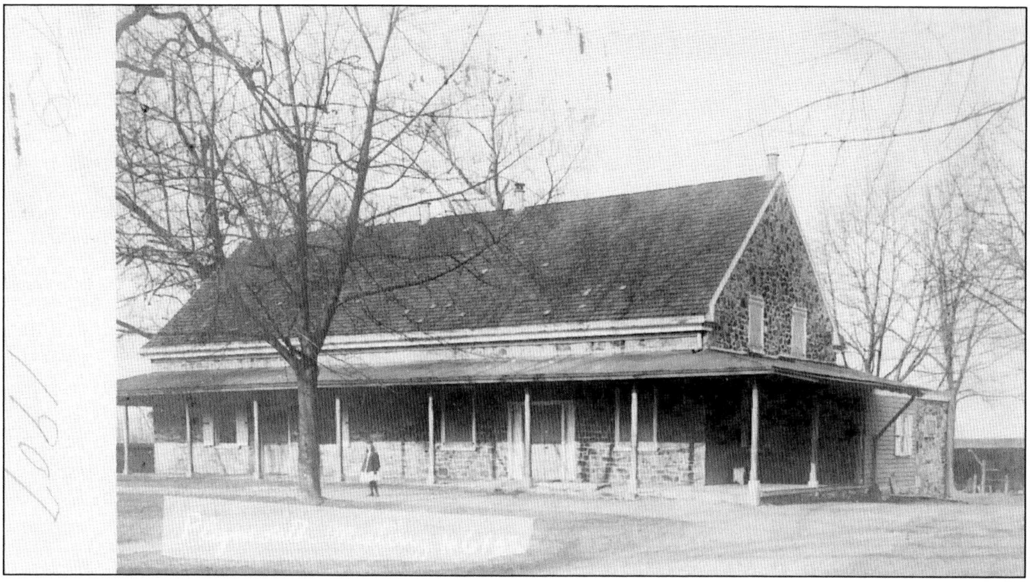

PLYMOUTH MEETING. Plymouth Friends established a Quaker Meeting sometime *c.* 1710 in Plymouth Township. A meetinghouse was erected at the junction of the Germantown and Butler Pikes in the early 1700s. A fire destroyed the structure in 1867 and another one was erected on the same site. This view shows the second meetinghouse, which is still in use. The village of Plymouth Meeting grew around the meetinghouse and contains many historic buildings.

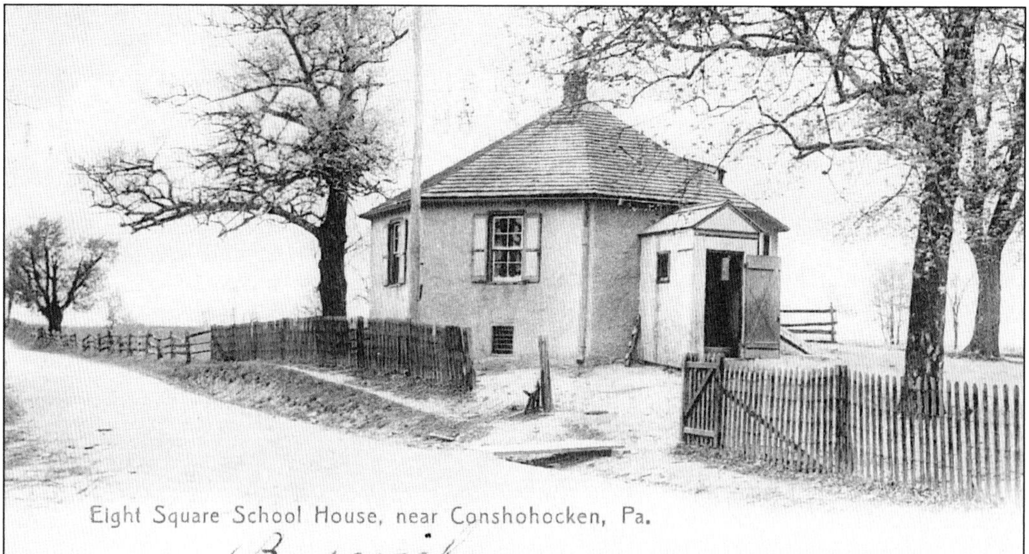

THE EIGHT SQUARE SCHOOLHOUSE IN PLYMOUTH. Eight-sided schoolhouses were in fashion in the late 1700s to the mid-1800s. This one was located on North Lane, north of Butler Pike, where apartment buildings now stand. Though it did not survive, the Philadelphia region has several still standing, including ones located at Newtown Square, Chadds Ford, Wrightstown, and Diamond Rock near Paoli. (Graham and Johnson postcard.)

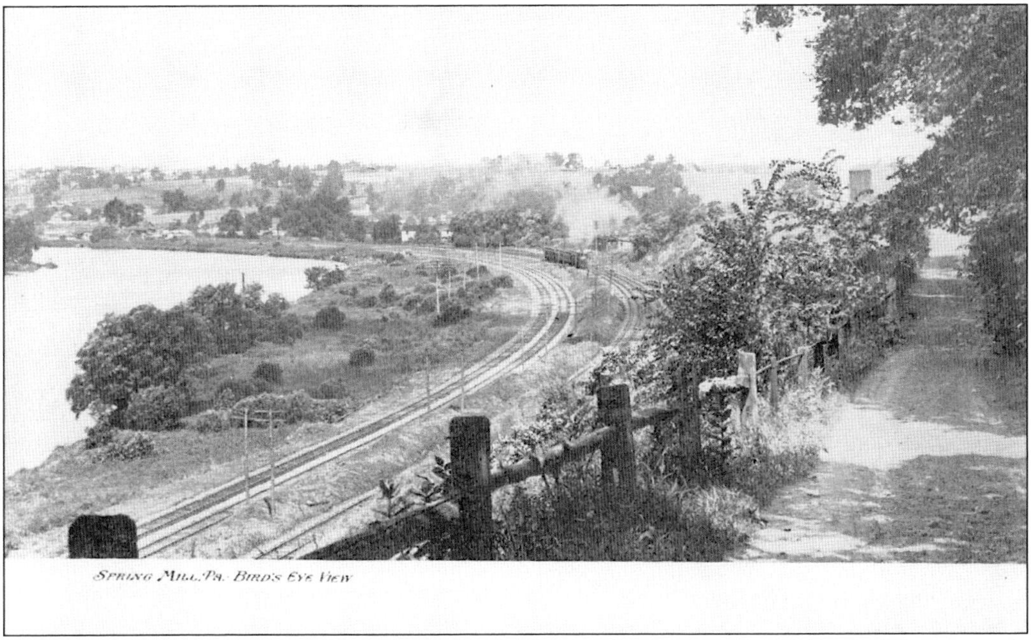

SPRING MILL—A BIRD'S-EYE VIEW. Spring Mill is a village along the Schuylkill River, south of Conshohocken in Whitemarsh Township. This scene is looking north along River Road. (World Post Card Company postcard.)

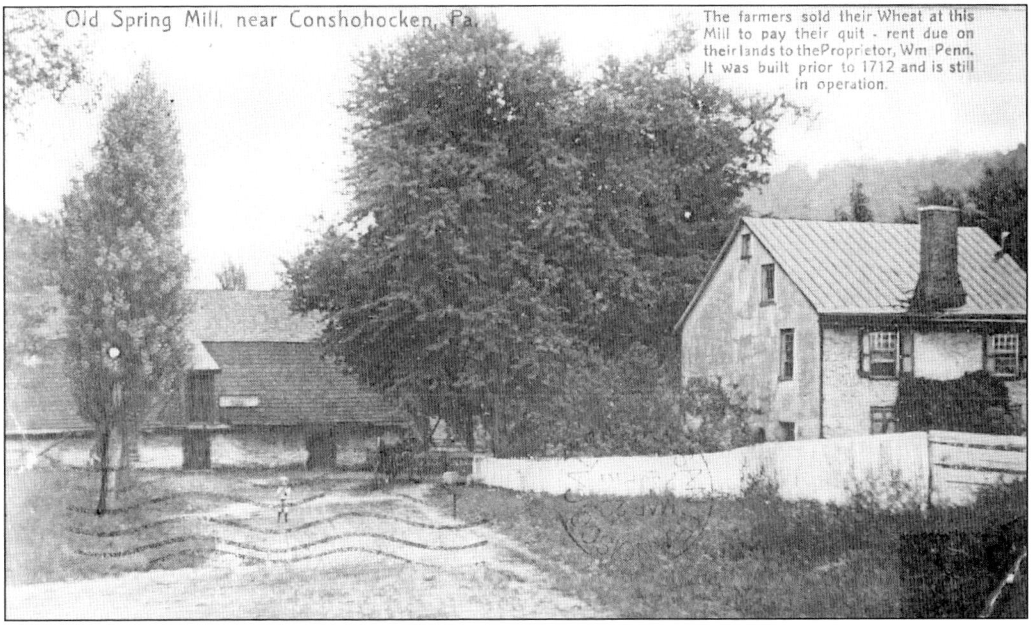

THE OLD SPRING MILL, NEAR CONSHOHOCKEN. The Spring Mill was located off Hector Street where Spring Mill Creek empties into the Schuylkill River in Whitemarsh Township. The mill was built c. 1715 and was a prominent landmark in Colonial times. Although this 1908 view shows the mill and mill house, today only the house is standing. (Graham and Johnson postcard.)

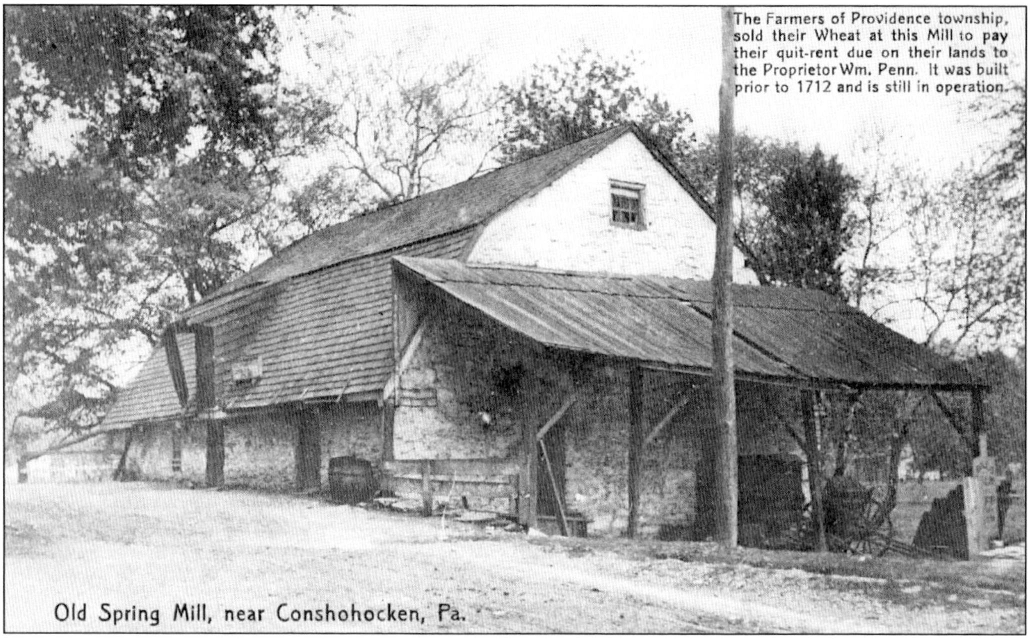

THE OLD SPRING MILL. This is a close-up view of the Spring Mill. This might very well be the building that dates from *c.* 1715. Even in this 1908 view, the mill looks quite old. (Graham and Johnson postcard.)

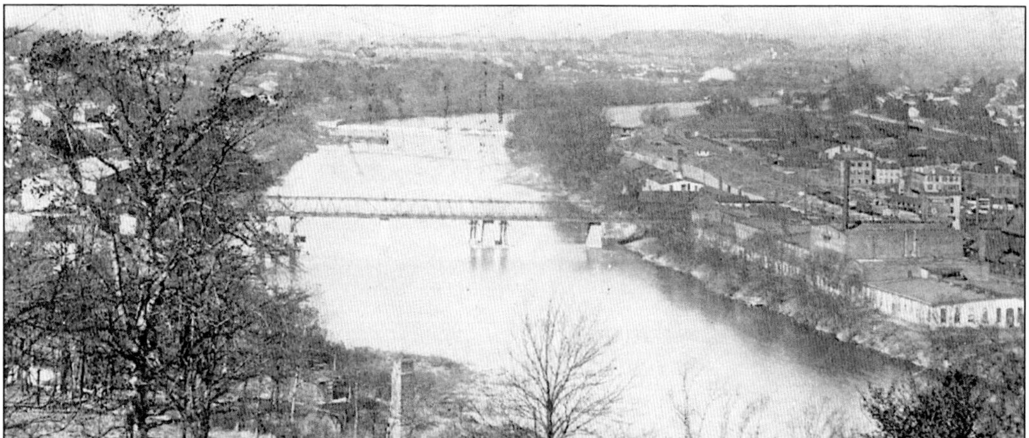

A RIVER VIEW FROM THE MATSON FORD BRIDGE IN CONSHOHOCKEN. Matson Ford, established in the 1740s by the Swedish settler Peter Matson, was a historic river crossing used by the American Army during the Revolutionary War in 1777 and 1778. The first bridge built on this site was a wooden covered bridge in 1840. In 1872, the steel bridge pictured in this 1906 view was built.

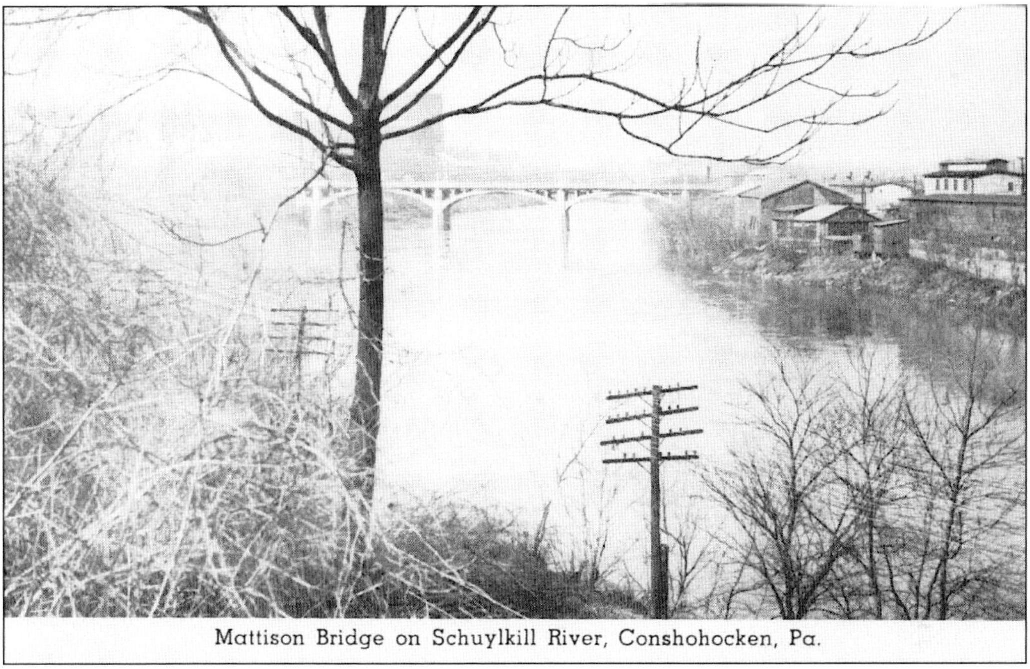

MATTISON BRIDGE ON THE SCHUYLKILL RIVER IN CONSHOHOCKEN. The bridge pictured in this 1950s postcard, built in 1921 and made of concrete, replaced the 1872 steel bridge. This is not "Mattison" Bridge as written on the postcard but the "Matson Ford Bridge."

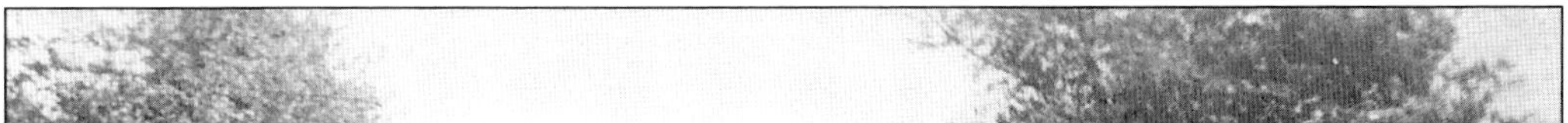

FAYETTE STREET LOOKING FROM FIFTH AVENUE IN CONSHOHOCKEN. This is a 1907 view of the tree-lined Fayette Street from Fifth Avenue. The Schuylkill Valley Traction Company trolley ran the entire length of Fayette Street. Schuylkill Valley ran trolleys between towns along the Schuylkill River corridor from 1895 until 1908. From 1908 until 1933, Reading Transit operated the old Schuylkill Line. (Graham and Johnson postcard.)

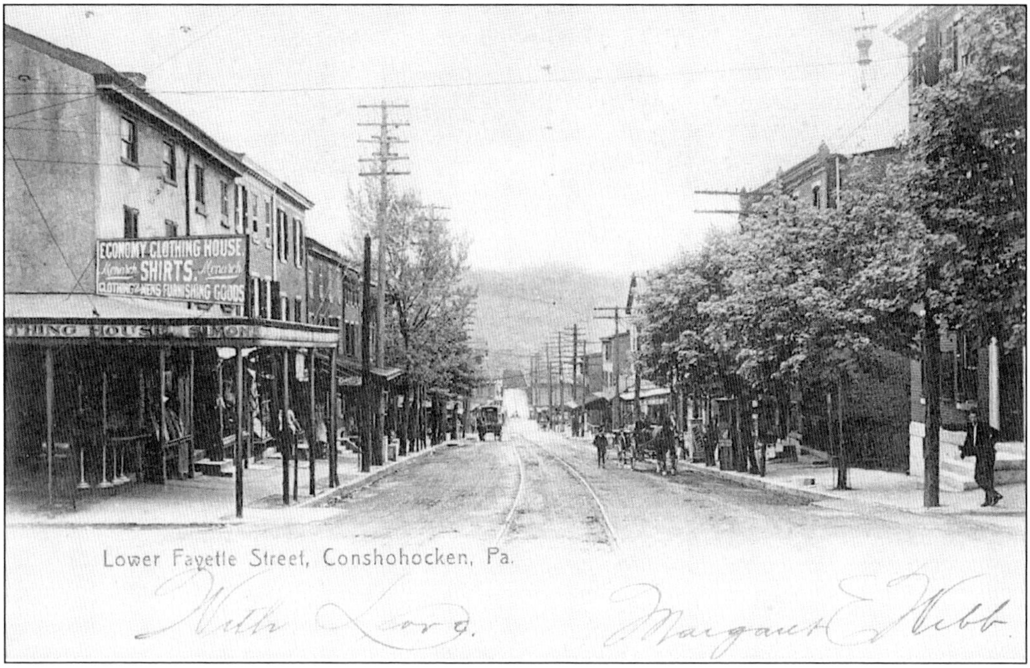

LOWER FAYETTE STREET. This 1906 view shows the old business district of Conshohocken looking southeast. The old 1872 steel bridge over the Schuylkill can be seen at the bottom of the street. Fayette Street has been widened since this view was made, and many of the structures seen here are no longer standing. (Graham and Johnson postcard.)

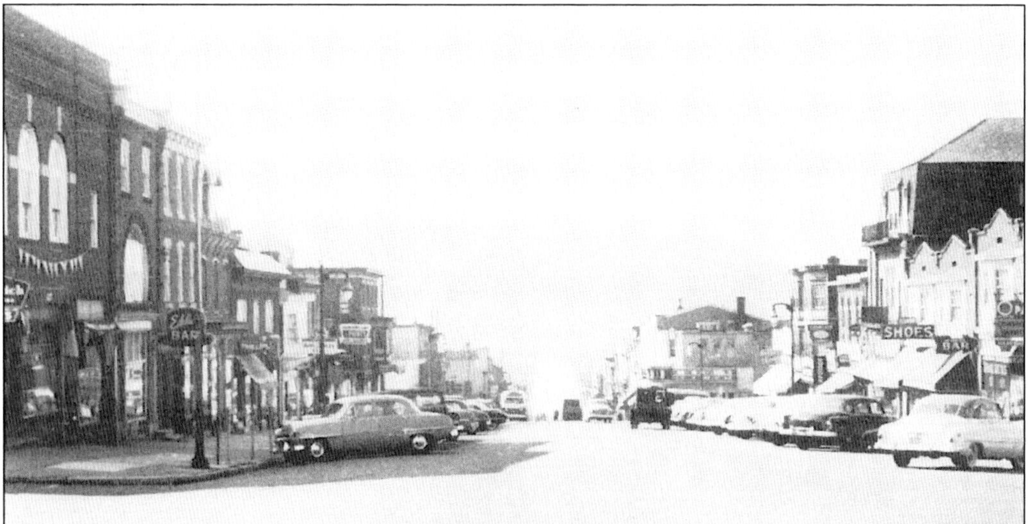

FAYETTE STREET. Although this view dates from only c. 1953, changes made to this street are evident today. Looking southeast toward the river, automobiles are no longer permitted to park diagonally along Fayette Street. Conshohocken still retains its business district with many small stores along Fayette Street. (Art-Glo Post Card Company postcard.)

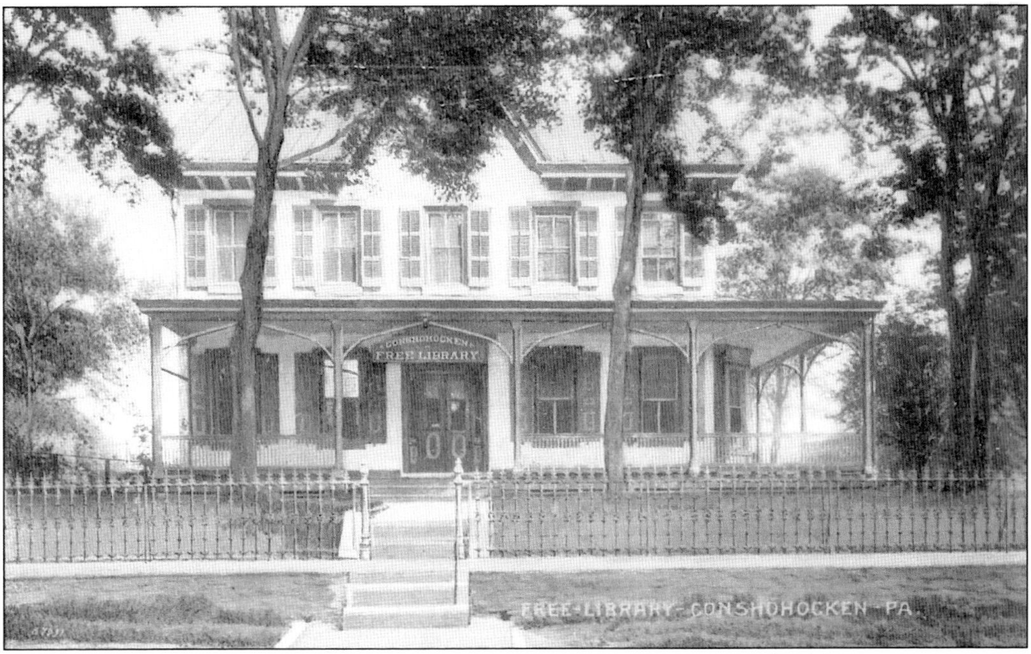

FREE LIBRARY IN CONSHOHOCKEN. Once a private home, this building was given to Conshohocken Borough for use as a public library in 1910. Located on Fayette Street at Third Avenue, it has been the Conshohocken Free Library since then. The beautiful Victorian architecture of the original home has been preserved. (Graham and Johnson postcard.)

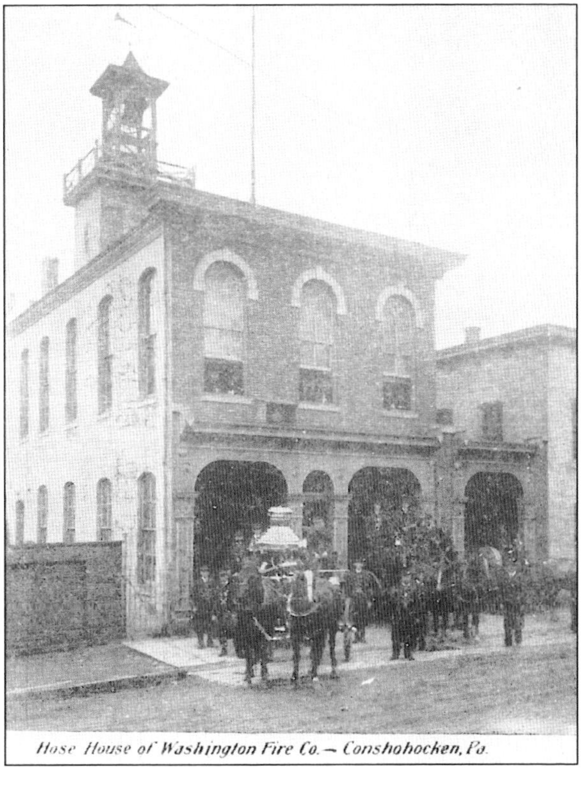

Hose House of Washington Fire Co.— Conshohocken, Pa.

THE HOSE HOUSE OF THE WASHINGTON FIRE COMPANY. Conshohocken's first fire company, the Washington Hose and Steam Fire Engine Company Number 1, has been in existence since 1874. The first fire house, built in 1877, had additions and changes made in 1883, 1908, and 1962. This is most likely the 1883 building, since the postcard pre-dates the 1908 addition.

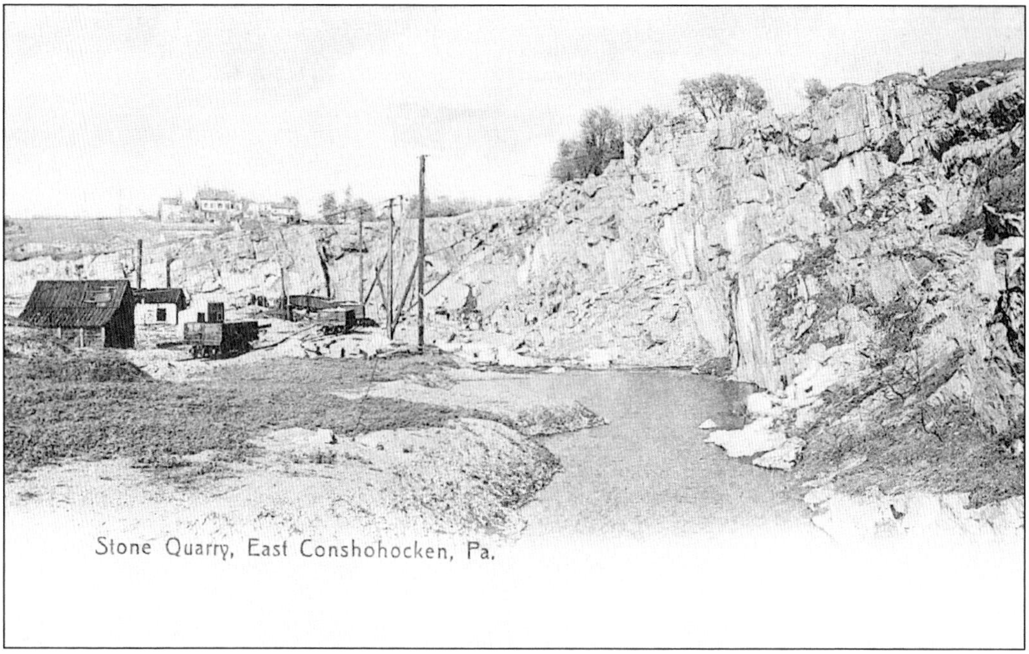

THE STONE QUARRY IN EAST CONSHOHOCKEN. The area from King of Prussia to Conshohocken was known for its fine stone and marble. King of Prussia marble was famous during Colonial times. Quarries, like the one pictured here, surrounded the Conshohocken area. Some of the stone used for Independence Hall was quarried at Conshohocken. (Graham and Johnson postcard.)

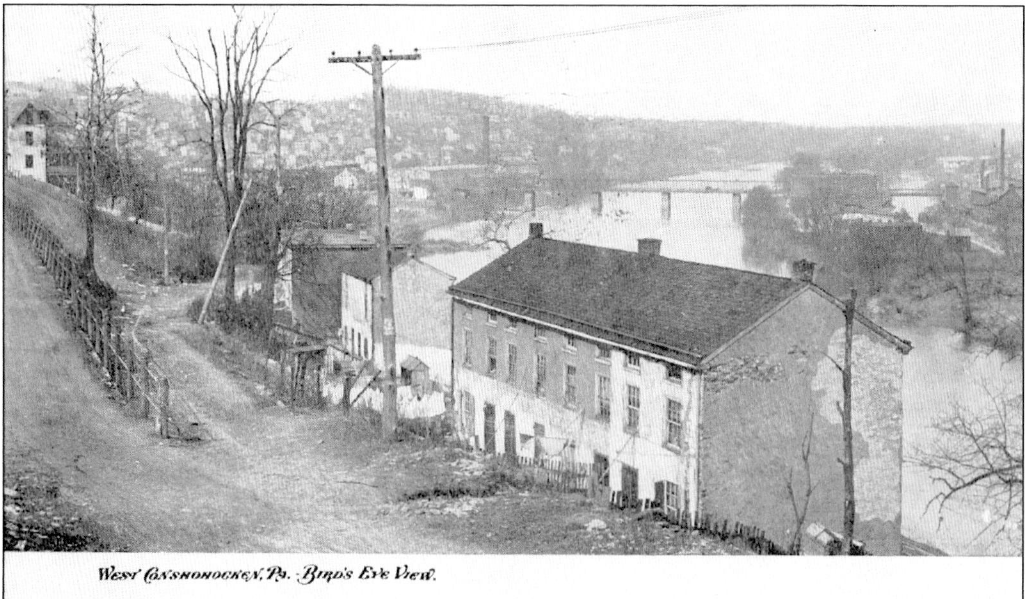

WEST CONSHOHOCKEN—A BIRD'S-EYE VIEW. This 1906 view shows the Schuylkill River, the Matson Ford Bridge, and West Conshohocken from the hills along the river looking north. The Schuylkill Expressway is located at this site. (World Post Card Company postcard.)

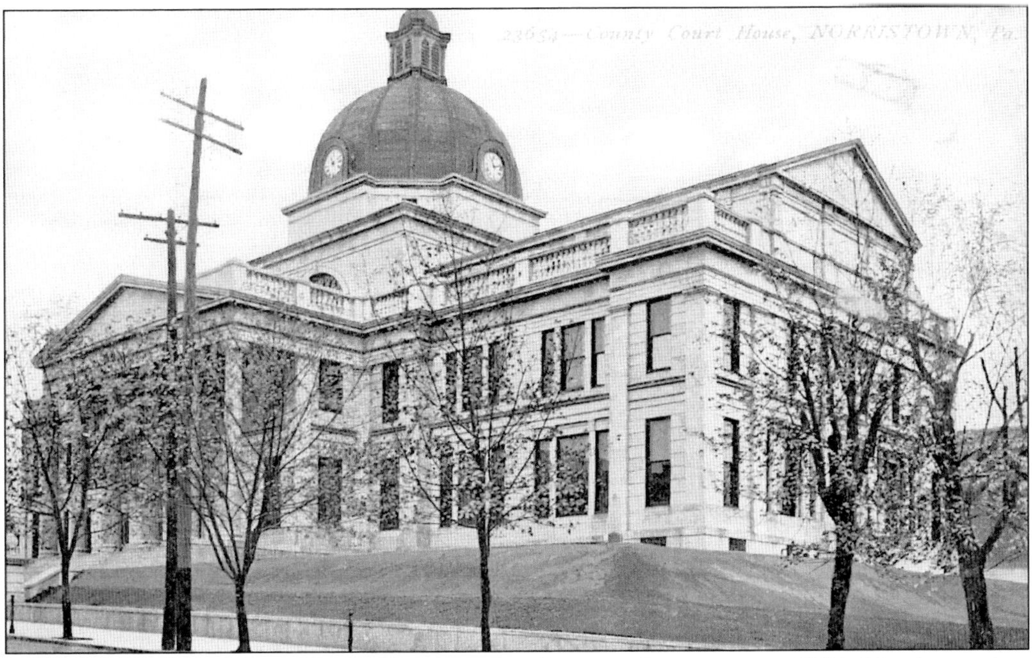

THE COUNTY COURTHOUSE IN NORRISTOWN. From its beginning in 1784, Norristown has been the county seat of Montgomery County. The original courthouse was built 1787–91. The present courthouse was built in 1856. The marble found throughout the building is the famous King of Prussia marble, which is found in many old buildings in the area.

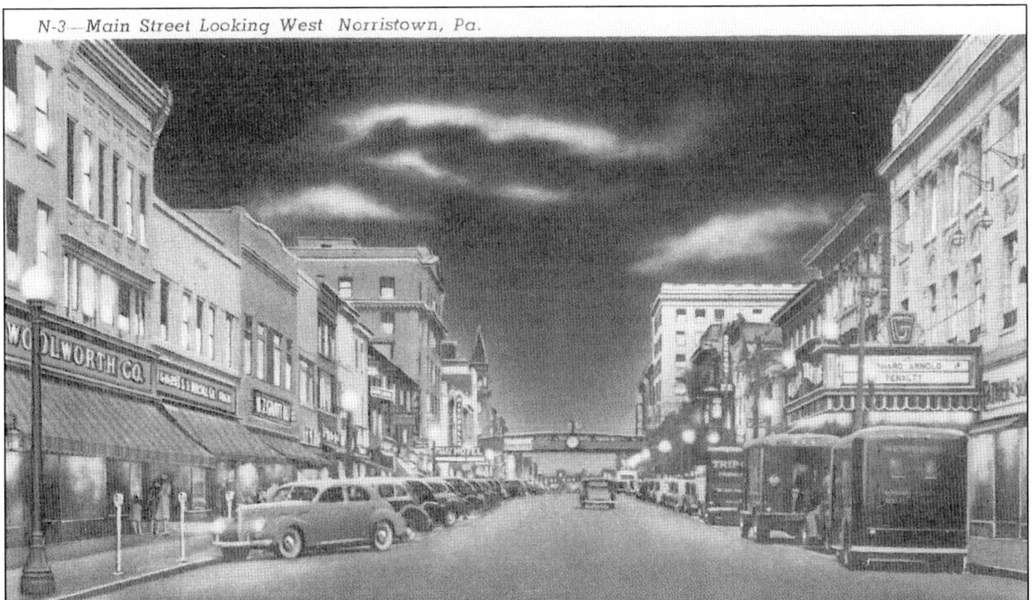

MAIN STREET, NORRISTOWN, LOOKING WEST. Ridge Pike becomes Main Street within Norristown Borough. This view shows a busy Main Street in the 1940s. Sadly, much of this business district is gone and Norristown suffers from urban decay, though some new redevelopment projects have been planned.

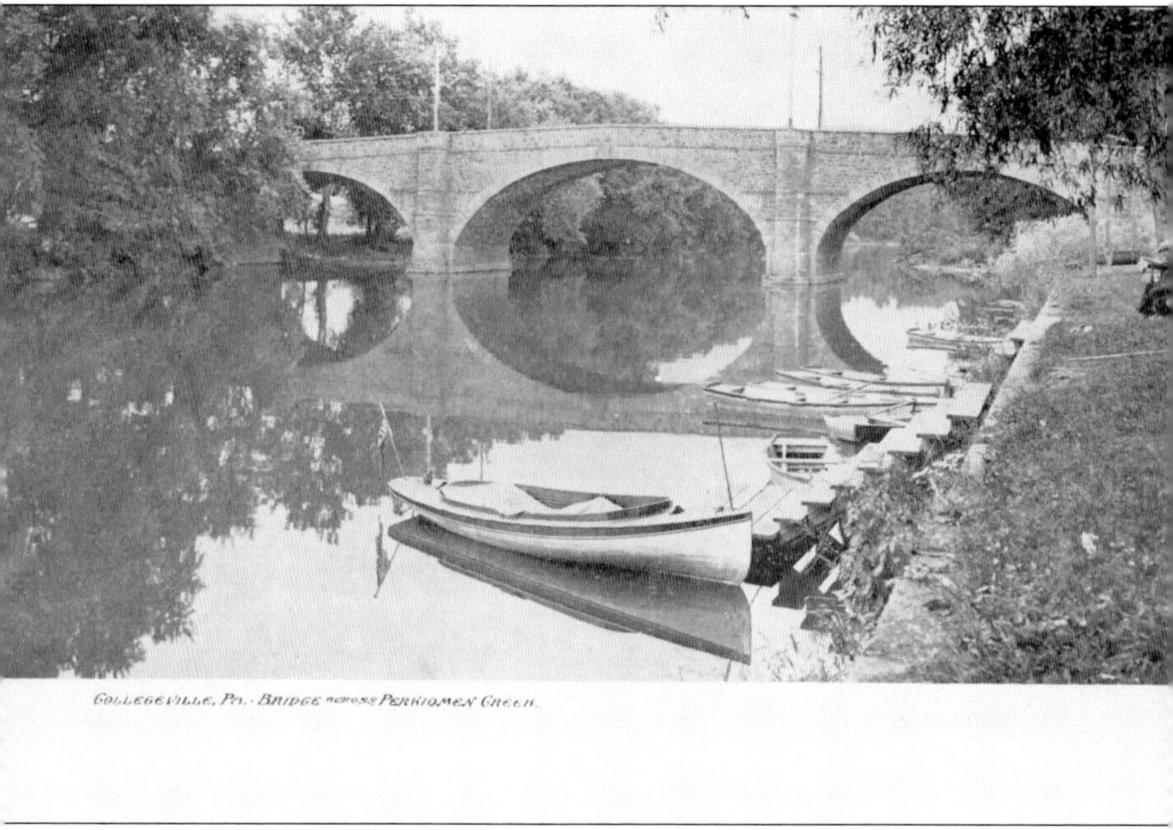

THE BRIDGE OVER PERKIOMEN CREEK IN COLLEGEVILLE. The Perkiomen Bridge was built in 1798 and is still in use today, making it one of the oldest spans in the county. Directly to the east of the bridge, the Germantown Pike ends at Ridge Pike, marking the end of that historic road. Ridge Pike continues west toward Pottstown. (World Post Card Company postcard.)

Six

Old Gulph Road and Lancaster Pike

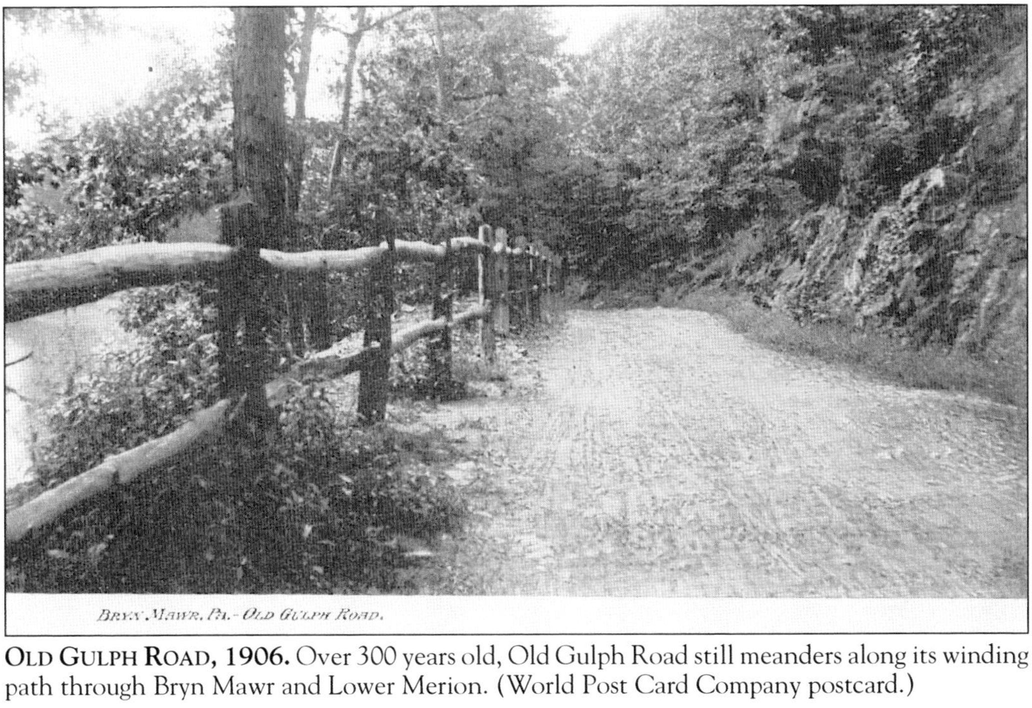

Old Gulph Road, 1906. Over 300 years old, Old Gulph Road still meanders along its winding path through Bryn Mawr and Lower Merion. (World Post Card Company postcard.)

LANCASTER PIKE
OLD GULPH ROAD

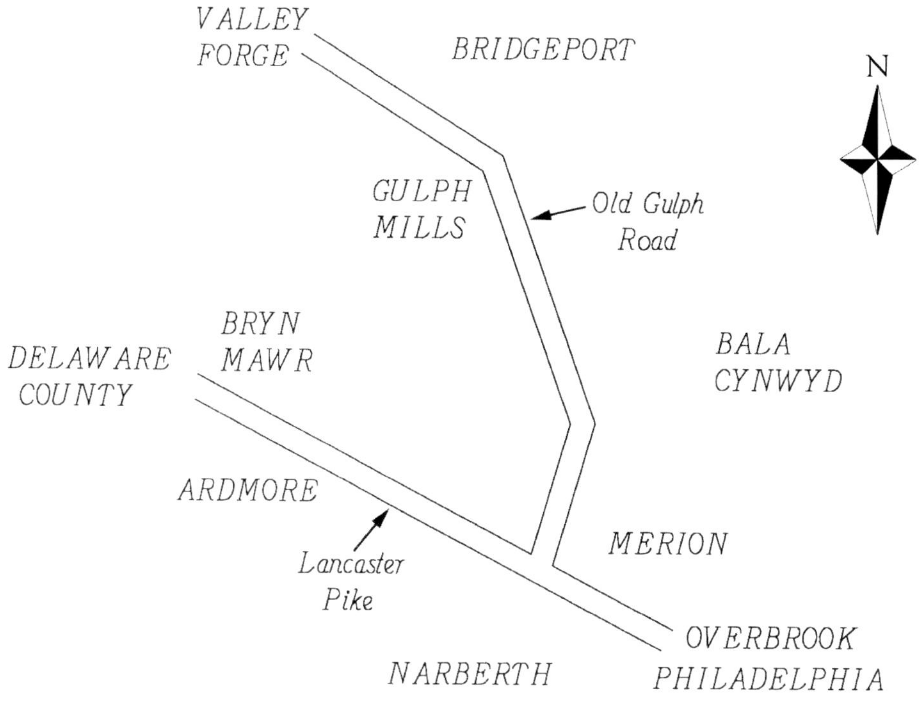

LANCASTER PIKE. Lancaster Pike begins near the Market Street Bridge over the Schuylkill River in Philadelphia. Early sections of this road date from 1687. In the early 1700s, Lancaster County was created and a road was opened to connect Lancaster City with Philadelphia. In 1792, Lancaster Pike became the first toll turnpike in the U.S. Much of today's roads follow that original path. Only a small section of Lancaster Pike is in Montgomery County. This area in Lower Merion Township is lined with fascinating and historic treasures that make the Main Line communities of Ardmore, Bryn Mawr, Merion, and Narberth very unique.

OLD GULPH ROAD. It, along with sections of Montgomery Avenue, was most likely one of the first roads leading out of Philadelphia to the west. A log house with a "1690" date stone and the 1704 Harriton mansion in Lower Merion help illustrate the age of this old winding trail. The Gulph Road of today begins at Montgomery Avenue and meanders toward Gulph Creek and Gulph Mills to King of Prussia, ending at Route 23 in Valley Forge.

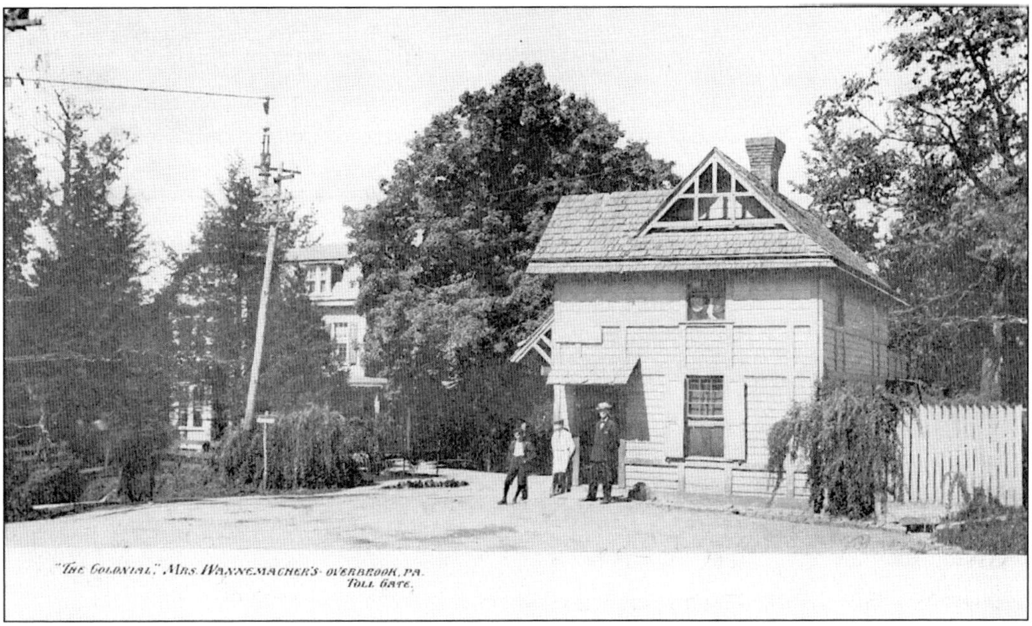

"THE COLONIAL" MRS. WANNAMACHER'S TOLLGATE. The tollgate stood on Lancaster Pike, west of the City Line Avenue intersection in Lower Merion Township. The St. Charles Seminary grounds presently occupy this site. (World Post Card Company postcard.)

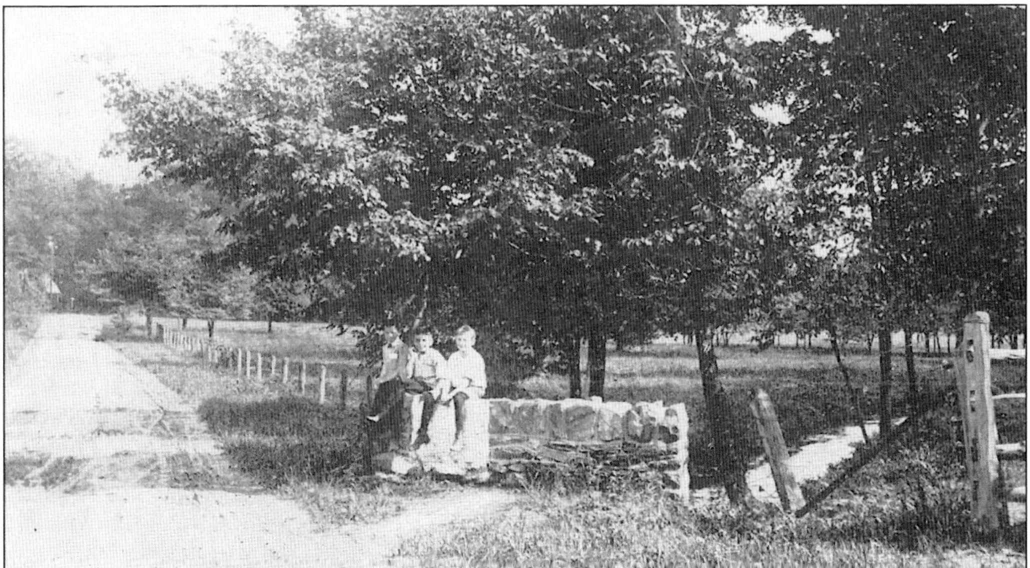

WINDSOR AVENUE IN WYNNEWOOD. Narberth Park now occupies this site at the corner of Wynnewood Road and Windsor Avenue. This scene is looking east from Wynnewood into Narberth Borough. (World Post Card Company postcard.)

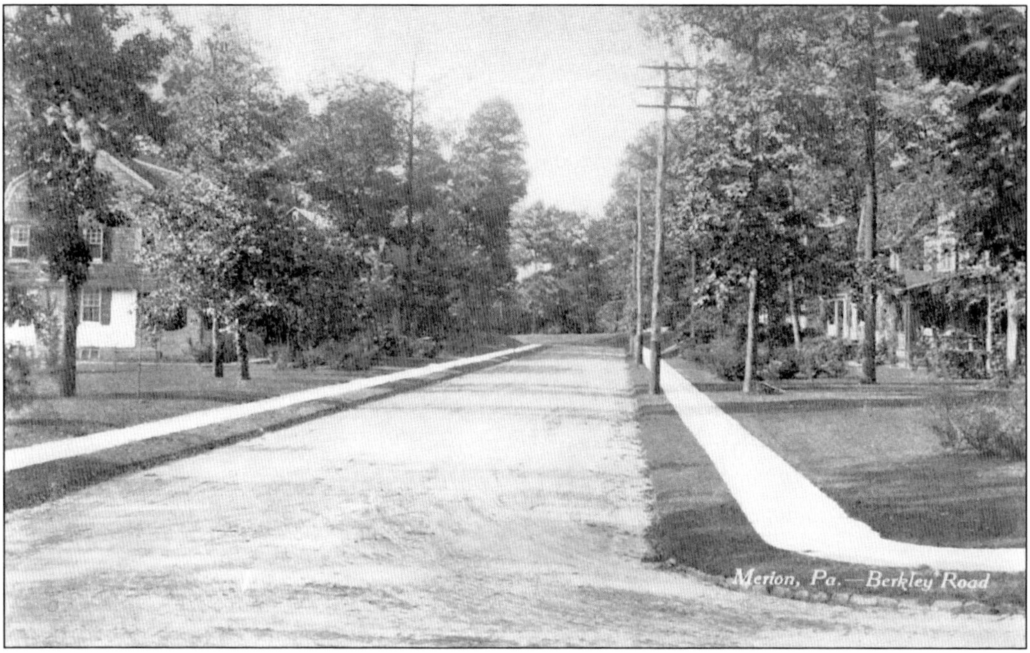

BERKLEY ROAD. This is a 1908 view looking north from Hazelhurst Avenue in Merion, which has always (and still does) contained beautiful residential sections like this. (World Post Card Company postcard.)

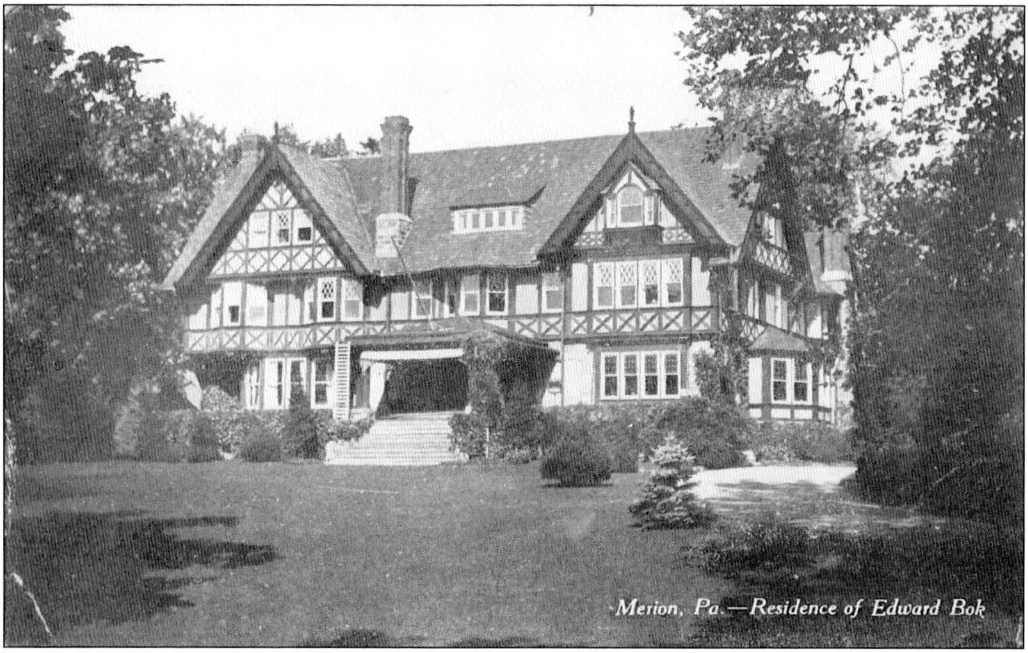

THE RESIDENCE OF EDWARD BOK IN MERION. The Bok Residence built on North Highland Avenue in Merion is a fine example of a Tudor Revival mansion. Bok made his money as the editor of the *Ladies Home Journal*. Merion has a collection of very fine mansions that were built for the wealthy elite of Philadelphia. (World Post Card Company postcard.)

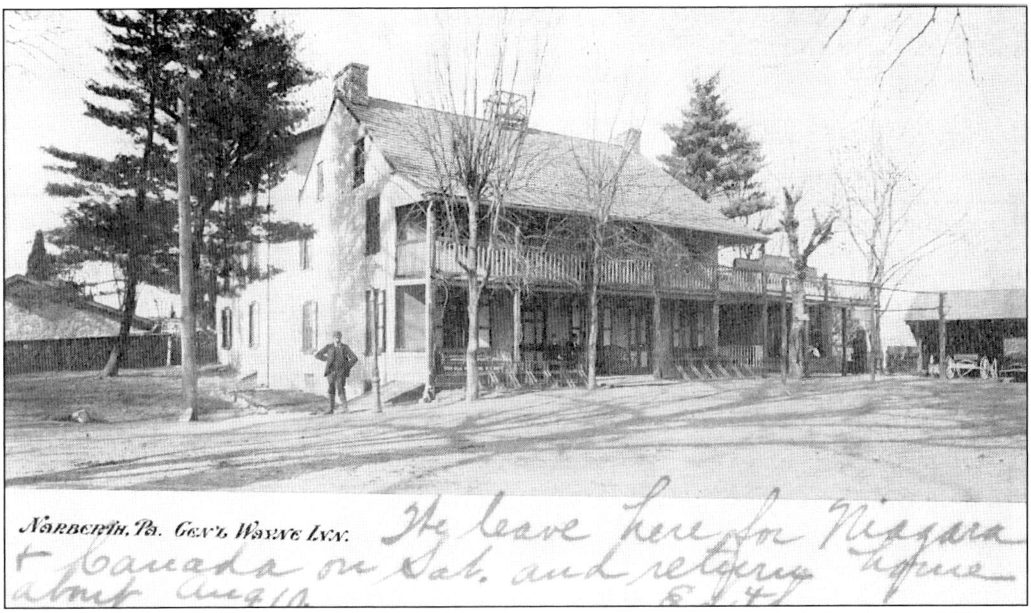

General Wayne Inn in Narberth. A tavern since 1704, it was named the General Wayne Inn in 1795 after the Revolutionary War General Anthony Wayne, who was born near Lancaster Pike in Chester County. The inn has quite a storied past, including documented ghosts and, in recent times, a murder. Situated on Montgomery Avenue, next to the Merion Friends Meetinghouse, together they constitute very historic Colonial landmarks in this region. (World Post Card Company postcard.)

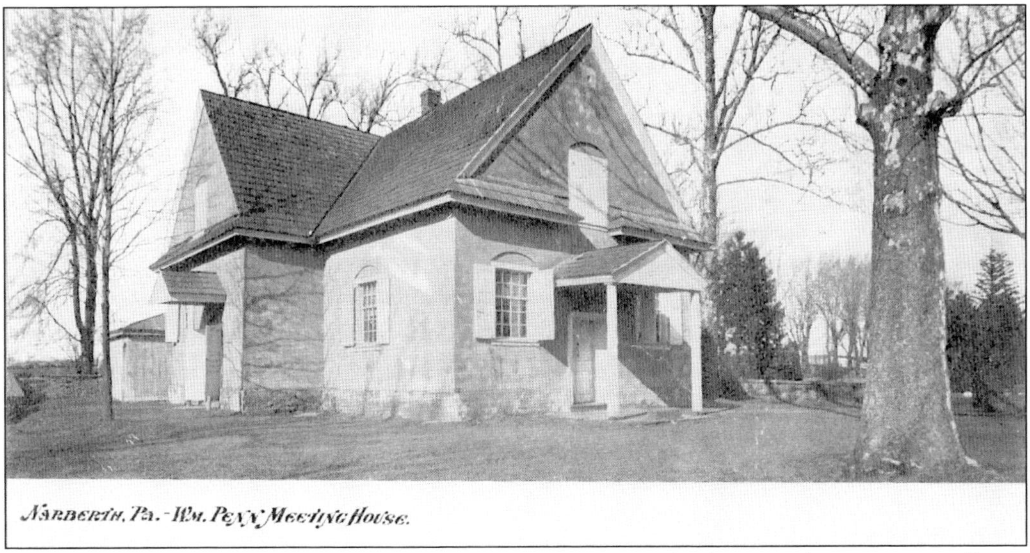

The William Penn Meetinghouse in Narberth. Dating back to 1695, it was originally on a section of the Gulph or Meetinghouse Road, which extended out from Philadelphia. Today it can be seen on Montgomery Avenue. It was thought that William Penn worshiped here, hence the name on this postcard; however, its rightful name is The Merion Friends Meetinghouse. It is the oldest Quaker meetinghouse in Pennsylvania and its cross-like floor plan is unique in comparison to the usual square or rectangular design of these buildings. (World Post Card Company postcard.)

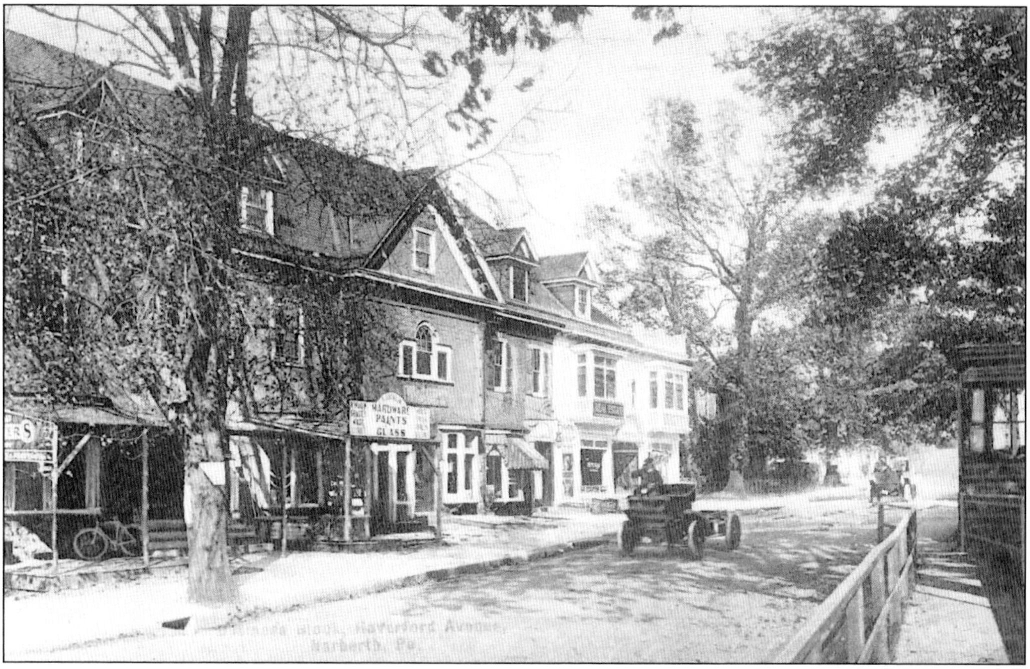

THE BUSINESS BLOCK ON HAVERFORD AVENUE. Narberth was incorporated as a borough in 1895. This 1915 view shows the main business block across from the railroad station. A big fire destroyed some of these buildings in 1940. Today, Narberth has a very quaint, small-town, business district. (Moore postcard.)

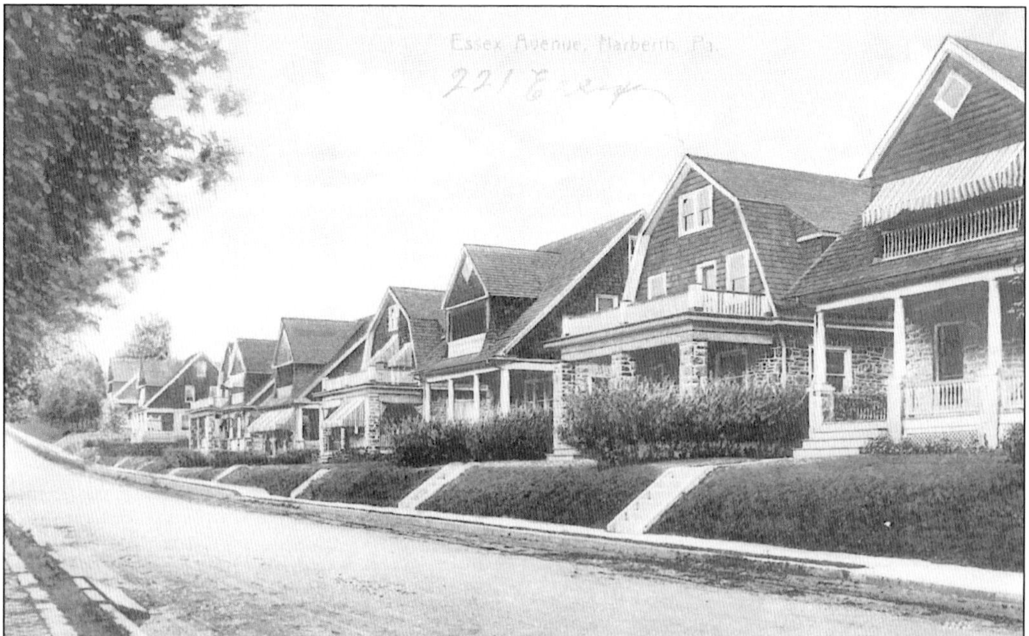

ESSEX AVENUE. Along with a small business district, Narberth also has beautiful residential sections, such as Essex Avenue, shown here *c.* 1915 looking north from above Windsor Avenue. These homes still stand. (Moore postcard.)

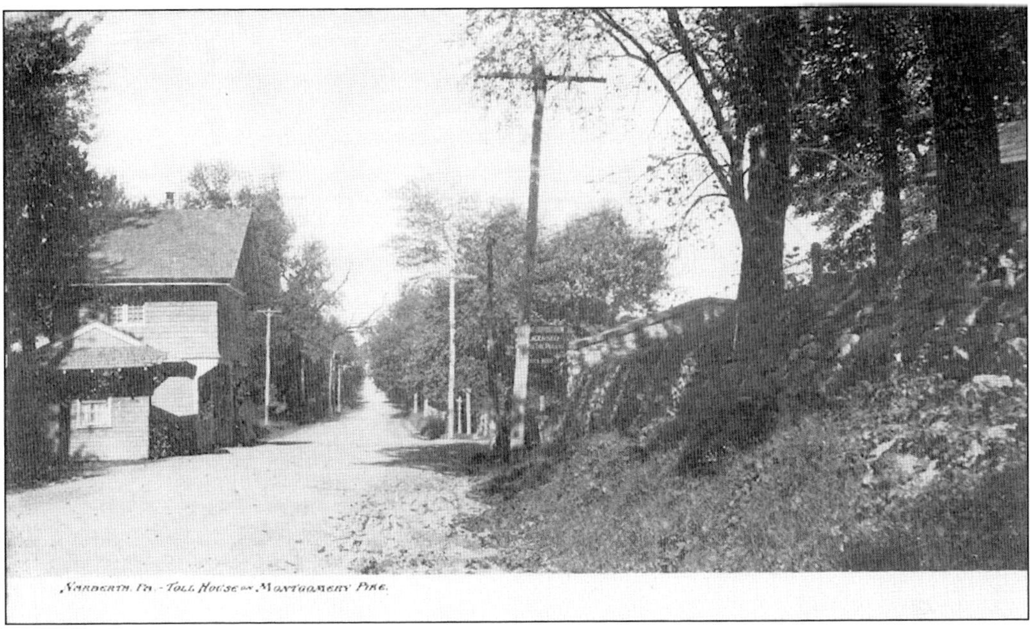

A Tollhouse on Montgomery Pike in Narberth. This scene is looking west on Montgomery Avenue in front of the Merion Friends Meetinghouse at Meetinghouse Lane. There is not a vehicle in sight, which is quite a comparison to today's four-lane road. Tolls were eliminated in 1914. (World Post Card Company postcard.)

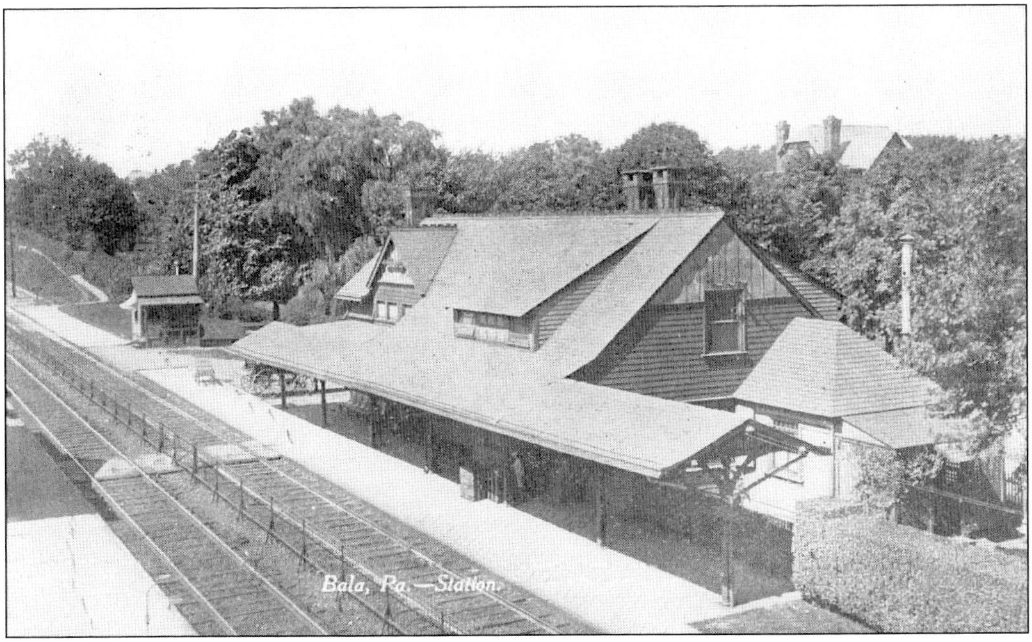

The Bala Train Station, 1910. Shown here in a view taken from the City Line Avenue overpass, the station is still in use, though this building is gone. (World Post Card Company postcard.)

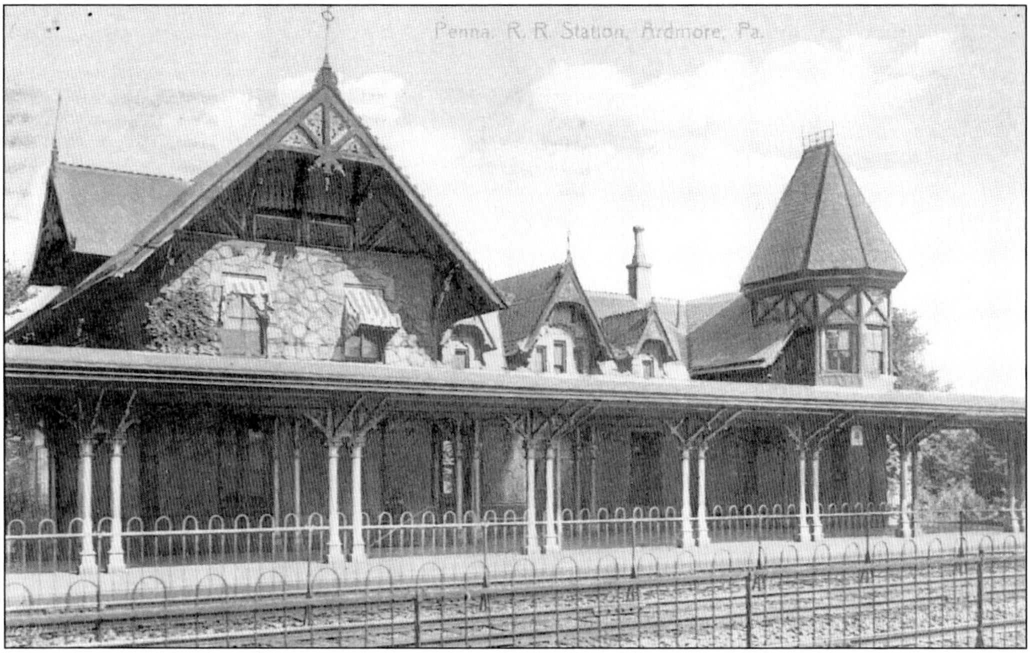

ARDMORE STATION C. 1915. The Pennsylvania Railroad was responsible not only for building train stations, but also for helping to develop the areas along its Main Line branch. Ardmore Station, though no longer standing, was built in 1870 of attractive stone and fanciful woodwork. It is easy see that the Main Line had some of the handsomest stations around. (Moore postcard.)

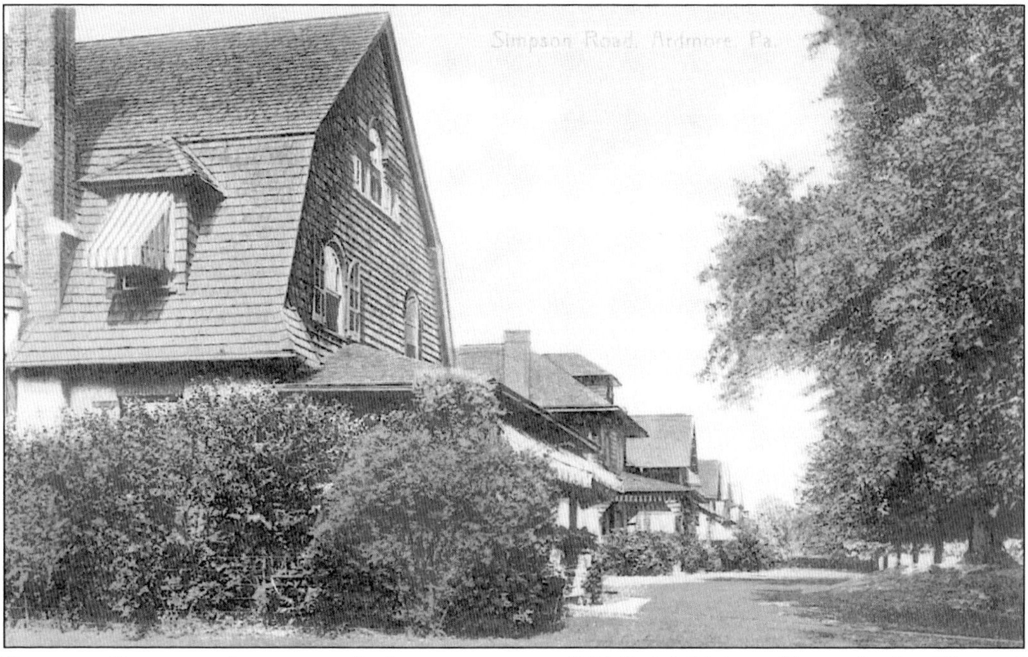

SIMPSON ROAD IN ARDMORE. Ardmore was one of Philadelphia's earliest suburbs. Pictured here are beautiful homes along Simpson Road between Athens Avenue and Argyle Road. All the homes are different and most shown here are still standing. (Moore postcard.)

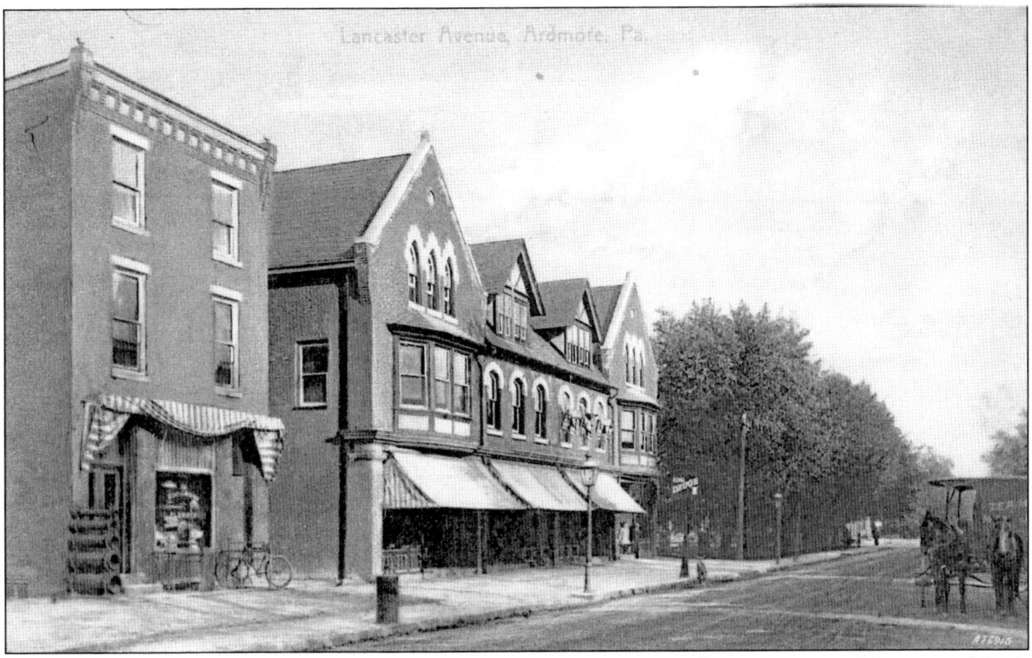

LANCASTER AVENUE IN ARDMORE. This 1910 view shows Ardmore's original business block along Lancaster Avenue. Looking east from Ardmore Avenue, these buildings are still in use but the trees to their right are gone and are now occupied by businesses. (Moore postcard.)

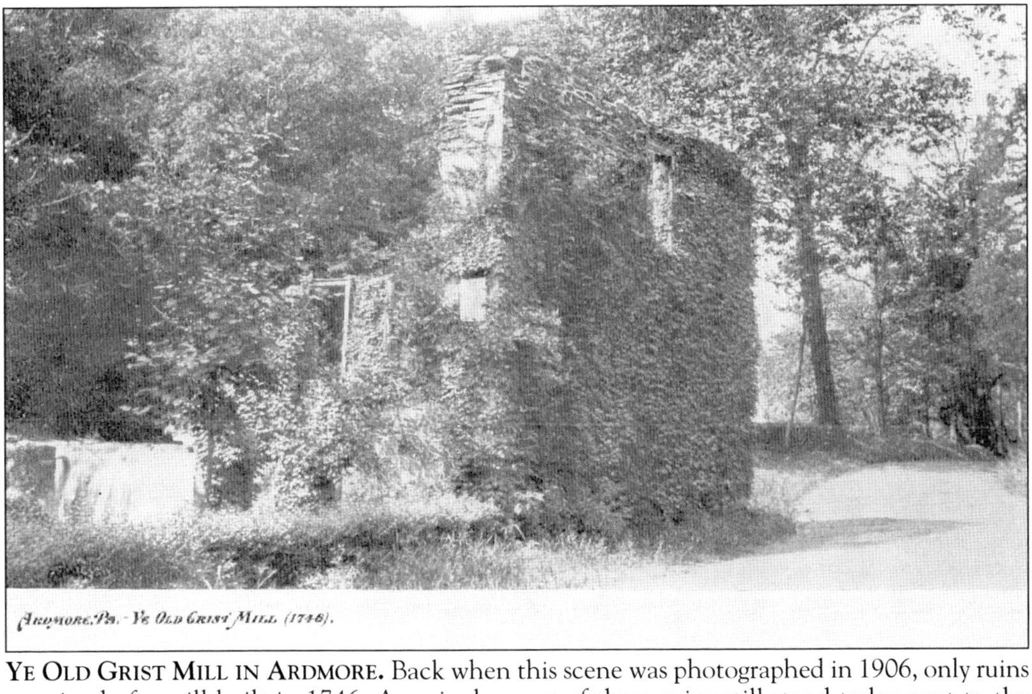

YE OLD GRIST MILL IN ARDMORE. Back when this scene was photographed in 1906, only ruins remained of a mill built in 1746. Amazingly, most of these ruins still stand today next to the dam on Mill Creek, on Old Gulph Road above Mill Creek Road, near Gladwyne. (World Post Card Company postcard.)

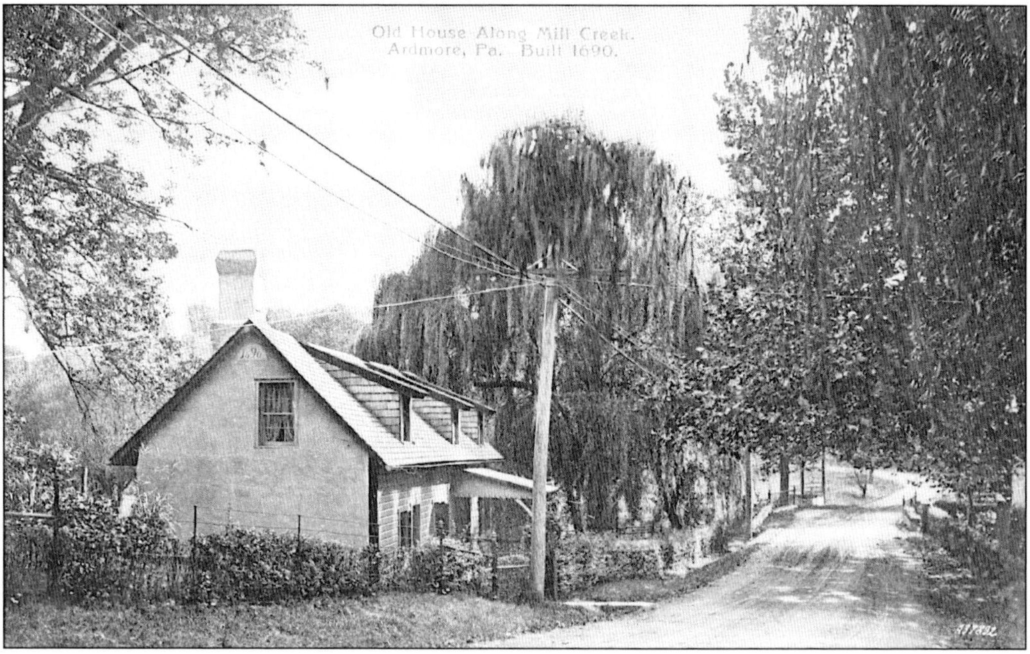

AN OLD HOUSE ALONG MILL CREEK IN ARDMORE. At the intersection of Old Gulph and Mill Creek Roads stands this house bearing a date stone of 1690. This is possibly the oldest date stone in the Philadelphia region. The 1907 view is looking east on Mill Creek Road from Gulph Road. Aside from the road being paved today, very little has changed. (Moore postcard.)

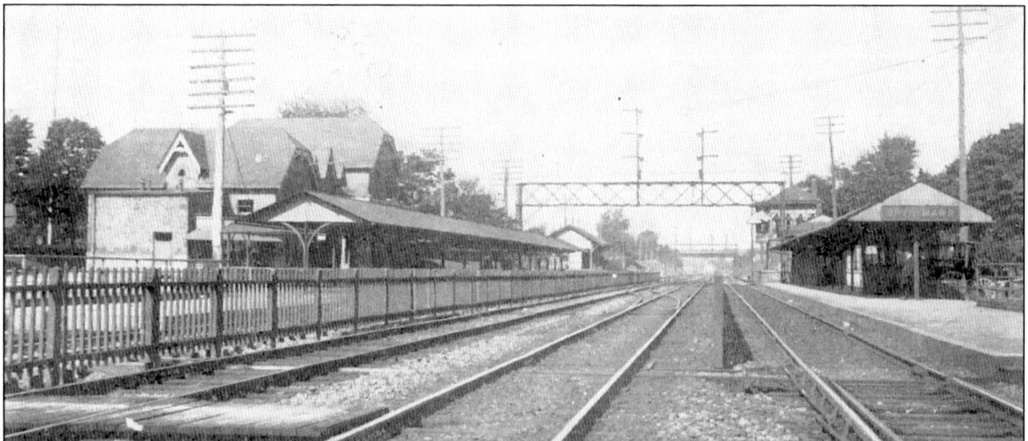

BRYN MAWR STATION. This is an interesting view of Bryn Mawr Station from the railroad tracks. Like Ardmore, Bryn Mawr was beautifully designed to attract commuters into Philadelphia. Bryn Mawr Station was built in 1869 and is currently used as a restaurant. (World Post Card Company postcard.)

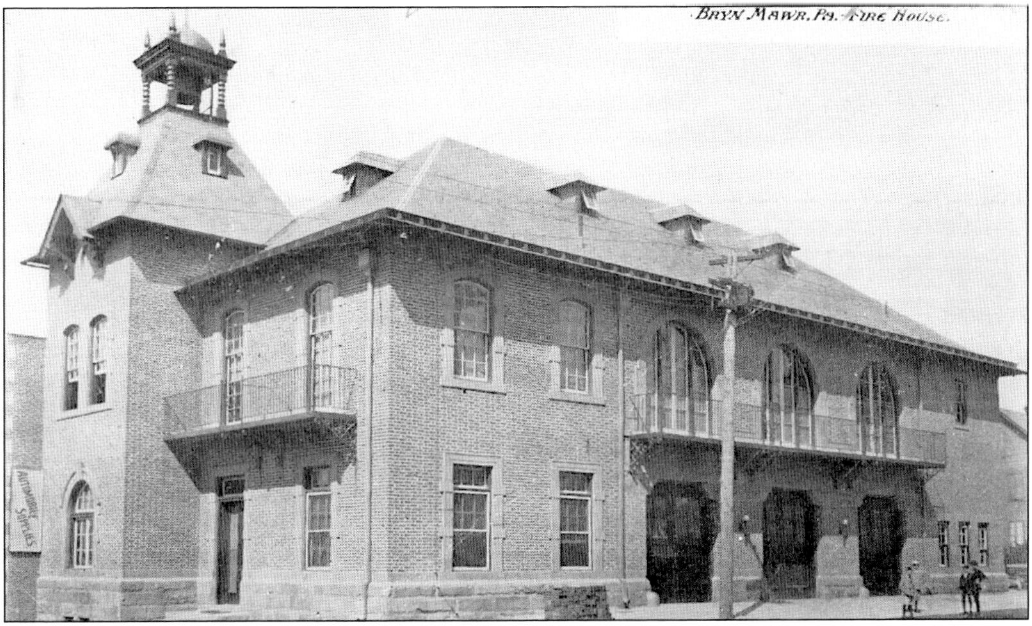

THE BRYN MAWR FIREHOUSE. Built in 1903 on the intersection of Lancaster and Merion Avenues, the structure is an excellent example of turn-of-the-20th-century firehouse architecture, which emphasized design and function. The bell tower is particularly attractive and, fortunately, the building remains basically unchanged from this 1905 view. (World Post Card Company postcard.)

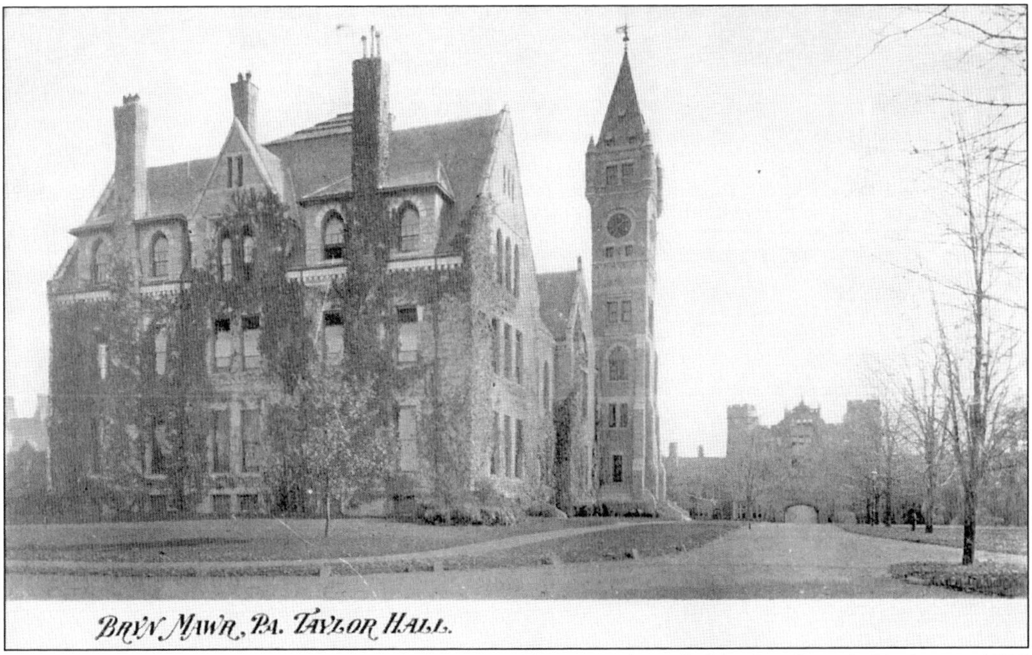

TAYLOR HALL IN BRYN MAWR. Bryn Mawr College was founded by Dr. Joseph Taylor in 1880 for the education of women. The college contained many attractive buildings, including Taylor Hall, named for the college founder. (World Post Card Company postcard.)

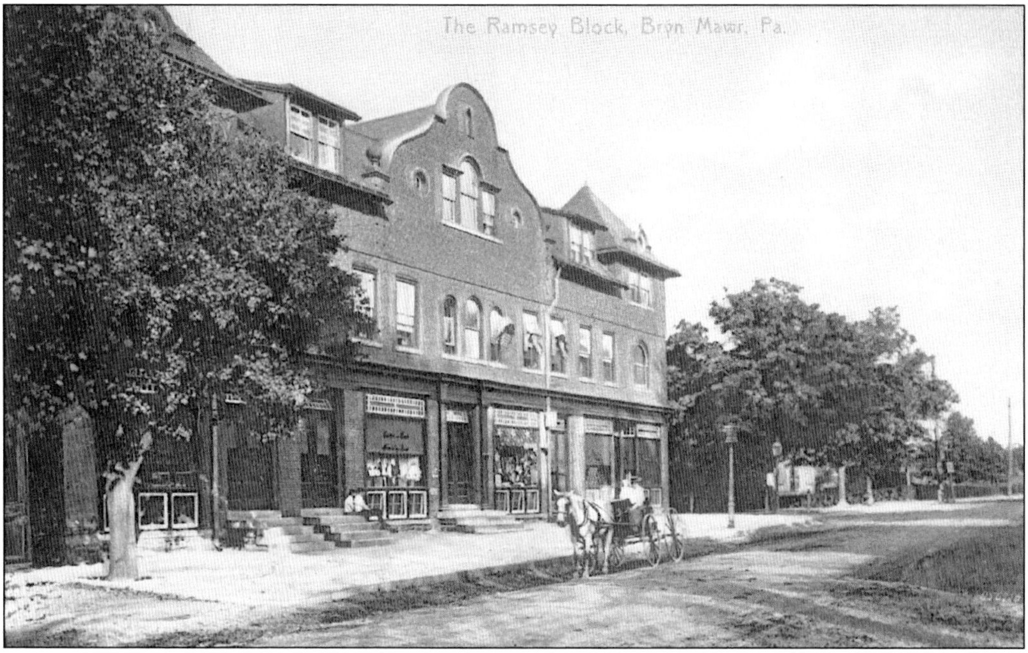

The Ramsey Block in Bryn Mawr. William Ramsey was Bryn Mawr's first postmaster in 1874. His block, including his store, was located on the intersection of Lancaster at Bryn Mawr Avenues. (Moore postcard.)

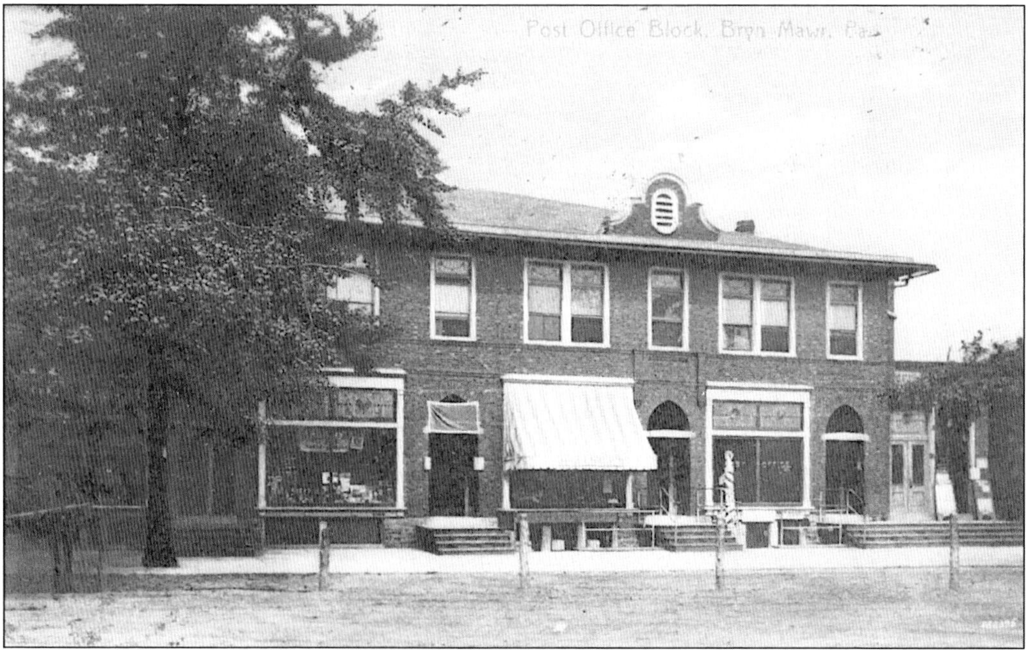

The Post Office Block in Bryn Mawr. This handsome building housed the Bryn Mawr Post Office in the early 20th century. As the town grew, the post office needed to expand to a larger building. This building still stands, though the portion to the left of the awning is gone. The right section contains a pharmacy and is located on Bryn Mawr Avenue between Lancaster Avenue and the railroad. (Moore postcard.)

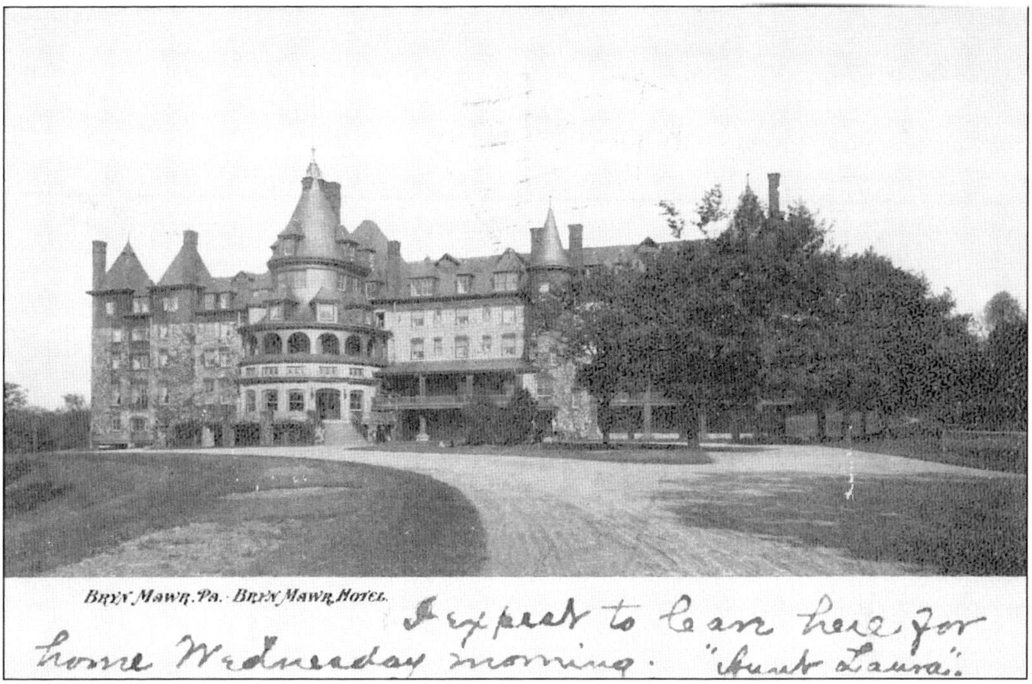

THE BRYN MAWR HOTEL. The Pennsylvania Railroad helped to establish a number of hotels along the Main Line in the late 1800s. One such place was near Bryn Mawr Station on Montgomery and Morris Avenues. Originally built in 1871, it was destroyed by fire *c.* 1890 and later rebuilt to become the Baldwin School. (World Post Card Company postcard.)

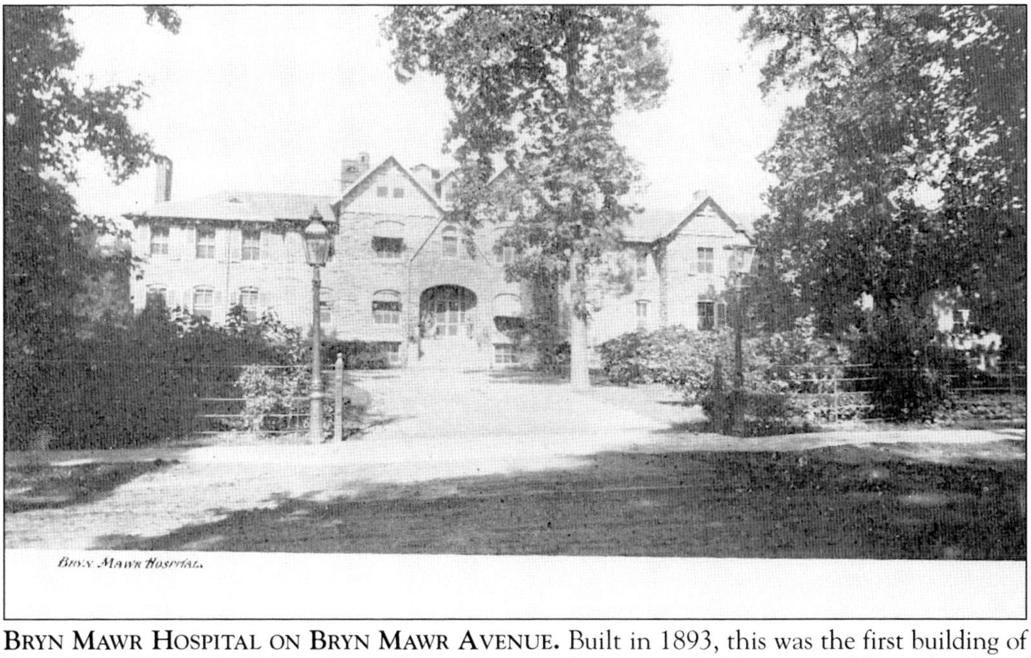

BRYN MAWR HOSPITAL ON BRYN MAWR AVENUE. Built in 1893, this was the first building of Bryn Mawr Hospital. Although it still stands, it is today surrounded by new and larger buildings that make up the Bryn Mawr Hospital complex. (World Post Card Company postcard.)

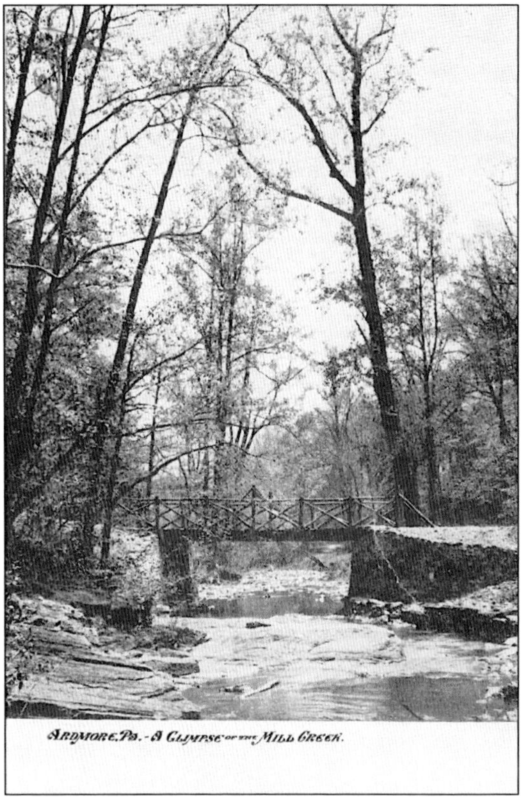

A GLIMPSE OF MILL CREEK IN ARDMORE. Mill Creek, which once had mills operating along its banks, is the main tributary in Lower Merion. It meanders through the central part of the township, forming deep valleys with scenic hills, before entering the Schuylkill River. (World Post Card Company postcard.)

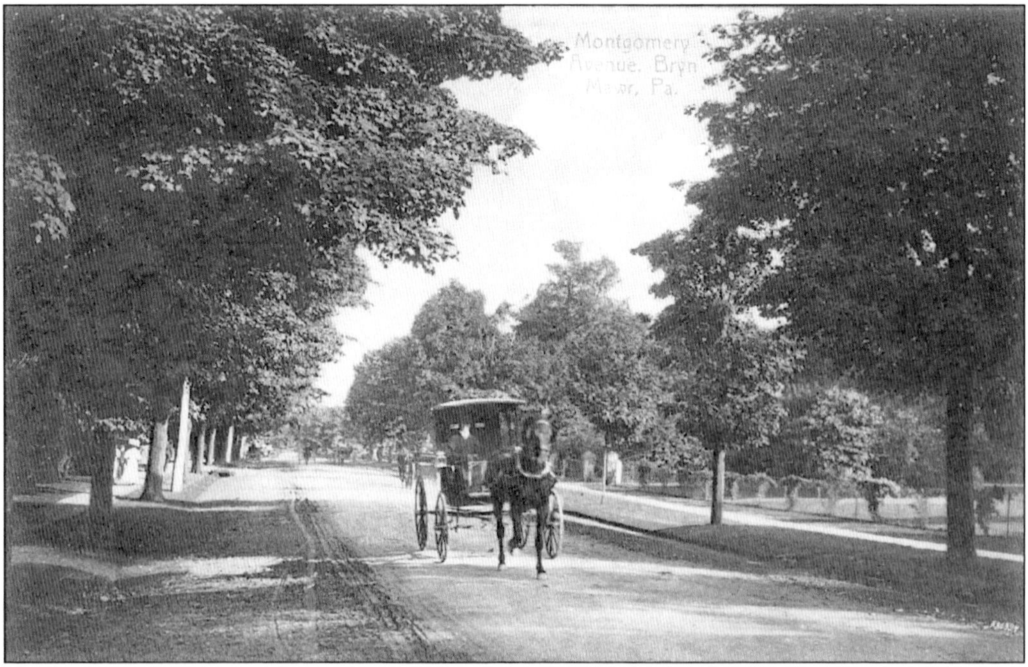

MONTGOMERY AVENUE IN BRYN MAWR. This 1910 view shows an almost vacant Montgomery Avenue. Today, of course, it is a major artery through the Main Line. (Moore postcard.)

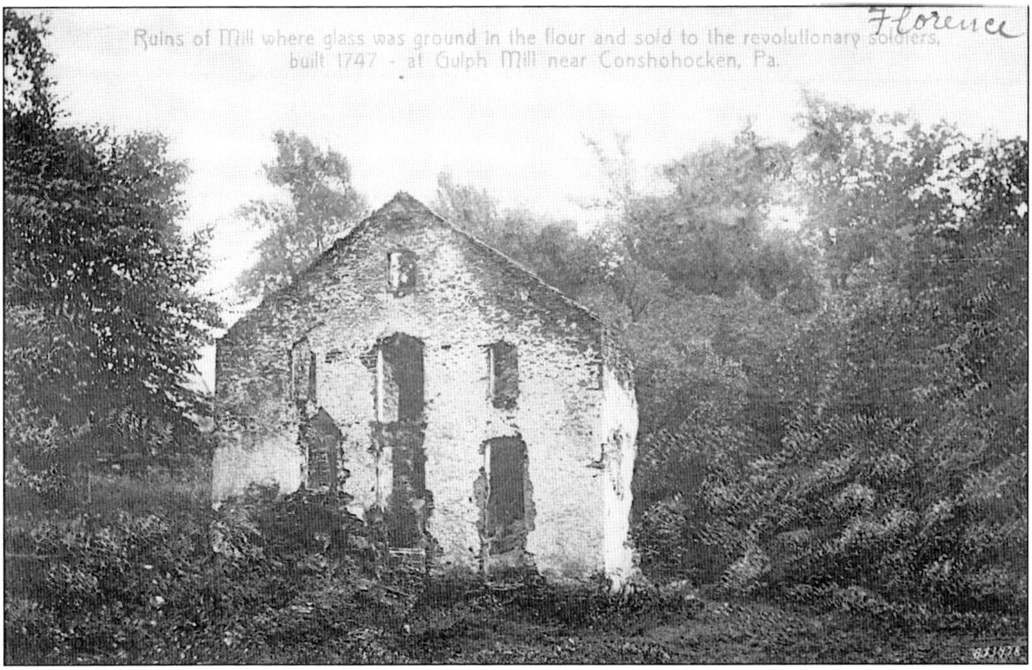

THE RUINS OF A MILL NEAR CONSHOHOCKEN. Shown here are the ruins of the Gulph Mill, built in 1747. The American Army camped at Gulph Mills from December 13 to December 19, 1777, en route to Valley Forge via Gulph Road. Nothing remains of the mill, but Gulph Mills Village still exists and retains its old historic buildings. The Schuylkill Expressway cuts through Gulph Mills and there are on and off ramps for Gulph Road. (Graham and Johnson postcard.)

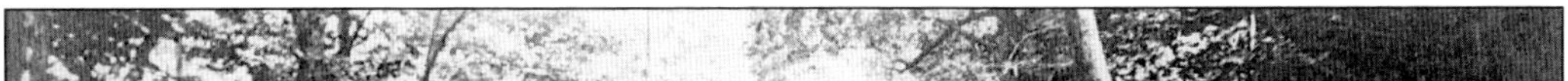

GULPH CREEK AT THE GULPH MILL NEAR CONSHOHOCKEN. Most creeks in Montgomery County were picturesque places with beautiful old trees and historic lure, including Gulph Mills Creek. Located in Upper Merion Township, its water powered the historic Gulph Mills. The creek flows through the village of Gulph Mills before emptying into the Schuylkill. An older Native-American name for this stream was Balligomingo. (Graham and Johnson postcard.)

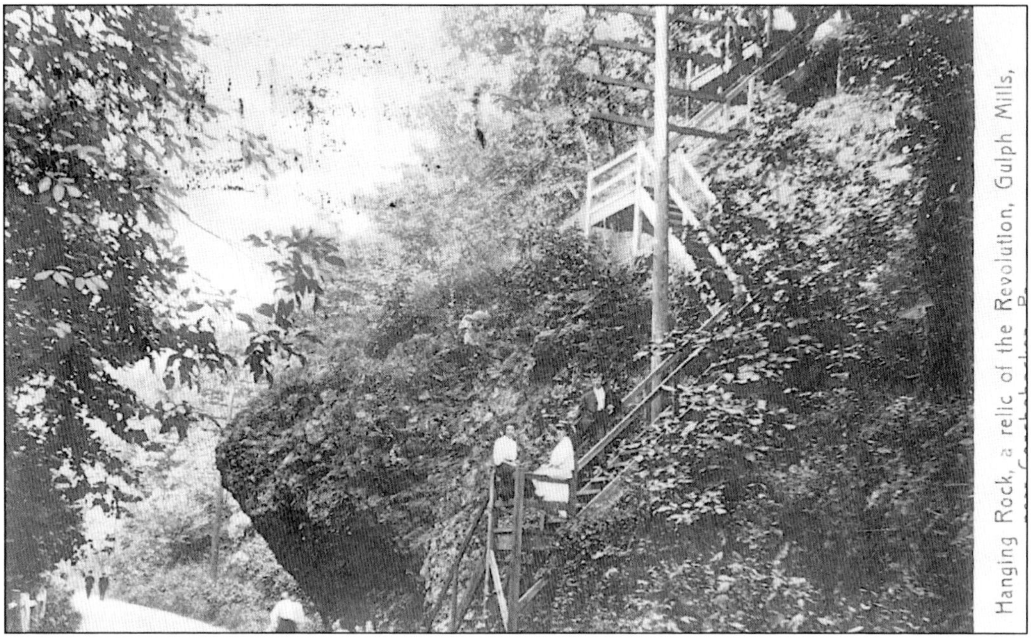

A RELIC OF THE REVOLUTION. Hanging Rock is located on Gulph Road north of Matson Ford Road at Gulph Mills. Legend states that George Washington sought shelter under the rock during a storm on his way to Valley Forge. This 1906 view shows the rock with steps and a lookout at the top. It appears that it was a curiosity to the local folks. The rock still overhangs the busy Gulph Road. (Graham and Johnson postcard.)

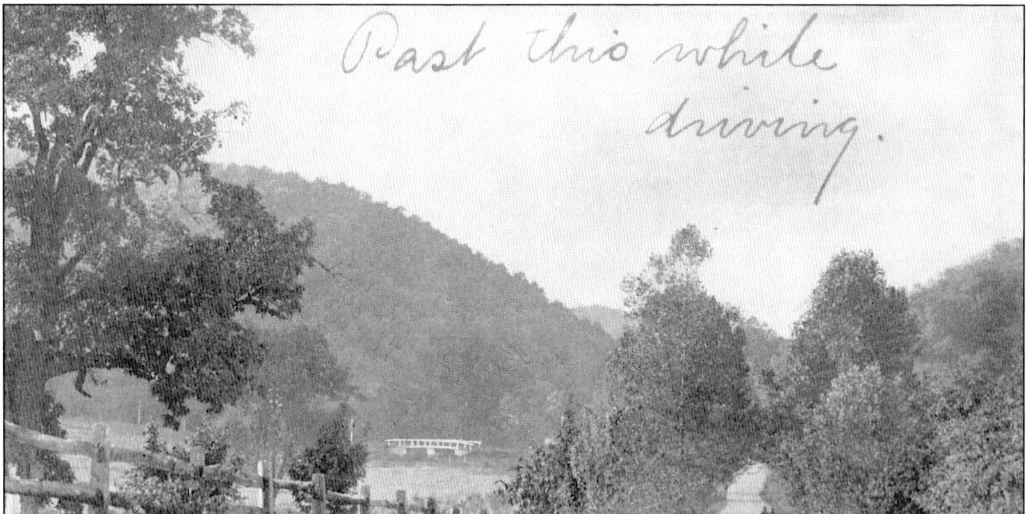

VALLEY FORGE. This is a view along Gulph Road, between Gulph Mills and Valley Forge. Both locales had a number of large hills and scenic areas. (World Post Card Company postcard.)

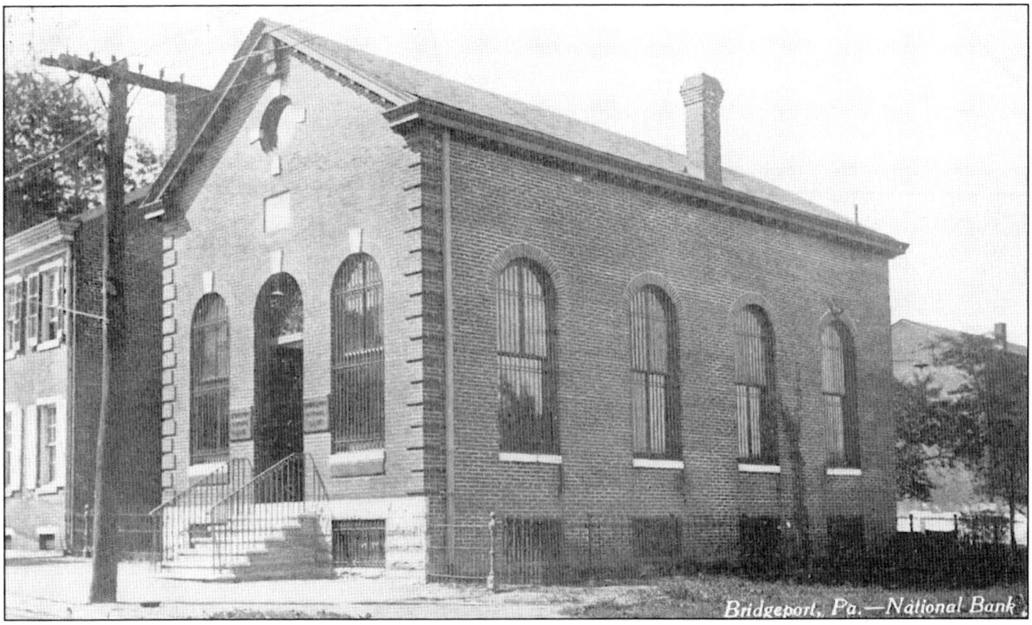

THE BRIDGEPORT NATIONAL BANK. The borough of Bridgeport was incorporated in 1851, and as it grew, so did its institutions, such as the Bridgeport National Bank. Founded in 1906, it aided in financing many town projects. This is its first building, located on DeKalb Street. In 1928, the present bank building was erected at Fourth and DeKalb Streets. Presently, in 1999, it is unoccupied. (World Post Card Company postcard.)

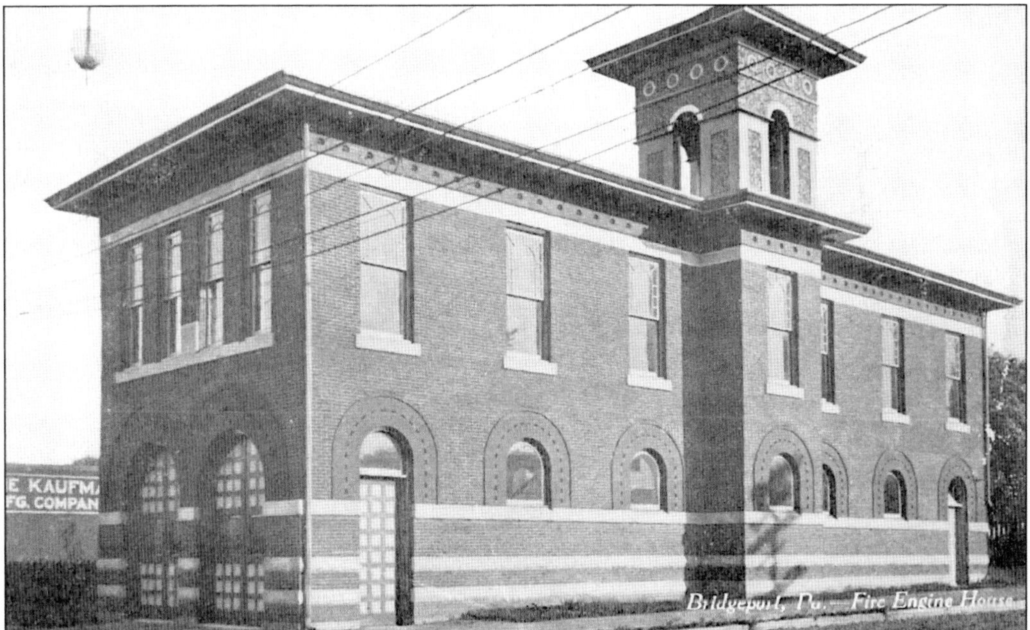

THE FIRE ENGINE HOUSE. Bridgeport Fire Company Number 1 was founded in 1891. This building, at Fourth and Mill Streets, was erected in the 1890s. The firehouse still occupies the site, though the building has been completely rebuilt without the second floor. An 1892 date stone appears above the front bays. (World Post Card Company postcard.)

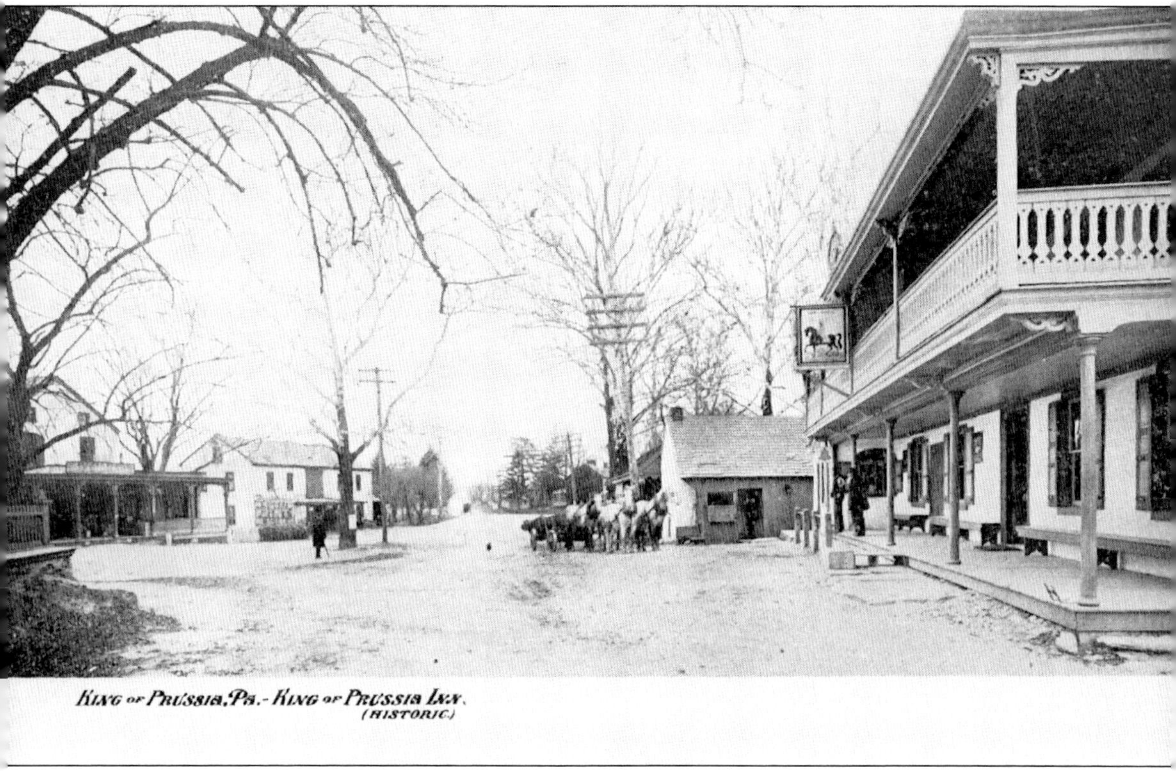

THE KING OF PRUSSIA INN. Situated on an island between north and southbound traffic on Route 202, the King of Prussia Inn is a historic gem dating back to 1719. Before roads were widened, the King of Prussia Inn faced DeKalb Pike, or Swedesford Road, where it crossed Gulph Road. Many Revolutionary War leaders have been visitors to this famous inn due to its proximity to Valley Forge, including Washington, Lafayette, Von Steuben, DeKalb, and many others. This 1906 view shows the village of King of Prussia looking north. The giant King of Prussia Mall would occupy all land on the left-hand side of the road. Plans call for the further widening of Route 202 and the King of Prussia Inn will have to be moved. A fund-raising effort has been established to move the inn to a spot of protected land on South Gulph Road. (World Post Card Company postcard.)

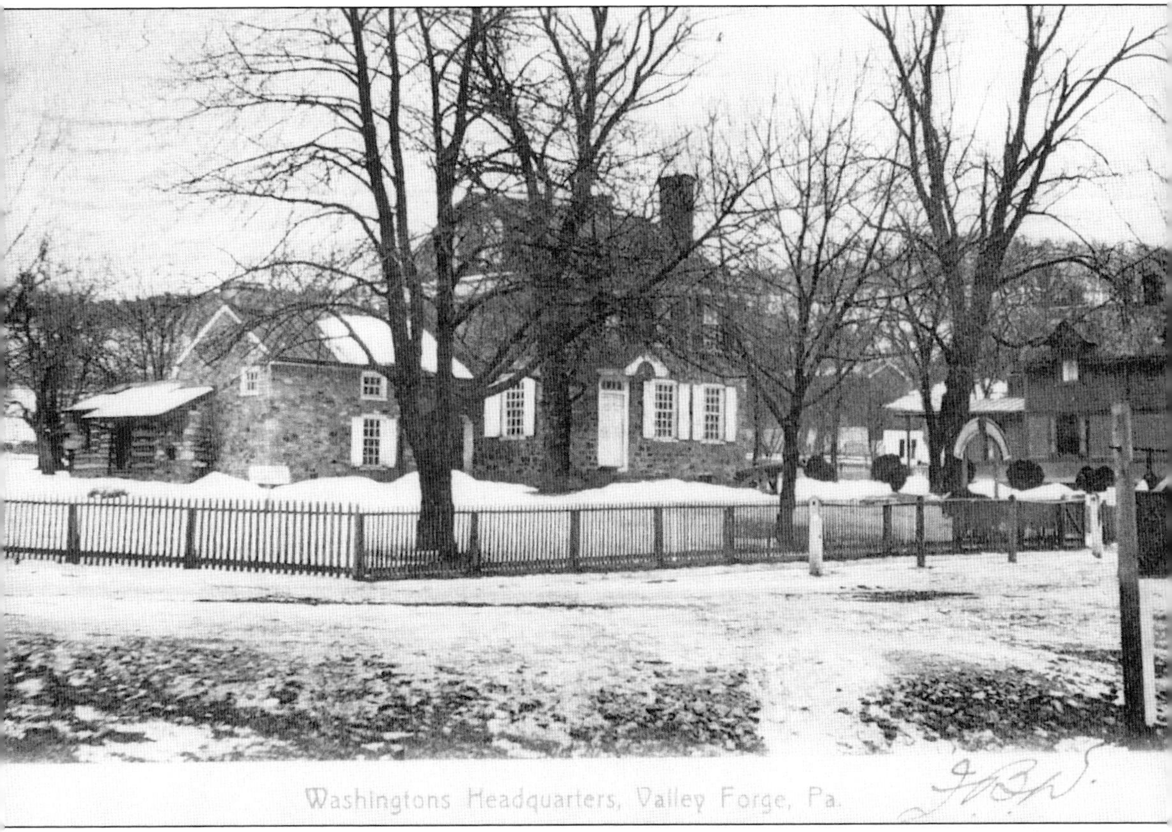

WASHINGTON'S HEADQUARTERS IN VALLEY FORGE. The Potts family built this house near the Schuylkill River and Valley Creek in Upper Merion Township in 1765. They also constructed a forge nearby, which would later become known as Valley Forge. George Washington stayed in this house during the winter encampment of 1777–78. The northern terminus of Gulph Road is just a short distance south of here. The Potts House was purchased in 1879 by a group of patriotic citizens who dedicated it as a museum and historic shrine to the public, making it one of the earliest attempts to preserve old important buildings. Today, the house is a landmark in Valley Forge National Historic Park and is open to the public. (S.J. Parker postcard.)

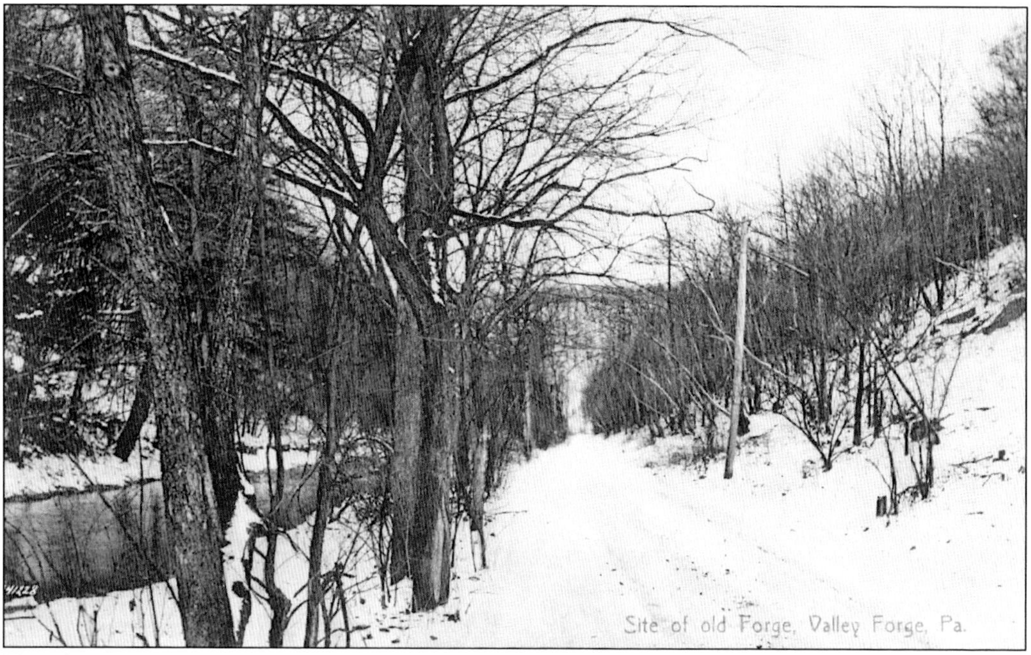

The Site of the Old Forge. The original forge was built along Valley Creek in the mid-1700s. The forge has long been gone, but the picturesque Valley Creek has changed little over the years. Many early postcard views of Valley Forge depict snow-covered winter scenes in an attempt to evoke images of the long, harsh winter of 1777–78. (S.J. Parker postcard.)

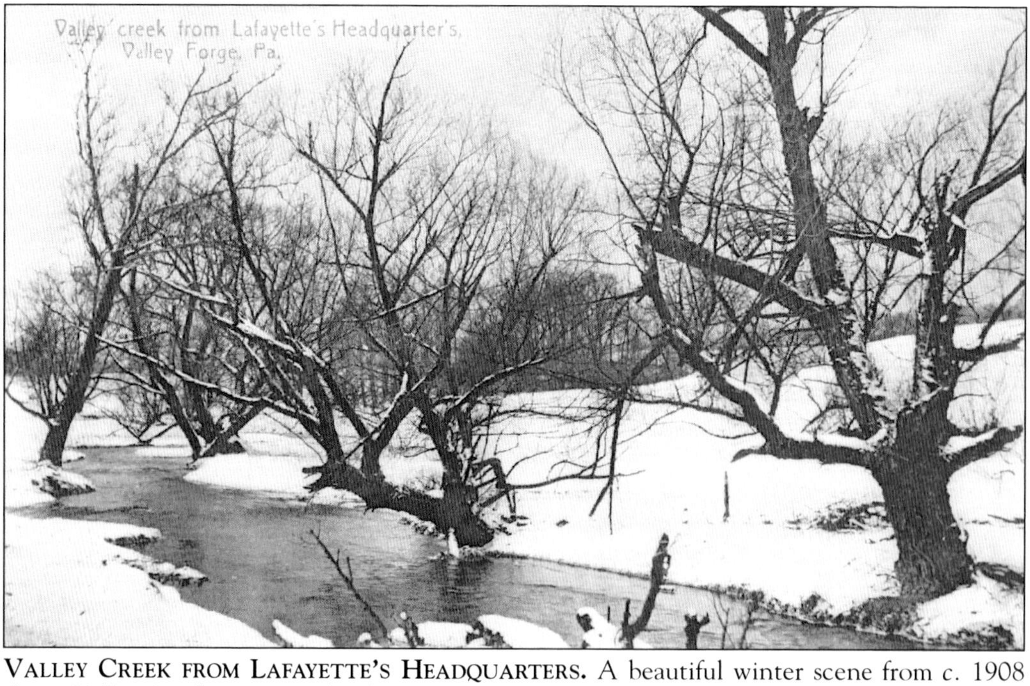

Valley Creek from Lafayette's Headquarters. A beautiful winter scene from c. 1908 shows Valley Creek. Fortunately, this area has been preserved in Valley Forge National Historic Park. (S.J. Parker postcard.)

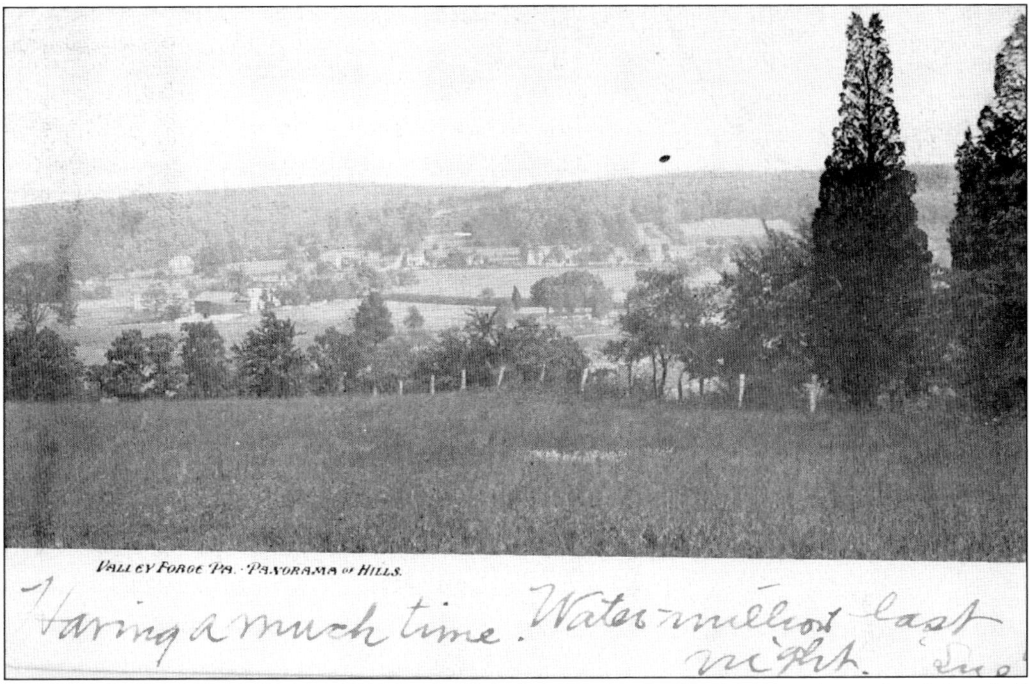

A PANORAMA OF HILLS. The hills around Valley Forge are the highest along the Schuylkill River south of Reading. It is no wonder that General Washington selected this place as a fortification and winter encampment. One strategy used by Washington was to select areas where hills were located to avoid surprise attacks and to keep a watch on the British Army. (World Post Card Company postcard.)

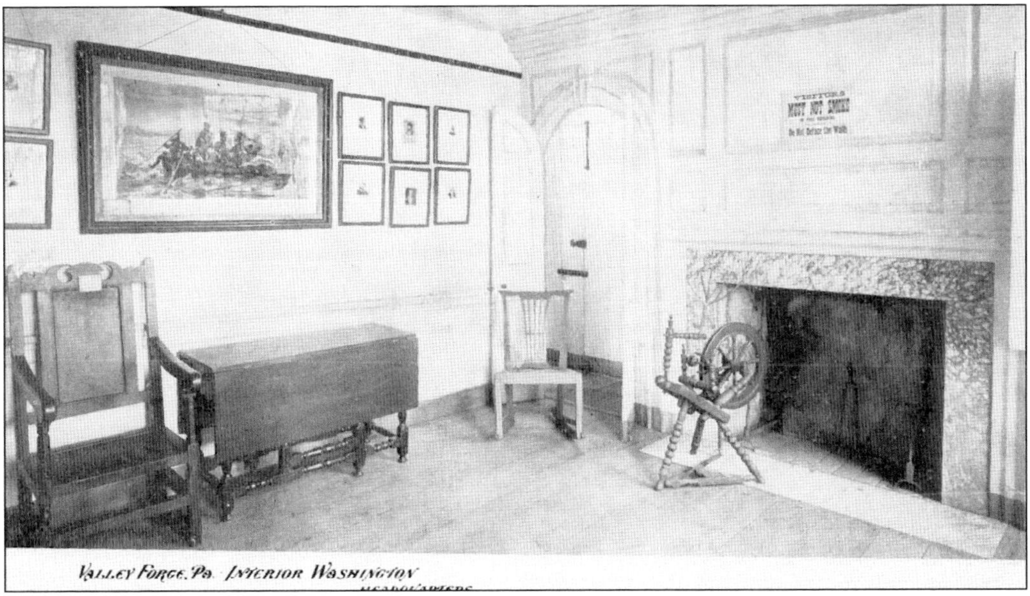

The Interior of Washington's Headquarters. When this picture of Washington's headquarters in Valley Forge was taken in 1905, the home would have been open to tourists. The room shows an old fireplace and antique furniture, including a spinning wheel and pictures depicting patriotic scenes. (World Post Card Company postcard.)

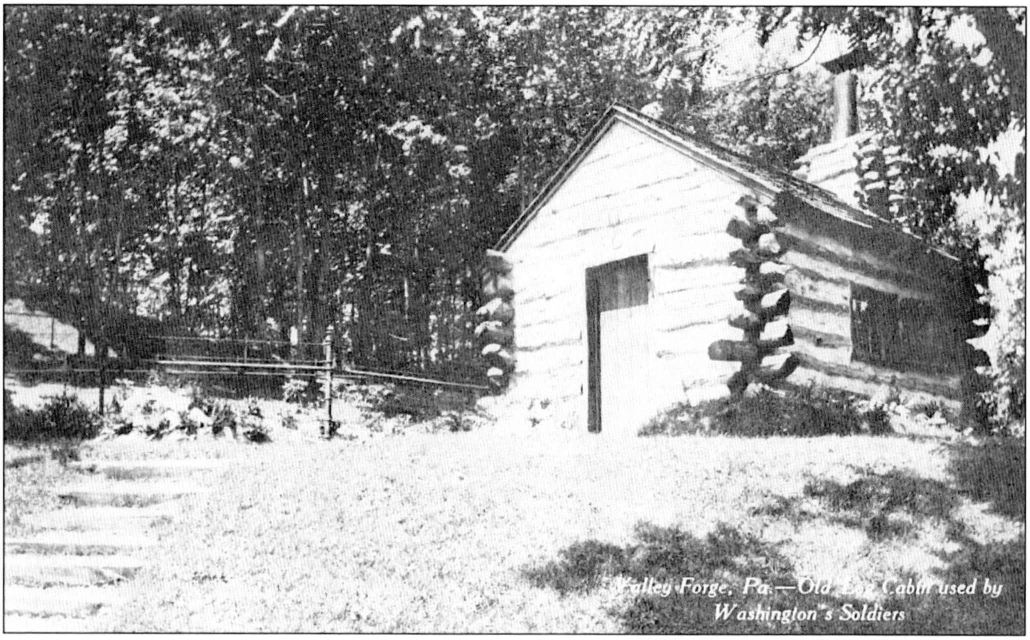

THE OLD LOG CABIN USED BY WASHINGTON'S SOLDIERS. In some instances, information on postcards is not historically accurate. No log huts or cabins survived, even when this view was made *c.* 1908. Log cabins were re-created in Valley Forge Park beginning *c.* 1905, so it is doubtful that Washington's soldiers used the one as indicated on this card. (World Post Card Company postcard.)

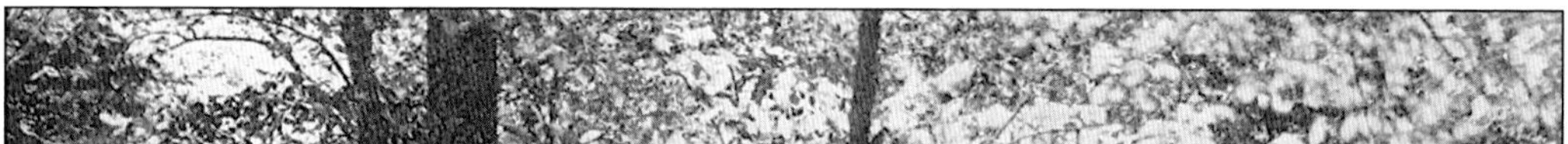

VALLEY CREEK. Located near the border of Montgomery County is the Knox Covered Bridge, which carries Yellow Springs Road over the Valley Creek in Valley Forge Park. Built in 1865, covered bridges were once part of the landscape in Montgomery County. Aside from this one, all covered bridges in the county have been replaced. (World Post Card Company postcard.)

Seven

MISCELLANEOUS AREAS

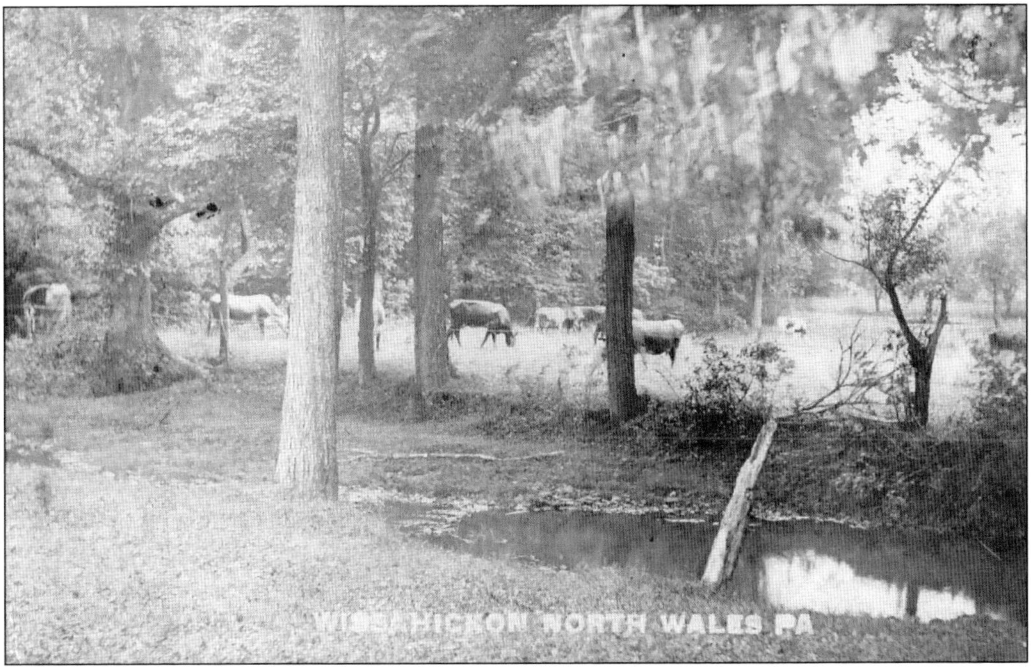

WISSAHICKON CREEK. This 1907 view shows Wissahickon Creek near North Wales, possibly near its source, a spring near the present Montgomery Mall. Notice that the creek is relatively small compared to other views in this book. Eastern Montgomery County once had numerous scenic views with farms and farm animals, a way of life that has almost vanished. (John Bartholomew postcard.)

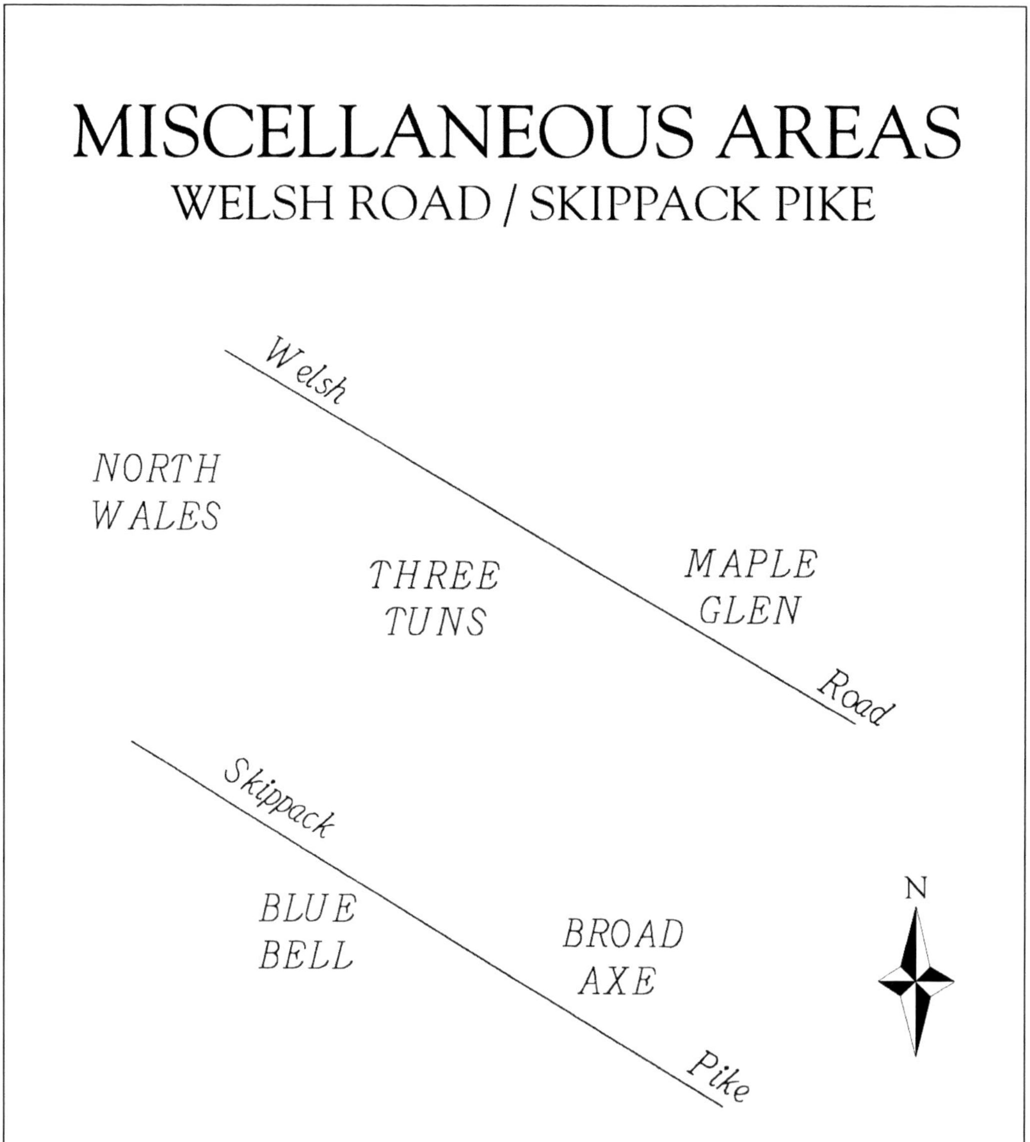

Welsh Road and Skippack Pike. Welsh Road and Skippack Pike are historic roads, but neither one linked Center City Philadelphia with other areas. Instead, they served mostly as rural roads connecting different settlements. Welsh Road was laid out in 1711 and, as its name suggests, connected the Welsh settlements in Gwynedd with mills near Huntingdon Valley and Holmesburg. Skippack Pike begins at Bethlehem Pike at Whitemarsh, and runs to Skippack Township and points west.

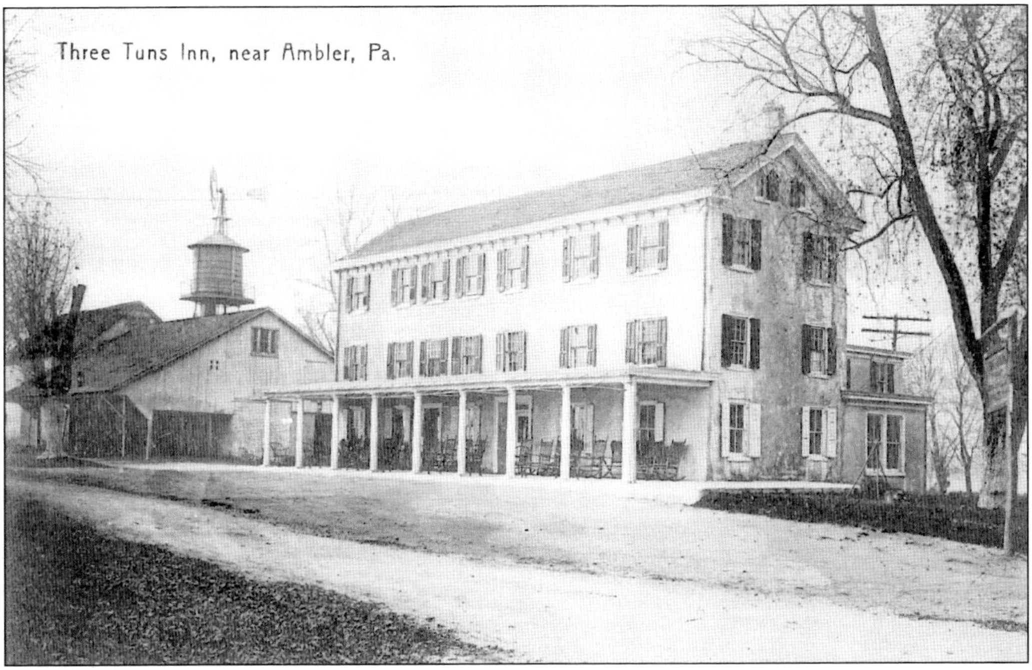

THREE TUNS INN. The village of Three Tuns was located at the intersection of Norristown Road and Butler Pike. Named for the tavern "The Sign of the Three Tuns," the village consisted of a few houses, a school, and a store. Built in 1803, the tavern was destroyed by fire in 1948. (Rees C. Roberts postcard.)

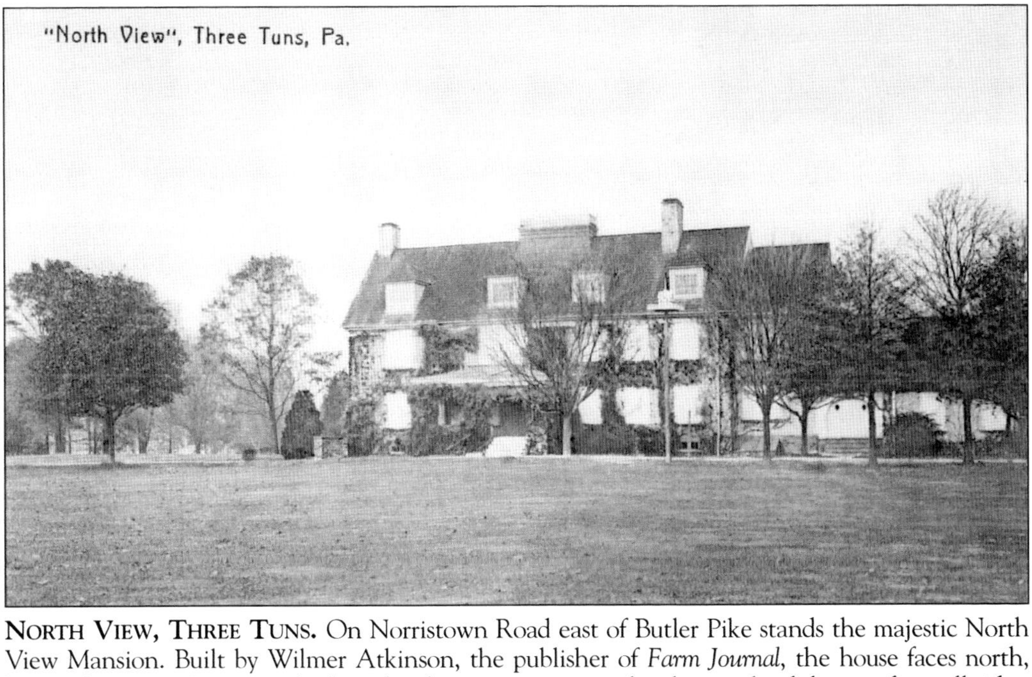

NORTH VIEW, THREE TUNS. On Norristown Road east of Butler Pike stands the majestic North View Mansion. Built by Wilmer Atkinson, the publisher of *Farm Journal*, the house faces north, hence the name. Prior to suburban development, it was said to have splendid views from all sides. Today, the mansion and grounds look unchanged from this 1910 view. (Rees. C. Roberts postcard.)

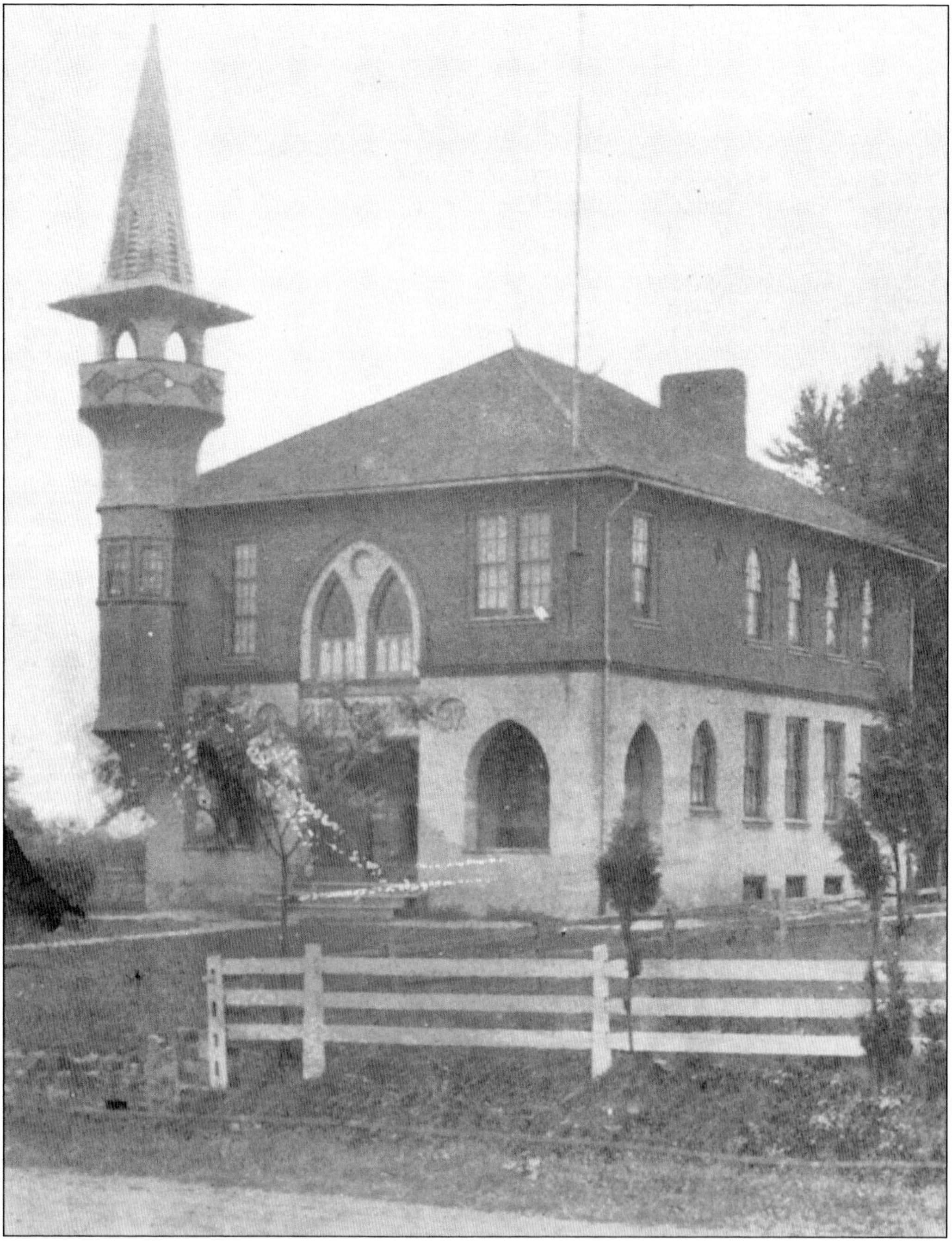

THE CENTRAL HIGH SCHOOL. On the corner of Skippack Pike and School Road stands Whitpain High School. Built in 1895, the two-story-building contained grade levels from first to eleventh. It was used for various grade levels until the 1960s. Presently, the uniquely styled building looks very similar to this 1906 view—with the exception that the steeple has been removed. The Wissahickon Valley Historical Society currently occupies the building. (World Post Card Company postcard.)

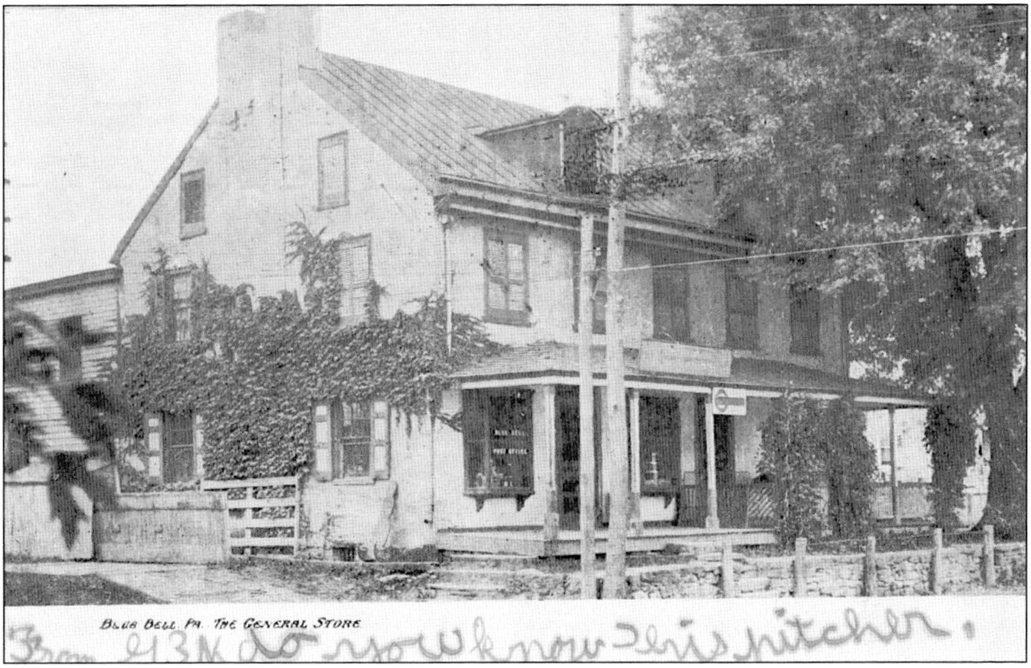

THE BLUE BELL GENERAL STORE. The Blue Bell Inn, which stands at the intersection of Skippack and Penllyn-Blue Bell Pikes, is said to date from 1743. It is now a popular restaurant, though it was used for many different purposes over the years. When this postcard was made, the building was the general store and post office for Blue Bell. It is said that its name originated from another inn that bore the sign of a blue-painted bell. (World Post Card Company postcard.)

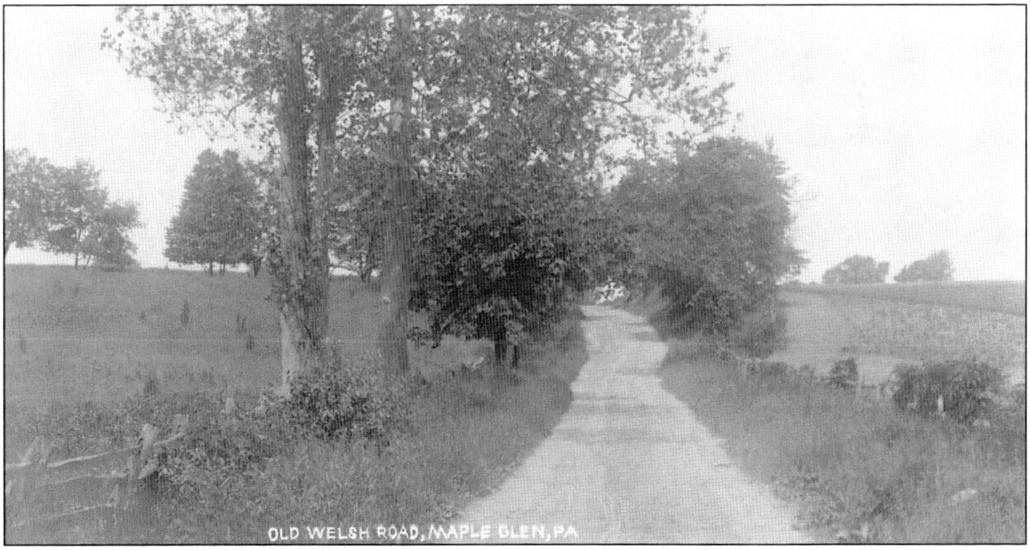

OLD WELSH ROAD IN MAPLE GLEN. In Maple Glen, a village on the border of Horsham and Upper Dublin Townships, Norristown Road, Limekiln Pike, and Welsh Road meet. This W.W. Miller view mailed in 1913 shows the typical rural setting and beautiful country that once dominated the region. Today, Welsh Road is quite busy and is a major east-west road in the county.

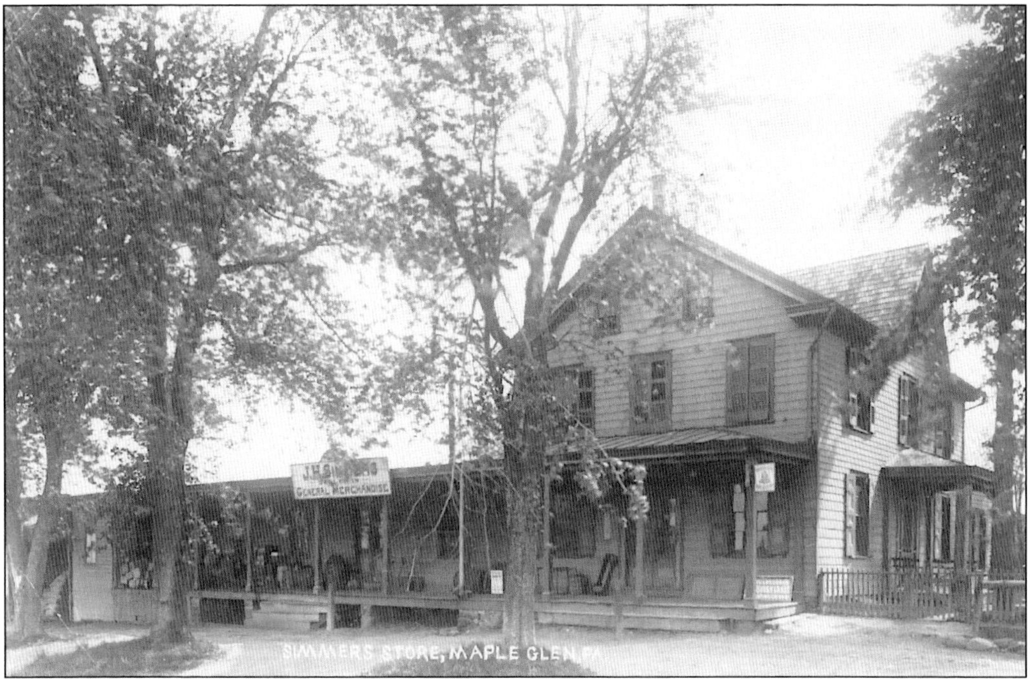

SIMMERS STORE IN MAPLE GLEN, C. 1910. At the northeast corner of Limekiln Pike and Norristown Road stood J.H. Simmers General Merchandise Store. Stores like this were the center of life in small villages like Maple Glen. The store was torn down in the mid-1960s and a gas station now occupies the site. (W.W. Miller postcard.)

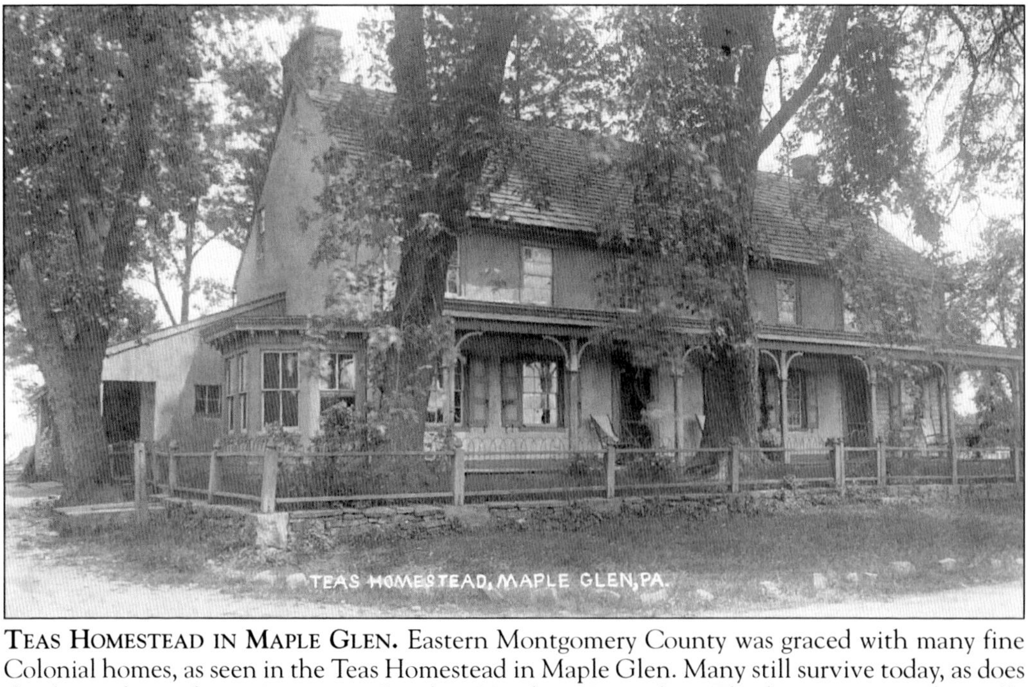

TEAS HOMESTEAD IN MAPLE GLEN. Eastern Montgomery County was graced with many fine Colonial homes, as seen in the Teas Homestead in Maple Glen. Many still survive today, as does this home located on Norristown Road in Horsham Township. The house remains basically unchanged from how it appears in this 1910 postcard by W.W. Miller of North Wales.

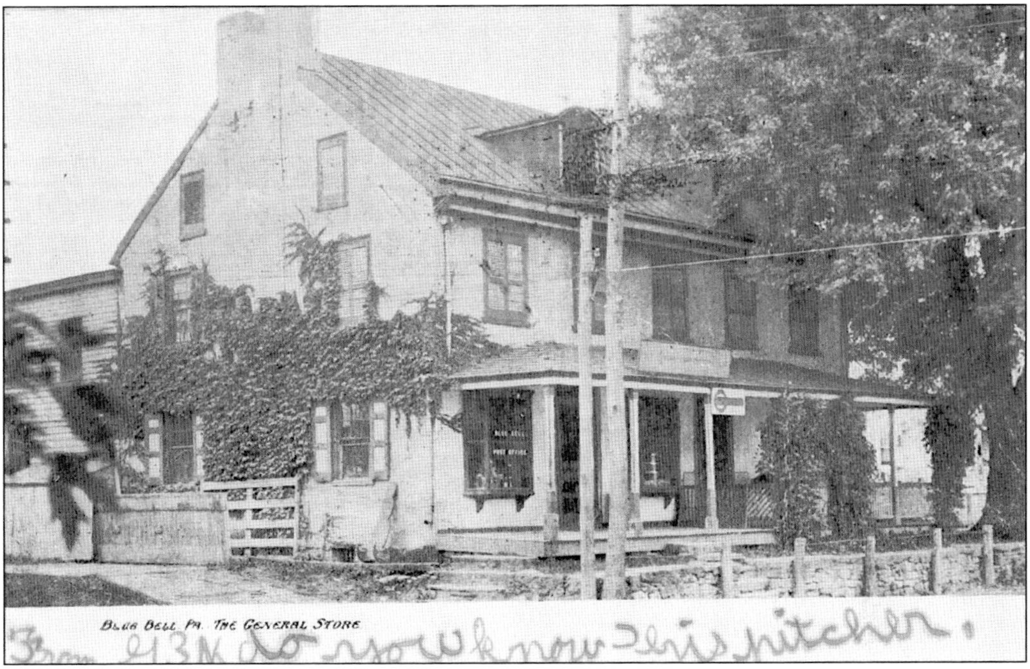

THE BLUE BELL GENERAL STORE. The Blue Bell Inn, which stands at the intersection of Skippack and Penllyn-Blue Bell Pikes, is said to date from 1743. It is now a popular restaurant, though it was used for many different purposes over the years. When this postcard was made, the building was the general store and post office for Blue Bell. It is said that its name originated from another inn that bore the sign of a blue-painted bell. (World Post Card Company postcard.)

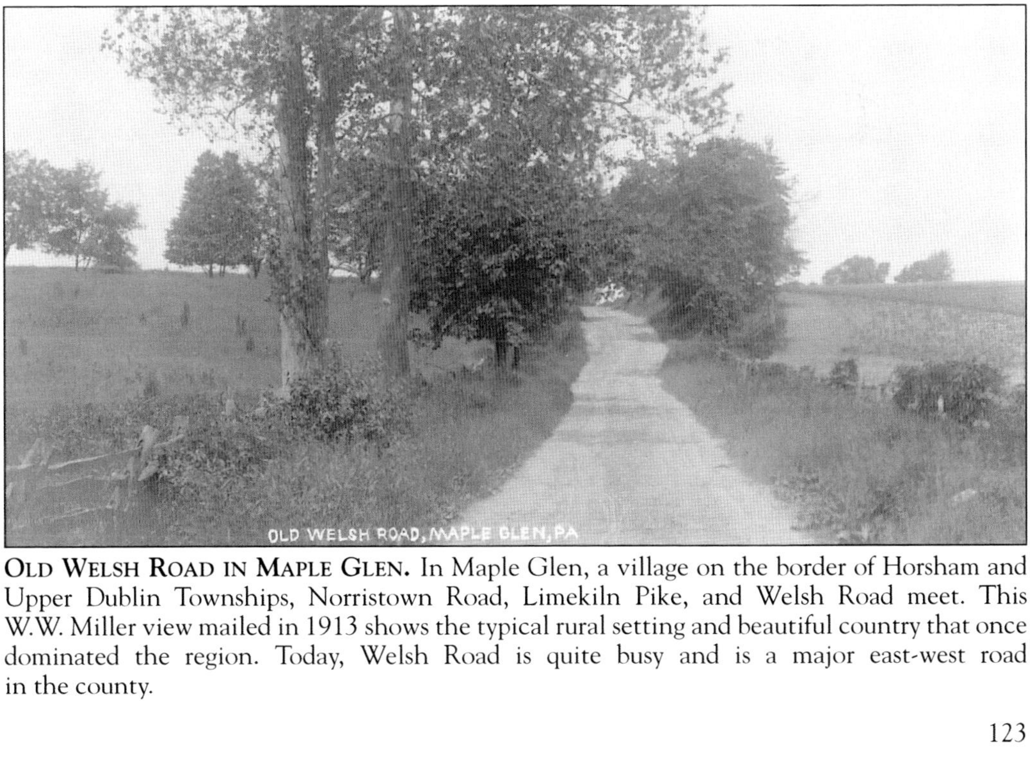

OLD WELSH ROAD IN MAPLE GLEN. In Maple Glen, a village on the border of Horsham and Upper Dublin Townships, Norristown Road, Limekiln Pike, and Welsh Road meet. This W.W. Miller view mailed in 1913 shows the typical rural setting and beautiful country that once dominated the region. Today, Welsh Road is quite busy and is a major east-west road in the county.

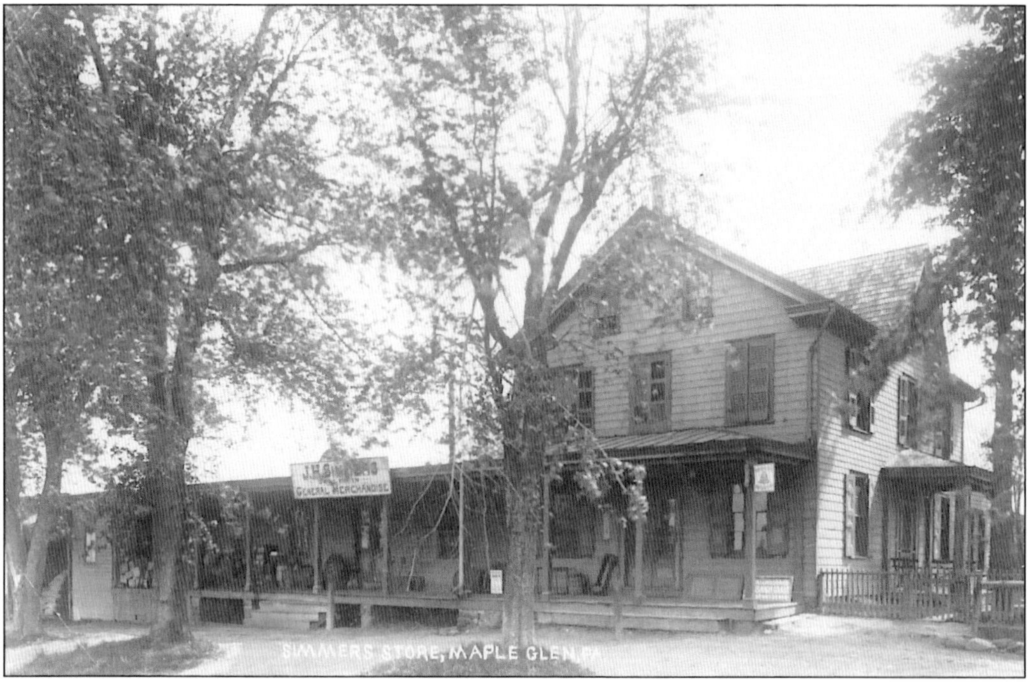

SIMMERS STORE IN MAPLE GLEN, C. 1910. At the northeast corner of Limekiln Pike and Norristown Road stood J.H. Simmers General Merchandise Store. Stores like this were the center of life in small villages like Maple Glen. The store was torn down in the mid-1960s and a gas station now occupies the site. (W.W. Miller postcard.)

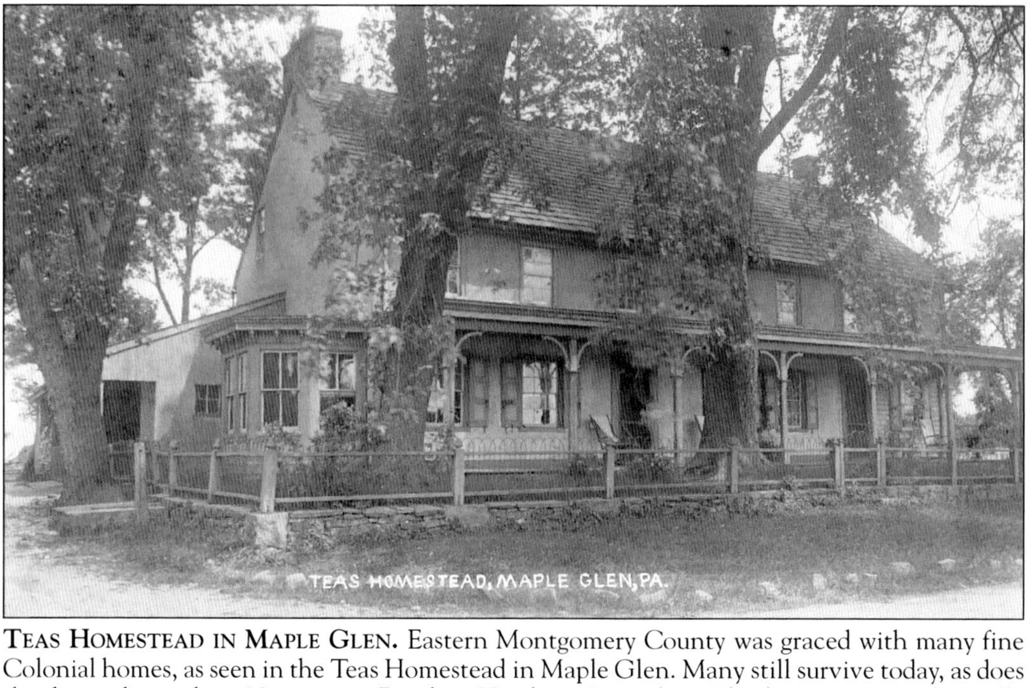

TEAS HOMESTEAD IN MAPLE GLEN. Eastern Montgomery County was graced with many fine Colonial homes, as seen in the Teas Homestead in Maple Glen. Many still survive today, as does this home located on Norristown Road in Horsham Township. The house remains basically unchanged from how it appears in this 1910 postcard by W.W. Miller of North Wales.

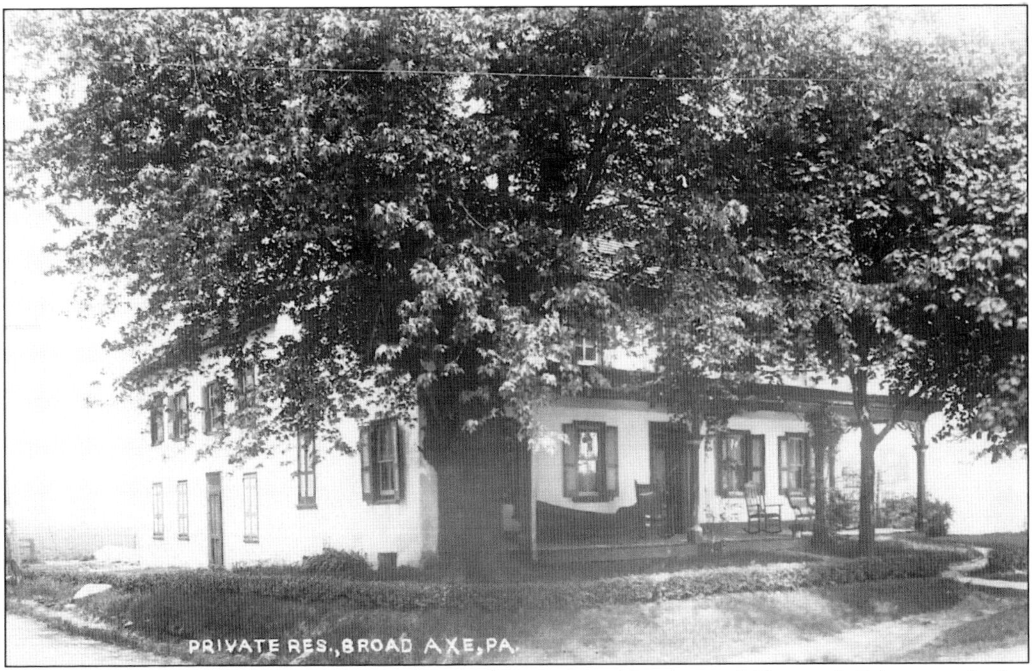

A Private Residence in Broad Axe. At the corner of Butler and Skippack Pikes stands the Broad Axe Tavern. Most likely built in the mid-1700s, it has been enlarged numerous times. The tavern gave its name to the small crossroads village in Whitpain and Whitemarsh Townships. This view shows a rather old, unidentified house in or near Broad Axe. (W.W. Miller postcard.)

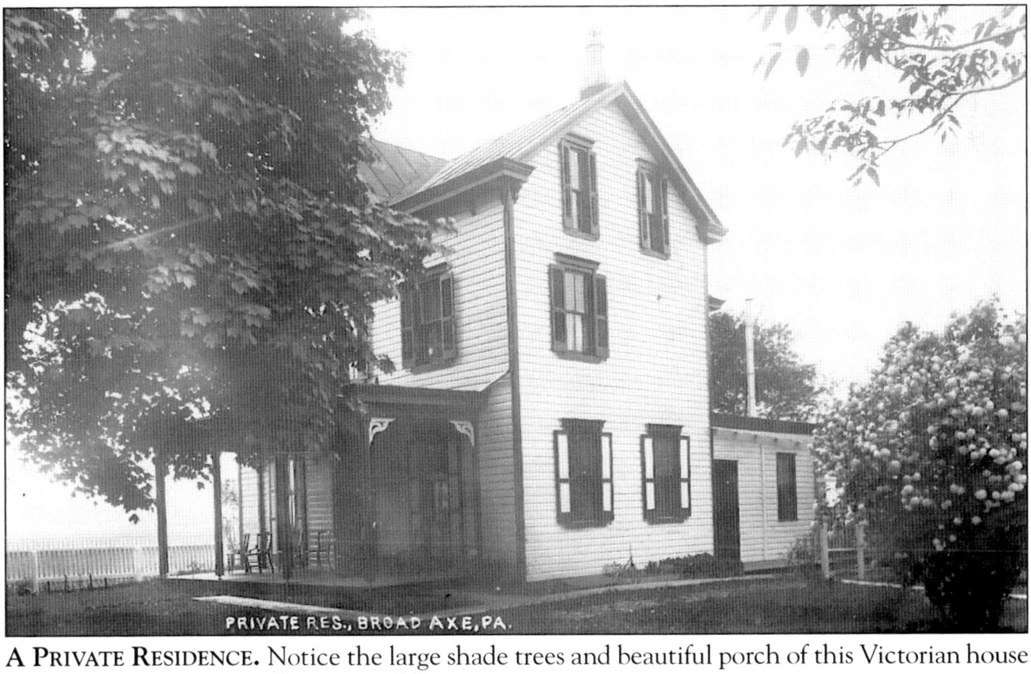

A Private Residence. Notice the large shade trees and beautiful porch of this Victorian house in Broad Axe. (W.W. Miller postcard.)

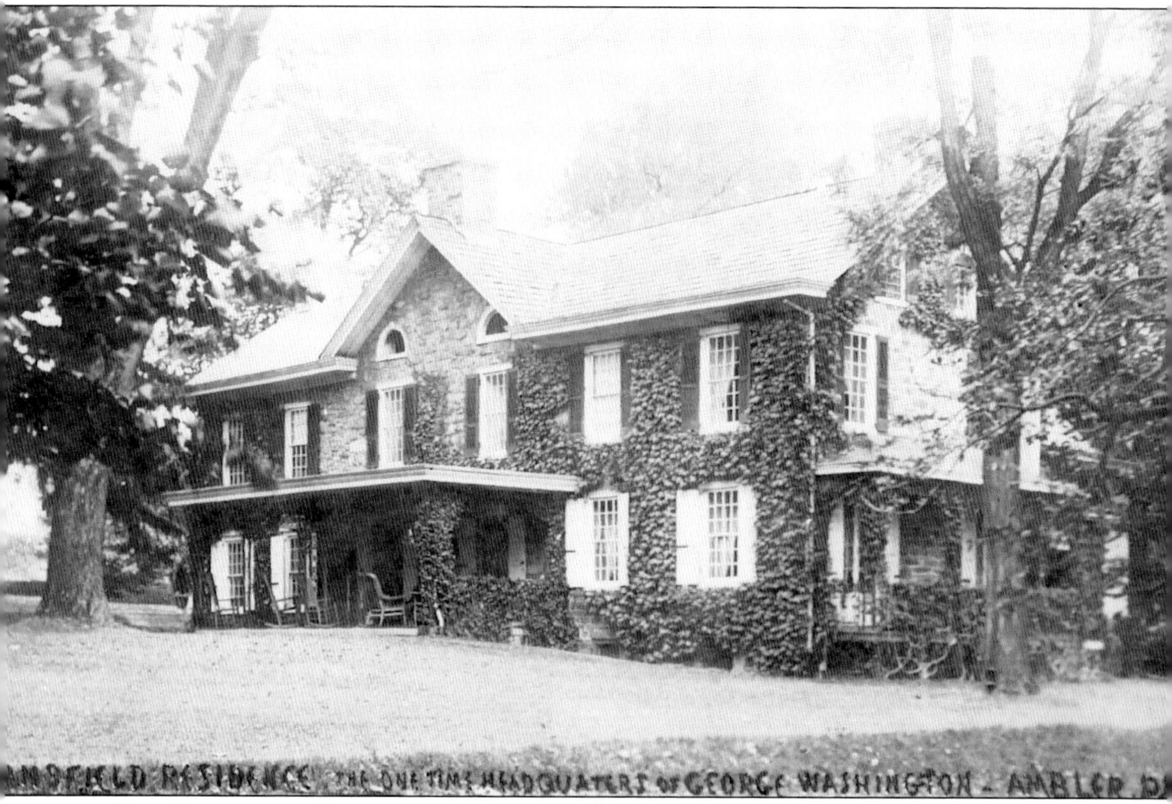

THE DAWESFIELD RESIDENCE. A mile north of Skippack Pike on Lewis Lane in Whitpain Township stands Dawesfield. Washington stayed here during the Whitemarsh Encampment from October 21 to November 2, 1777. Built in 1728 by Abraham Dawes, the home and grounds are beautifully maintained. The privately owned house is historically and architecturally significant. Huge old trees, a barn, and outbuildings are also on the property. (Sliker postcard.)

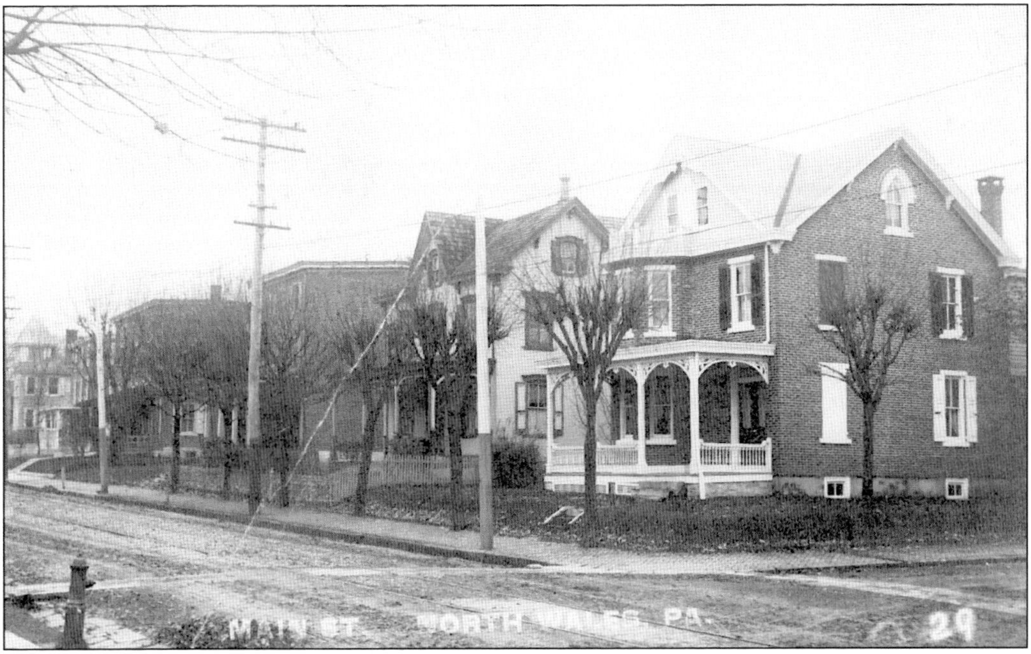

MAIN STREET IN NORTH WALES. This view is looking south on Main Street from Elm Street. Only the first three buildings in this 1910 view are still standing. The building on the corner is presently a funeral home. (John Bartholomew postcard.)

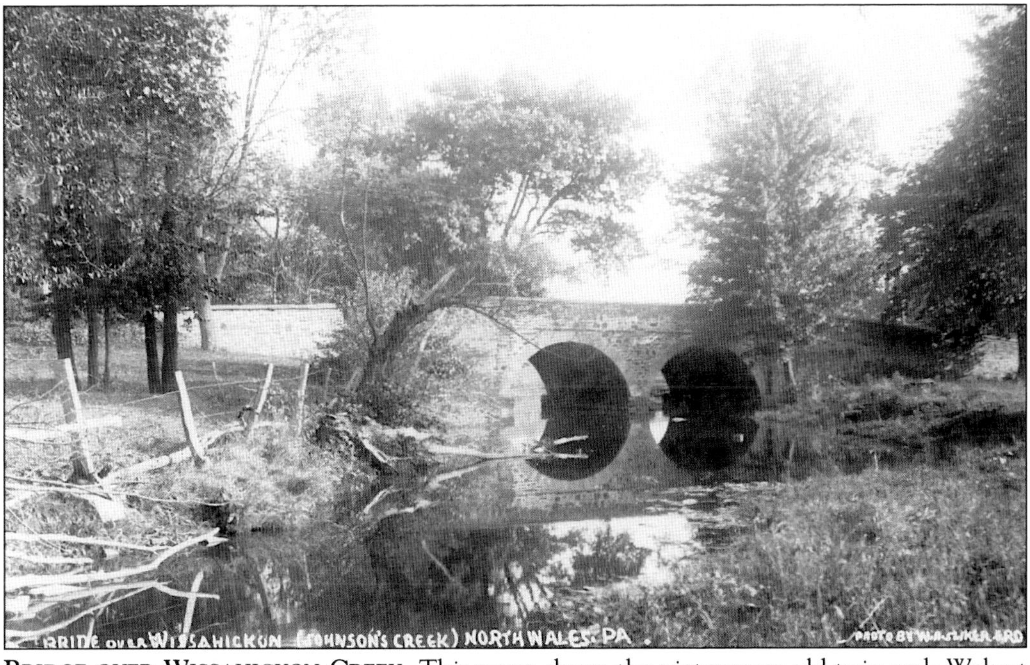

BRIDGE OVER WISSAHICKON CREEK. This scene shows the picturesque old twin arch Walnut Street/North Wales Road Bridge. Many early county bridges were of this type, constructed from stone found nearby. The bridge is no longer standing. (Sliker postcard.)

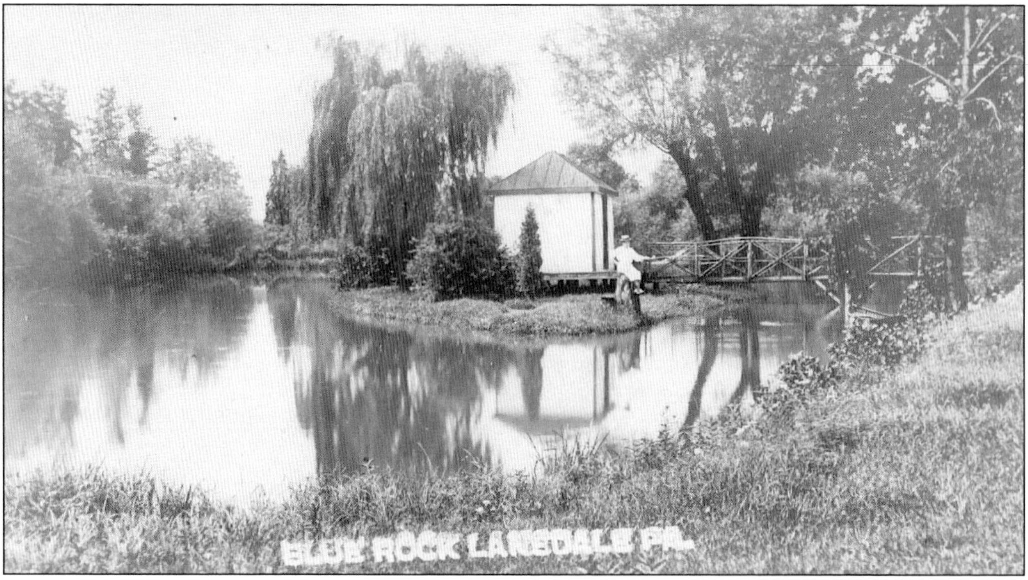

BLUE ROCK. Blue Rock was an area where Wissahickon Creek was dammed, creating a scenic pond. Located near East Main Street at the Wissahickon in Lansdale, it was a pretty spot for a picnic or canoe ride. A shopping center and homes now occupy the site. (Bartholomew postcard.)

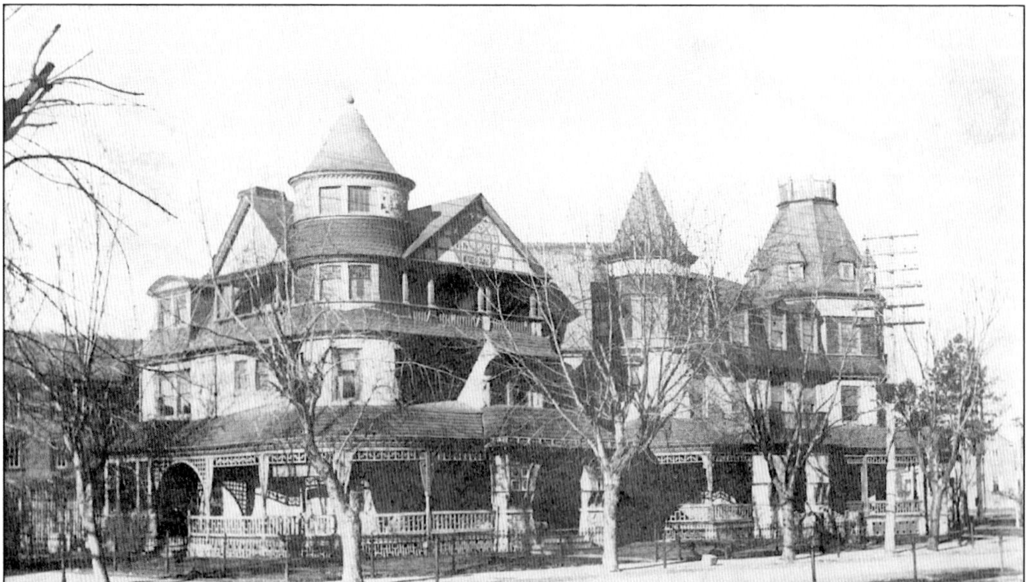

THE HOTEL TREMONT IN LANSDALE. A landmark in the center of Lansdale for over 100 years, the Hotel Tremont stood at the corner of Broad and Main Streets. Remodeled froman old home into a hotel in 1893, the beautiful Victorian-style building is no longer standing. In the late 1990s, it was torn down and replaced by a Rite-Aid Pharmacy. (John Bartholomew postcard.)